University of Stirling Library, FK9 4LA
Tel: 01786 467220

POPULAR LOAN

This item is likely to be in heavy demand.
Please **RETURN** or **RENEW**
no later than the date on the receipt

People-Centred Businesses

Also by Johnston Birchall

BUILDING COMMUNITIES, THE CO-OPERATIVE WAY

CO-OP: The People's Business

CO-OPERATIVES AND THE MILLENNIUM DEVELOPMENT GOALS

DECENTRALISING PUBLIC SERVICE MANAGEMENT (*with C Pollitt*)

REDISCOVERING THE COOPERATIVE ADVANTAGE: Poverty Reduction
Through Self-help

THE INTERNATIONAL CO-OPERATIVE MOVEMENT

Also edited by Johnston Birchall

HOUSING POLICY IN THE 1990s

THE NEW MUTUALISM IN PUBLIC POLICY

People-Centred Businesses

Co-operatives, Mutuals and the Idea of Membership

Johnston Birchall
Professor of Social Policy, Stirling University

palgrave
macmillan

First published 2011 by
PALGRAVE MACMILLAN

Palgrave Macmillan in the UK is an imprint of Macmillan Publishers Limited, registered in England, company number 785998, of Houndmills, Basingstoke, Hampshire RG21 6XS.

Palgrave Macmillan in the US is a division of St Martin's Press LLC, 175 Fifth Avenue, New York, NY 10010.

Palgrave Macmillan is the global academic imprint of the above companies and has companies and representatives throughout the world.

Palgrave® and Macmillan® are registered trademarks in the United States, the United Kingdom, Europe and other countries

ISBN 978-0-230-21718-8   hardback

This book is printed on paper suitable for recycling and made from fully managed and sustained forest sources. Logging, pulping and manufacturing processes are expected to conform to the environmental regulations of the country of origin.

A catalogue record for this book is available from the British Library.

A catalogue record for this book is available from the Library of Congress

10   9   8   7   6   5   4   3   2   1
20   19   18   17   16   15   14   13   12   11

Printed and bound in Great Britain by
CPI Antony Rowe, Chippenham and Eastbourne

For Bernadette

Contents

List of Tables

1
People-Centred Businesses

We are at the Treasury in Whitehall. I sit at a very large table with a group of chief executives discussing corporate governance. From where I am sitting I can see St James's Park and, through a rear window, the roofs of several government ministries. I am among powerful people in a powerful place; they are the top people in the worlds of banking and insurance, and they have been invited by the government to share their views on how financial services companies should be governed. There is an air of expectation; civil servants sit to one side recording every nuance of our conversation. We discuss several issues to do with good governance, including the old controversy over whether the European tradition of having a supervisory board and a management board is superior to the British and American tradition of having just one unified board. We spend some time discussing the kinds of skills board members need in order to be effective. This is a few years before the global banking crisis, but we have a sharp discussion about risk and whether board members can assess the risks their managers are taking. We get on to the subject of executive and non-executive directors, the point at issue being how many of each a board should have if it is to be effective. The general opinion seems to be that there should be a balance, but some lean towards having more executive directors on the board than non-executives. This means they want the managers of the company to be in control rather than the owners. I find this idea quite alarming, but say nothing.

They take it in turns to describe how their own companies deal with this issue. The recently retired chief executive of a large life insurance company explains 'In our company we have a tradition that 'non-execs' are in the majority on the board. I don't know why'.

> *Finally I find my voice. 'That's because you are a mutual; if the non-execs were not in a majority then you would cease to be member controlled. You see, in theory you are owned and controlled by your members, who are the customers. They vote the non-executives on to the board.' I pause to let this sink in, and then sum up: 'If non-execs were not in a majority you would no longer be a mutual'.*
>
> *He looks puzzled and says 'I never thought of that'.*

The purpose of this book is to explain why that highly-paid and experienced executive missed such an obvious point about his own company, and to evaluate the importance of the point he had missed. There is a whole class of business organisation that is owned not by investors, or the public, or a particular entrepreneur, but by those who *benefit directly* from its activities: end-users or customers, other companies who supply to or are supplied by the business, or its employees. This is, to put it simply, a *member-owned business*, and it is quite distinct from an *investor-owned* business.

The art of seeing

Why did the former chief executive not see what was plainly in front of his eyes? To answer this question it is worth making a slight detour into this question of 'seeing'. When we look at something the eyes are not the only organ that we use. Obviously, the brain interprets what we see and makes sense of it. Also, we do not see everything that comes into our vision but select what is important to us and, in a sense, *choose* to process that information rather than any number of other possible sensory perceptions. As humans, we complicate matters by using language, and we put labels on objects as part of a process of deciding what is important to us. For example, look at how an ornithologist will travel for hundreds of miles to catch a glimpse of a rare warbler that most of us would just see as a dull brown bird. Look at how a trained botanist will search for ages in a forest to find a rare orchid that we would just see as another wild flower. The process of naming changes how we see things. Why should an otherwise intelligent and experienced manager not have seen into the nature of the organisation he had been leading? – Because the label 'mutual' was not important to him. He had not been trained to see it, and had not been equipped with the precise kind of language needed to value what he saw.

His ignorance would have been easier to excuse if it had been displayed perhaps 15 years earlier, when hardly anyone could define a mutual. The demutualisation debate, which began in the early 1990s in the UK with the conversion of building societies to investor-owned companies, had the effect of sharpening business analysts' vision; they began to ask what it was that was being destroyed, and whether something valuable was being lost in the process (Drake and Llewellyn, 2001; Birchall, 2000). The idea of member-ownership also came into focus in a perverse way, when failings in governance came to light in the life mutual, Equitable Life, and policyholders began to appreciate that their membership of the company gave them strong rights to participate (Birchall, 2001).

What are we looking at?

So what is a member-owned business? What does it look like? How can we distinguish it from other forms of ownership? To save time, let us begin by labelling it an *MOB,* as opposed to an *IOB* which is an investor-owned business. The crucial distinction is between a business that is people-centred, and one that is money-centred. Henry Wolff put this well in a book he wrote in 1907 about co-operative banks. He said:

> *The joint stock company is a union of money units, each of which carries a vote. The co-operative society is a union of persons. These persons do not, like the shareholders in a joint stock bank, join together to earn a profit out of others. They combine not as dealers but as customers* (Wolff, 1907: 50).

What sort of persons can be members of an MOB? Here is a simple classification. Apart from the investors of capital, there are three main stakeholders in a business: its consumers, the producers who supply inputs to or take the outputs from the business, and its employees. In an MOB, usually one of these other stakeholders is put at the centre of the business. This gives us three classes: consumer-owned, producer-owned and employee-owned businesses. The advantages to stakeholders of co-operating are obvious; together they can channel the value added from the business to themselves rather than to investor-owners or to 'middlemen'. Consumer-OBs provide people with consumption goods at the lowest possible price and with a guarantee of good value, and so make their income go further. Producer-OBs enable self-employed people and family businesses to gain the strength in numbers they need to survive in the market. Employee-OBs provide people with an income, but also are a way of gaining control over the conditions under which they labour, providing what the International Labour Organisation calls 'decent work'.

Of course, it is not quite that simple. There are three complications. First, though most MOBs are 'single-stakeholder' in nature, the people who join them can have more than one identity, being at the same time producers as well as consumers, or employees as well as customers. Farmers are both producers and individually consumers, and so agricultural supply co-operatives often provide them with consumer goods as well as farm inputs. Some of the people who need banking services have their own businesses, and so have both business and personal accounts. The employees of consumer co-operatives are also customers, and so are allowed to become members (though there are rules that prevent them from being in a majority on the board). Second, in some MOBs more than one type of person can join. Insurance mutuals that set out to insure farmers often extend into general assurance for householders. Credit unions often have in membership individual customers and small businesses. Savings and loan societies often have two categories of member; savers and borrowers. Third, a few MOBs are multi-stakeholding. They deliberately offer different categories of membership to more than one stakeholder. The Eroski retail co-operative in Spain has employee and customer members. The social co-operatives in Italy that provide care services to disabled and vulnerable people are, by law, required to offer membership to employees, service users and carers. However, multi-stakeholder-OBs are quite rare; probably because in taking such different interest groups into membership they increase the costs of governance (see Hansmann, 1996). A straight forward definition of an MOB follows: it is

> *a business organisation that is owned and controlled by members who are drawn from one (or more) of three types of stakeholder – consumers, producers and employees – and whose benefits go mainly to these members.*

We can use this classification to list the different types of MOB in the same way that scientists identify individual genera within a class, and species within a genus (see Table 1.1). If a new species of MOB were to evolve, we ought to be able to fit it into an existing genus or class. Also, if an MOB allows some ownership by investors or government, or has some of the features of an MOB and some of another type, it can usefully be called a hybrid.

Table 1.1   A suggested taxonomy of member-owned businesses

Class	Genus	Species	Hybrids
Consumer-owned	General retailing	Consumer co-ops: food, staple goods	Jointly-owned business with other retailers
Consumer-owned	Specialist retailing	Consumer co-ops: pharmacy, funerals, travel, garage services, etc	Joint ventures
Consumer-owned	Insurance	Friendly societies, mutual assurance, life insurance, health insurance	
Consumer-owned	Housing	Market value housing co-ops, non-equity co-ops	Community housing associations (Scotland)
Consumer-owned	Utilities	Electricity, water, telecoms co-ops	Joint ventures with local govt
Consumer-owned	Education	Child care co-ops, co-operative schools (Sweden)	Schools with multi-stakeholder governance, foundation health trusts (England)
Consumer- *and* producer-owned	Banking	Co-operative banks, credit unions, savings and credit co-ops	Mutual savings banks (USA)
Producer-owned	Retailer-owned wholesaler	Supermarkets, hardware stores, pharmacy	Jointly-owned business with wholesalers
Producer-owned	Shared services for self-employed, small business & professionals	A wide variety, including taxi drivers, artisans, market traders, dentists co-operatives	Minority producer-ownership in an IOB
Employee-owned	Continuum: simple labour co-ops to conglomerates	A wide variety of sectors	Employee share-ownership schemes

There is one more set of terms to be explained. MOBs are called variously, *co-operatives, mutuals*, and *economic associations*. These terms are almost synonymous but not quite. Co-operatives trace their origins to the 'Rochdale Pioneers' who opened a consumer-owned store in a small industrial town in the North of England in 1844. As we shall see further in Chapter 3, their 'Rochdale principles' were adopted by cooperative movements in many other countries and from the 1920s onwards codified and updated by a representative body, the International Cooperative Alliance (ICA). These principles have been enshrined in cooperative laws around the world, and applied not only in consumer but also producer and worker-owned businesses that share a distinct cooperative identity. The latest revision was in 1995, when the ICA provided this definition of a co-operative:

> *An autonomous association of persons united voluntarily to meet their common economic, social and cultural needs and aspirations through a jointly owned and democratically controlled enterprise* (ICA, 1995).

The ICA also provided seven principles: voluntary and open membership; democratic member control; member economic participation; autonomy and independence; education, training and information; cooperation between co-ops and concern for community (Birchall, 1997, Ch.10).

Mutuals do not have such a strong social identity; their history is much more mixed and less obviously heroic, and they cannot be said to constitute one movement. However, some types of mutual do have a distinguished history and a social movement ethos. British friendly societies were such a movement until sidelined by the state in social insurance after the Second World War. In France the term 'mutuality' carries a much stronger meaning than elsewhere, and is more like that of a cooperative. There are three important differences between a cooperative and a mutual. First, the term mutual is usually applied to financial MOBs; their purpose is to raise funds from their customers in order to provide them with services such as savings and loans, various types of assurance, health insurance, pensions, housing mortgages and so on. They do this through recycling money within a closed system that does not include – or need – outside investors. Second, a mutual can have different stakeholders taking part in governance. Building society customers can be savers or borrowers, or both, while pension customers can be on a with-profits or a fixed interest basis. Their rights in the business have to be allocated carefully, but otherwise governance is similar to that of a co-operative. Third, mutuals insist that customers become members, while co-operatives often also have dealings with customers who are not members.

Just to complicate things further, some demutualised businesses still carry the word 'mutual' in their name even though they are investor-owned and have no right to! Also, there is a class of business organisation that is semi-mutual; savings banks often see their customers as 'members' but do not allow them a share in governance; they are governed by a self-perpetuating board of trustees and so are much more like charities. In the USA they are called mutual savings banks, but they are only mutual in one sense, that there is no separate set of investors to take the profits. Finally, consumers can get together to make investments, and provided they have an equal vote as persons they are entitled to call their business a *mutual* investment club. Such investment mutuals are providing a service to their members that just happens to be one of helping them to invest capital.

The third term, economic association is the broadest of the three terms, carrying no ideological 'baggage' or set of universal rules by which it is distinguished from other types. It is usually applied to farmer associations, and is useful in distinguishing MOBs that do not conform to co-operative principles. As we shall see in Chapter 9, in developing countries new forms of farmer association are being promoted that avoid a cumbersome and intrusive bureaucracy set up to regulate co-operatives. They represent a fresh start, and can be registered in the flexible legal status of a company or association. Also, collective action by producers can result in new forms of association that do not conform to co-operative principles. In India, groups of farmers have evolved successful ways of managing water courses for irrigation by linking investment and returns to the amount of water used. This gives a more dominant role to richer farmers than would a co-operative, but it works much better than officially-sponsored water co-ops (Shah, 1996).

Does ownership matter?

Of course, we have to face the possibility that, like the small brown bird that excites the birdwatcher but for most people remains just a small brown bird, the question of business-ownership is not all that interesting. Learning to *see* it may not be important. Economists tend to emphasise other dimensions that are more important, such as the type of market sector, the intensity of competition, market imperfections, transaction costs, the quality of management, or the impact of new technology. It is entirely possible to analyse the life insurance market or the retail supermarket trade without discussing financial mutuals or consumer co-operatives. Also, firms that survive in sophisticated regional or global markets have common characteristics, such as a reliance on managers to make most decisions and a need to expand beyond national borders in order to meet the competition; a meat packing company owned by Finnish farmers may look very like a meat packing company owned by investors.

However, there are strong arguments for the importance of ownership. First, it brings benefits to one stakeholder rather than another. If a firm is owned by investors, they can appropriate the profits and benefit from increases in share values. Nobody else can do so. If, on the other hand, it is owned by the employees, or by customers, or by other firms that rely on it for their business, they take the profits (though they do not benefit from share value as usually shares are not traded). Further, they can decide not to pursue profit but to give priority to other aims; consumers may value the quality of the product, employees' decent working conditions and producers the quality of inputs to their businesses or effective marketing of their products. The contrast is seen strongest in retail financial services, where there is no reason for seeking investors with capital when customers supply all the capital the firm needs and take all the benefits. Demutualisation has been seen in this light; the main benefit of retaining mutuality is argued to be the prevention of profit-taking by a separate group of investors (Hansmann, 1996).

Second, ownership gives control over the business to one stakeholder rather than another. There are always conflicts of interest between different stakeholders. They cannot all maximise their return from the business. If some interests were not excluded from ownership the business would lack direction and the costs of governance would be too high. More positively, giving ownership to stakeholders who rely on the business not just for profit but for their livelihood, or to meet basic needs, or to pursue their own business aims, enables the business to be 'people-centred' rather than money-centred (Parnell, 1995). There are some reservations though. In modern business organisations managers have a lot of power regardless of the ownership form the organisation takes; it can be argued that a 'managerial revolution' has taken place that makes ownership less relevant. In consequence, ensuring effective governance is a problem for all types of business except those owned by individual owner-managers.

Third, there are always costs incurred in bringing one set of stakeholders or another into ownership. Stakeholders who are left outside have to rely on contracts that carry transaction costs, while those on the inside have to bear the costs of governance. Member-ownership provides a different mix of costs that, under the right circumstances, makes a firm more competitive. For instance, mutual life insurers have an inherent advantage over investor-owned equivalents, as they do not have to decide how to allocate profits between with-profits policyholders and investors. Clearly, other things being equal, policyholders will gain from controlling the business as members. Related to this is the cost of regulation. In potentially monopolistic industries such as supply of utilities, and in sectors that rely on long-term contracts such as provision of pensions, investor-ownership needs heavy regulation by governments to safeguard the interests of customers. Mutual water companies and electricity co-operatives align the interests of customers more closely with the aims of the business.

Fourth, the existence of a member-owned sector has wider systemic effects. It can be argued that markets that include MOBs provide more choice to consumers, help prevent monopoly and monopsony, provide room for innovation (particularly in ethical trading), and generally keep investor-owned businesses competitive. The demutualisation of the building society sector in UK was opposed by members who began to realise the value of mutuality, but also by critics who warned of the dangers of an investor-dominated banking system (Drake and Llewellyn, 2001). The UK Co-operative Bank has been able to innovate, abolishing bank charges on current accounts and challenging other banks to follow suit, and refusing to lend to businesses its members regard as unethical (Birchall, 2001). Consumer co-operatives in the UK and Italy have led the way in developing fair trade products (Lacey, 2009).

Finally, anyone who doubts the importance of ownership should note how struggles over demutualisation have intensified – it is now clear that it is 'fought out' by interested parties who have a lot to gain by the outcome. The recent crisis in the banking sector shows that the loss of MOBs has long-term effects; lending practices by banks have become riskier, because their time horizon has been much shorter and incentives to take risks much higher than in the mutual sector. The ultimate illustration of this is in the demise in the UK of Northern Rock and Bradford and Bingley, both sound building societies that were bankrupted by their managers a few years after they became investor-owned banks.

How important is the member-owned sector?

If different types of business, classified by ownership type, were like the little brown bird in our metaphor, they would be all the more valuable for being small and rare. However, in business there is no virtue in being either! What would make the MOB sector more or less important? First, it ought to be large in size relative to the market it is operating in, that is, have a significant *market share*. What 'significant' means depends on the market. If there are only a few big players, as in UK food retailing, the Co-operative Group's 8% of the market is significant. If there are many small players, as in Japanese food retailing, the consumer co-operative share of the market is equally significant at around 2%. Here are some statistics on MOB market share. Producer co-operatives have a large share of the market in many countries. For instance, they have 99% of milk production in Norway; 95% in New Zealand and 80% in the USA. They have 71% of fishery in Korea and 40% of agriculture in Brazil. Consumer co-ops are the market leaders in Italy, Switzerland, Singapore and Japan, and strong in the Scandinavian countries and Atlantic Canada. They have 55% of the retail market in Singapore, 36% in Denmark and 14% in Hungary, as well as 8% in the UK (Birchall, 2008). The share of the insurance market is also high; the International Co-operative and Mutual Insurance Federation has 184 insurance companies in membership from 70 countries, who together have 7% of the world's premiums.

Even the smaller MOB sectors have a large market share in some countries. Much of the housing built in Norway and Sweden in the second half of the last century has been co-operative, and it has also proved popular in the USA with higher income dwellers and with retired people (most of the apartments in New York are co-ops). In Latin America and Japan, health co-ops are important. Unimed in Brazil is the biggest co-operative medical system in the world with 367 local member co-operatives operating in over 80% of Brazil's counties with 98,000 doctors in membership, serving 12 million patients. In the USA, over 1000 electricity co-operatives supply power to around 12% of households, mainly in rural areas. In Argentina 58% of rural electricity is supplied by co-ops, and they are also strong in telecommunications. In Bolivia they have proved they are a serious alternative to privatisation of water services to urban consumers.

Whether individual MOBs are themselves large is also important, as it is unlikely that a sector consisting only of small businesses will make an impact, particularly if some of its competitors are large in scale. Here are some statistics on the *size of MOBs*. Some of the world's biggest businesses are agricultural marketing co-operatives. They include CHS, a conglomerate of farmers, ranchers and primary co-ops that is ranked 166 in the Fortune 500 listing, and Fonterra Co-operative Group, one of the top six dairy businesses in the world and New Zealand's largest company. There are household names such as Sunkist, the world's largest marketing co-op in citrus fruits; Ocean Spray the largest producer of cranberry juice, and Land O'Lakes, the number one marketer of butter in the USA. Agricultural supply co-operatives are also very large. Zen-Noh in Japan is the top co-operative in the world in turnover, distributing farm inputs to three million farm households. Limagrain, based in France, is the world's fourth largest seed producer, while Growmark, in Northern USA and Canada, supplies fertiliser, biofuels, petroleum, seeds and animal feeds to a quarter of a million farmer members. DLG Group is the largest animal food company in Denmark, supplying farmers with inputs such as seeds, lime and fertilisers.

Co-operative banks are also very large. In France, Credit Agricole is the largest bank, with 28% of the customer banking market. It is owned mainly by over 2500 local banks federated in 39 regional banks. Rabobank has 50% of Dutch citizens in membership and is the largest agricultural bank in the world (OCDC, 2007). Then there are large banks based on the Raiffeisen and Volksbank networks in Germany, Switzerland and Austria, and in many other parts of the world. In virtually every developed country one or two co-operative insurers will be among the top ten: Nationwide Mutual is ranked 108 in the Fortune 500 in the USA; Folksam is dominant in Sweden; Ethias the second in Belgium; the Debeka group the fourth largest in Germany; Unipol the fourth in Italy, and so on.

MOBs are particularly strong in providing wholesaling for independent retailers. Rewe, based in Germany, is a group of independent retailers and chain stores operating 7330 stores, and is the third largest player in the European food trade. Edeka is the fourth largest, with 4100 stores. Intermarche, Leclerc and Systeme U are major players based in France. In the USA the Wakefern Food Corporation is the largest, with 43 members owning 200 Shoprite superstores. Associated Wholesale Grocers, the second largest, serves 1900 stores in 21 states. In New Zealand, three co-operative buying groups called Foodstuffs form the second largest grocery distributor. In Western Europe pharmacy chains are very strong; Noweda Apothek is the top pharmacy wholesaler in Germany, with 6000 member pharmacies, and Cooperativa Farmaceutica Espanola is the largest in Spain. MOBs are strong in provision of health care in countries where insurance-based provision allows for competition between suppliers. In the USA for example, some of the largest health providers are consumer co-operatives; the Group Health Co-operative in Puget Sound provides health care for 570,000 members, while Health Partners in Minnesota and Wisconsin has 630,000 members.

It is not just the size of individual MOBs that is important, but their concentration. This way of looking at MOBs is important, because many choose to federate in large groups rather than becoming one integrated business organisation. For instance, there is a large concentration of mutual banks in France, the largest being Credit Agricole but also including Credit Mutuel that has 3300 caisses federated into 18 regional federations. Then there are the Caisses d'Epargne, a group of over 400 local banks, and the Groupe Banques Populaires, which consists of 18 regional co-operative banks. In Quebec, the Mouvement des Caisses Desjardins consists of over 500 local caisses populaires, grouped in 11 regional federations. It has become the sixth largest financial institution in Canada, and the largest in Quebec, and it has had a profound effect on the regional economy. In the Emilia Romagna region of Italy there is a concentration of around 8000 independent producer co-operatives producing a wide variety of goods including fashion, ceramics and speciality cheeses. The Mondragon Corporation has grown out of a small group of worker co-ops in the Basque region of Spain to become the largest concentration of worker-owned businesses in the world. It now has 264 companies in membership, and has become Spain's seventh largest industrial company, with a workforce of over 100,000. North Italy also has a concentration of co-operatives of all types; there are 75,000 co-ops with 1.25 million employees, 6.5% of total employment, 7% of GDP, and with 16 ranked among the top 200 enterprises (ICA, 2010).

Another way of measuring the size of MOBs is through estimates of their membership. The membership organizations of the International Co-operative Alliance (ICA) have between them 800 million members in over 100 countries. What proportion of the population of each country are co-op members? ICA statistics quote one in two people in Finland and Singapore; one in three in Canada, New Zealand, Honduras, and Norway; one in four in the USA, Malaysia and Germany; one in five in Kenya; one in ten in Costa Rica; one in 11 in Colombia and so on. If we see each member as a representative of a household the figures become even more dramatic; more than one in two Finnish households have membership, one in three Japanese, one in four Indonesian, and so on. Such figures for developing countries are hard to find, but a recent study of 11 countries in Africa estimates that around 7% of Africans are co-op members and that the numbers are continuing to grow (Develtere et al, 2008).

Another way of measuring the scale of MOBs is through estimates of their share of country GDP. It varies widely, from 45% in Kenya, through 22% in New Zealand, 21% in Finland, 16% in Sweden and 13% in Switzerland, 8.6% in Vietnam, 7% in Italy, and 5.6% in Colombia.

Another factor is the longevity of the sector. Many MOBs trace their origins back to the 19th century or even earlier (Birchall, 1994). They may have gone through a long process of merger and consolidation, but they have proved their staying power. A related point is the robustness of start-ups. There is good evidence, for instance, that employee-owned businesses last longer and are less likely to fail than conventional small businesses (Birchall, 2009, Ch.11).

The advantages of diversity

One argument for MOBs that can be found in the business ecology literature is that there is a need for diversity. Hannan and Freeman say

the ability of society as a whole to respond to changing conditions depends on the responsiveness of its constituent organisations and on the diversity of its organisational populations (1989: 3).

Diversity is important because it affects the capacity of a society to respond to uncertain future changes. MOBs are a 'repository of alternative solutions to the problem of producing sets of collective outcomes' (Hannan and Freeman, 1989: 7). There are other ways of responding to a rapidly changing environment. IOBs can be reorganised but, because of inertia and the ability of existing coalitions of interest to block change, this will be costly and may not even be possible. New organisations can be created to deal with new problems, but start-ups are always fragile and have a much higher risk of failure than do established businesses. If we see the global economy as a kind of evolutionary, adaptive system then we can expect one type of business to thrive at the expense of another. However, if one type dies out completely then the stock of existing solutions will have declined. This almost happened with the UK building societies in the 1990s, but around 30% of the sector survived and is now showing that it has some inherent advantages over IOBs; mutuals are more risk-averse and so more trusted by consumers for relatively simple transactions such as residential mortgages and savings, and they have built-in advantages from not having to remunerate a separate group of shareholders (Drake and Llewellyn, 2001). They are able to compete with the investor-owned banks, and so their survival is good for the financial system as a whole (Llewellyn and Holmes, 1991).

MOBs are good in a crisis

only bank not affected

Further evidence of the sector's importance is pointed up by the current banking crisis. The massive public bail-out of private, investor-owned banks has underlined the virtues of a customer-owned co-operative banking system that is more risk-averse and less driven by the need to make profits for investors and bonuses for managers. Credit unions and co-operative banks all over the world are reporting that they are still financially sound, and that customers are flocking to bank with them because they are highly trusted. The point is an important one, because the co-operative banking sector is extraordinarily large; the World Council of Credit Unions has 49,000 credit unions in membership, with 177 million individual members in 96 countries. The International Raiffeisen Union estimates that 900,000 co-operatives with around 500 million members in over 100 countries are working according to the co-operative banking principles worked out in Germany by Friedrich Raiffeisen. The essence of co-operative banking is quite simple. It is that members, who include both savers and borrowers, use the co-op to recycle money from those who have it to those who need it, without anybody outside taking a profit and with interest rates set so that the system is self-sustaining.

Another crisis that has pointed up the advantages of MOBs is the recent increase in food and energy prices that will impact most severely on the world's poorest people. The World Bank estimates that food demand will double by 2030 as the world's population increases by another two billion people. There is an urgent need for developing countries to increase the output of food yet, as a recent World Bank Report has shown, the rural economy has been badly neglected (2008). The answer is to encourage farmers to mobilise collectively in associations that organise the supply, processing and marketing of crops and give them access to markets. Only in this way will they be able to increase the quantity and quality of outputs. Farmer-owned businesses are growing in most developing countries, but they need a lot more financial help and technical support if they are to reach their potential. India's dairy co-ops illustrate what can happen when a concerted effort is made over a long period of time: here, 100,000 dairy co-ops collect 16.5 million litres of milk from 12 million farmer members every day, making a massive contribution to India's food supply (OCDC, 2007).

Another crisis is the social exclusion and civil unrest caused by growing economic inequalities. The uneven effects of globalisation are felt everywhere, even in the world cities of London, New York and Tokyo, where an underclass services the global workforce. It is felt most in the mega-cities and remote rural areas of developing countries, where the problem is no longer one of economic exploitation by colonial powers but of indifference – they have been bypassed by the global system. The only way that a majority of people in the megacities (and a minority in the world cities) can get work is in an unregulated informal economy char-acterised by underemployment and poor wages. The only way they can begin to participate in the global economy and find decent work is through association, in credit co-ops that lend them money to start small businesses and shared service co-ops that support them in self-employment (Smith and Ross, 2006). The kind of financial 'deepening' that the World Bank envisages will only be achieved through MOBs; unlike NGOs that have a reputation for project-based lending that is unsustainable, co-ops consistently reach the poor in a sustainable way (World Bank, 2007).

Along with these crises is the looming prospect of the Millennium Development Goals not being met at their target date of 2015. This would mean the world has failed in its goals of eradicating extreme poverty and hunger, ensuring all children get primary education, ensur-ing gender equality, reducing child mortality and so on. There are good reasons for thinking that MOBs have in-built advantages in poverty reduction. The World Bank has identified three elements in an anti-poverty strategy: opportunity, empowerment and security. Because MOBs are economic associations, they provide the opportunity for poor people to raise their incomes. Because they are democracies with each member having one vote, they empower people to own their own solutions, and because they pool risks at the level of the enterprise and offer micro-insurance they increase security (Birchall, 2003). Also, there is now a great deal of evidence to show that they not only raise incomes but contribute directly to meeting several of the other MDGs (Birchall, 2004; Birchall and Simmons, 2009).

There is some evidence that even during conflicts MOBs can survive; in Sri Lanka and Nepal, they have been the only independent organ-isations allowed by both sides in the civil war zone. After conflicts, they often play a crucial role in restoring both economy and civil society. In East Timor, a network of 20,000 farmers has been formed that pro-cesses a third of the country's coffee for export (Bibby and Shaw, 2005). In Rwanda, after the genocide the credit union system was in ruins. It was rebuilt without regard to ethnicity, and now there are 149 unions with nearly 400,000 members. In Bosnia cheese co-ops, and in Monte-negro dairy co-ops, have encouraged displaced refugees to return, while in El Salvador electricity co-ops have boosted the local economy so ex-combatants can find work. Similar stories can be told of Guatemala, Lebanon, Azerbaijan, Serbia and Montenegro. There is also evidence of MOBs bridging longstanding ethnic divides; electricity co-ops in Bangladesh have a common membership among the 28 million users, and in India dairy co-ops treat members of different castes as equals.

The plan of the book

At this point it is hoped that the case has been made for the importance of 'seeing' this previously overlooked category of people-centred business that we call, for convenience, an MOB. Chapter 2 provides a comprehensive theory of what we might call the 'ecology' of member-owned businesses that explains why they began in particular places and at particular times, why they have survived or disappeared, and what might be their prospects for the future under the twin challenges of globalisation and world recession. It draws on a variety of theoretical perspectives such as business ecology, transaction cost economics, social capital theory, collective action theory, theories of market failure and so on. The end result is a quite comprehensive explanatory theory that can then be applied to each type of MOB in turn. Chapters 3 to 8 provide the main part of the book, presenting the history and ecology of each type of MOB in a series of stages from founding through growth to consolidation, decline and renewal. This main section uses the explanatory theory of Chapter 2 to explain why each type has developed in the way it has, and to identify organisational comparative advantages. It deals with issues such as demutualisation and the effects of globalisation on each sector.

Chapter 3 provides an analysis of consumer-ownership in retailing through consumer co-operatives, showing how the sector began in Britain and by the end of the 19th century had grown spectacularly all round the developed world. It shows how in several countries in Europe this form fell back under intense competition from IOBs, but is now enjoying a period of recovery and in some countries strong growth. It shows how the very large consumer co-ops are meeting the challenge of globalisation through joint buying but how, as in the IOB sector, expansion from one country to another remains problematic. It shows how issues such as fair trade with developing countries, ethical shopping, and the 'local food' movement are providing new impetus for this type of MOB. Harnessed to a member-relations strategy and tangible member benefits, these can enable even the largest consumer co-ops to be, to some extent, member-driven.

Chapter 4 analyses consumer-ownership in insurance, identifying three basic types: friendly societies (known in North America as fraternal societies), mutual insurance companies and secondary insurers owned by other types of MOBs. It traces the history of friendly societies, showing how there was enormous growth in most developed countries, followed by a period of state intervention in health care. Depending on which of four forms public policy took, in some countries their position as major providers of health insurance was consolidated, while in others their role was undermined and they began to decline. It then traces the history of mutual insurance companies in life and non-life insurance, analysing the reasons for, and effects of, the widespread conversion to IOBs. It finds that there is a persistent problem of lack of member-involvement in governance that partly explains the ease with which demutualisation occurred. Finally, it identifies a rather difficult to identify but very large sector, of secondary level insurers owned by other MOBs that seems to be doing rather well.

Chapter 5 distinguishes between house building and permanent housing co-ops, and then distinguishes further among permanent co-ops between full equity, limited equity and non-equity types. It traces their history in Norway and Sweden and New York where they have become dominant in apartment block housing, and in Western Europe and Canada where they have become significant minority tenures. It describes the interplay between different tenure forms, showing how sometimes co-ops offer an alternative to owner-occupation, sometimes to private or social renting. It explains under what circumstances collectively-owned housing can and cannot evolve.

Chapter 6 analyses several areas of consumer-ownership in public services, focusing on health care, education, utilities (water, electricity, telecoms, and transport), and leisure services. It tackles the difficult question of the relationship between member-ownership and public-ownership, demonstrating how governments have sometimes provided windows of opportunity for membership-based providers, but often have preferred a public monopoly (or in the case of utilities a private, regulated monopoly) that has prevented the MOB option from being tried. It discusses the question of how to design both public and member-ownership into the governance of service delivery agencies, suggesting that multi-stakeholding public benefit companies will be preferred to the simpler form of a consumer MOB. However, where a simple service has to be delivered on contract, the employee-owned business has potential.

Chapter 7 analyses consumer/producer-ownership in banking. First it traces the history of building societies, known in the USA as savings and loans. It assesses the impact of demutualisation and makes links between recurrent banking crises, the loss of MOB status and increase in risk. Then it traces the founding of co-operative banks in Germany and its subsequent spread throughout the world. It identifies three stages in growth; the first through Europe, the second (in the form of the credit union) through North America, and the third (driven by the World Council of Credit Unions) throughout most of the world. It then provides some statistical evidence for the consolidation of the older sectors in Europe and North America, showing that the co-operative form has achieved a remarkably large market share. It describes the impact of globalisation on co-operative banking, and assesses the effects of growing complexity and expansion across borders on member-governance. Then it shows how resilient co-operative banks are in the current financial crisis and draws lessons from member-ownership for the reconstruction of a global regulatory system for banking.

Chapter 8 analyses producer-owned businesses such as farmer co-ops, retailer-owned wholesalers and shared service co-ops. It assesses the impact that globalisation is having on the ownership structure of very large producer-owned conglomerates, providing a typology to explain the way farmer-ownership is evolving and, in some cases, becoming diluted. Then it discusses the complex relationship between retailer and wholesaler in the ownership of distribution systems, and brings into focus the rather hazy notion of a shared service co-operative. It analyses the history and ecology of employee-ownership, explaining why worker co-ops have such a mixed history of success and failure, and extracting lessons from the successes of Mondragon and North Italy. It traces the origins of more partial forms of employee-ownership in the USA. Finally, it provides some evidence on what effect the current recession is having on all these types of MOB.

Chapter 9 considers the particular problems of MOBs in developing countries. It accounts for the weaknesses of co-operative businesses, showing how in the postcolonial period they were first dominated by government and considered to be public sector organisations and then, from the 1980s onwards, subjected to all the rigours of privatisation and structural adjustment. The chapter shows that the international policy context is favourable, but that continued interference by governments and political parties keeps some traditional co-operative movements dependent. Case studies of Sri Lanka and Tanzania are introduced to show how new member-based social movements are emerging, particularly among women, and mainly in the credit sector. The argument for membership-based businesses is re-evaluated, and applied in particular to rural development and farm-based economies, with recognition that a new type of farmer association may be the way forward.

Chapter 10 reviews the comparative advantages and disadvantages of MOBs. It finds that the main weakness is a *lack of member-involvement*, made worse by the pressures of intensified market competition and globalisation, and ending in demutualisation. It finds, on the other hand, that their main strength is in the *idea of membership*. If this can be made more concrete and woven into the way that MOBs do business, it gives them a unique advantage over their competitors. The chapter identifies the need to nurture members through an explicit membership strategy to which managers and boards must give priority. It shows how such a strategy is built on a sound understanding of human motivation and an ability to discriminate between different types of member. It discusses the impact of membership on governance, recommends a two-tier board structure and identifies various dangers that would dilute the idea of membership. These range from a possessive individualism that is inimical to co-operation to its opposite; an over-idealistic view that sees it as the solution to more problems than it can possibly solve. The chapter identifies challenges such as the growing complexity of MOBs, the impact of transnational memberships and the ignorance of this type of business among young people. Borrowing a concept from evolutionary psychology, it suggests that a co-operative 'meme' is needed, a simple way of encapsulating the idea of membership that will enable it to spread among populations.

2
Theorising the Rise and Fall of Member-owned Businesses

Organisations are difficult to understand. They are comprised of people yet they survive even when the people within them change. They are a collective endeavour but in legal terms have the status of an individual 'person'. Metaphors such as a machine or an organism are both useful depending on what aspects of an organisation we want to see, but no one metaphor seems to capture it all. We need to be able to look at it in different ways; it has hard features such as structures and systems, soft features such as shared norms and values, overt features such as organisational charts and hidden features such as habits and routines. If we are to understand MOBs, we need to look at internal processes such as the relationships that exist between owners, managers and board members that determine their governance. We need to look at external processes such as the networks that exist between MOBs, or the regulatory environment a particular type of MOB finds itself in.

Some researchable questions

What are we focusing on; individual MOBs or whole sectors? Ecological theorists point out that there are four possible levels of analysis (Hannan and Freeman, 1989). First there are *individual organisations*. These are not all that interesting in themselves unless they are founder members of this type of MOB, or are big enough to be major players in a sector (such as the Co-operative Group in the UK, Rabobank in the Netherlands or Metsalitto in Finland). We study these not because they are particularly successful but because they represent a large part, or even in some countries the whole part, of an MOB population. In fact, we should beware of the kind of case study approach that focuses on the most successful or innovative business, as this can give a false picture of the population as a whole. Second, there is the *demographic level*, at which all the MOBs in a particular market are identified. Here we are interested in variations in vital rates for organisational populations. Examples would be the rise and decline of the building society sector in the UK or the mutual savings and loans sector in the USA. At the third level we are into *population ecology*, looking at the variation in vital rates for populations in relation to other populations; the environment that MOBs are in contains populations of other types of organisation within the same sector. Here we want to know how the different types compare in efficiency and effectiveness, and how distinctive they are from each other. Examples would be the home loans sector in the USA, where we would compare mutual versus investor-owned savings and loans, or the retail sector in Italy, where we would compare co-operatives with multiple chains. At the top level there is a *community ecology* of organisations. Here we are looking at a whole sector without being interested in organisational types. This level is not very important for our purposes, except where a whole industry is in trouble and this explains the demise of co-operatives. The cotton industry in parts of India or Tanzania would be a good example; here farmer co-operatives ceased to exist because the industry itself ceased to exist.

What are we interested in finding out? The main question is: How significant are member-owned businesses in the wider scheme of things? This can be broken down into three types of question. First there are the *how questions*: these are largely descriptive, and a good answer would tell the story of where and in what sector a particular type of MOB originated, how it grew, whether and to what extent it has declined or changed its character, or converted to another type. Second, there are the *why questions*; these are largely analytical and theoretical, and a good answer would explain why a particular type of MOB began, why it grew, why it has declined or had a new lease of life. Third, there are the *what questions*: these are normative, asking what a particular form has contributed to meeting people's needs, what has it done that is distinctive or innovative, or challenging, what has it contributed to the wider business environment. It also concerns what its current potential is in relation to contemporary issues such as environmental sustainability, poverty reduction, gender equality, fair trade and so on. All of these questions can be answered at the three levels (see Table 2.1).

In addition, we need to identify periods in the evolution of organisations; they are founded at some point in time, most of them grow, sometimes they decline, and they may die and cease to exist, or merge

Table 2.1   Some important questions

Level of analysis	The How Question	The Why Question	The What Question
Individual organisation	How has this organisation survived?	Why has it survived?	What is its wider significance?
Demography	How has the sector evolved?	Why has it evolved in this way?	What has it achieved?
Population ecology	How has it evolved in relation to competitor organisational types?	Why has it achieved its current market share?	What has it achieved in comparison with its competitors?

with other organisations, or convert to a different ownership type. Let us, for convenience, identify seven periods: founding, growth, consolidation, decline, death, conversion and renewal. For there to be a phenomenon to study, the first two periods need to have happened but the story from then on may include all sorts of twists and turns leading to inertia, death or renewal. A lazy way of understanding this would be to talk about organisational life cycles, as if MOBs were organisms that are born and grow, wear out and die. We will not be doing that here, because, although it is tempting to talk of organisations growing old and of inertia setting in, unlike organisms they can be renewed or transmute into another form.

Some useful explanatory theories

What theories are most useful in helping us to answer these questions? Organisational ecology seems promising, but it has three drawbacks. First, it remains very theoretical and there is a lack of empirical studies that make the distinction between different ownership types. Second, there are limits to the extent to which the evolutionary metaphor can be used to generate insights. Just as organisations are not organisms, nor are MOBs collectively a species to which ideas of natural selection apply. They are not the product of natural evolution but have been purposefully designed and can be redesigned. While the ecological view reminds us that change is difficult and that inertia is common, particularly in large, well-established organisations, it is not good at explaining the 'rebirth' of organisations. Nor should we just assume that because an organisation type survives it has adapted well or is the fittest (Hannan and Freeman, 1989), though it is safe to assume that the survivors are more fit than those that have died!

In the next few chapters we will be tracing the 'evolution' of different types of MOB, but using the term suggestively rather than trying to fit their history point by point into a framework derived from biological evolution. This is why we put heavy reliance on the work of historians, who are good at providing detailed accounts of what happened and when, who was involved and how a particular type took off. Historical accounts are important because they enable us to trace the lasting effects of the conditions under which an organisation was founded. An organisation's history strongly constrains its subsequent possibilities, and the social and economic conditions at founding have lasting effects. Theorists call this 'path dependence', which is as Hannan and Freeman put it 'a condition where the present possibilities depend on the previous trajectory of events' (1989: 11). In its weakest form, path dependency means no more than that 'where we are today is a result of what has happened in the past' (Margolis and Liebowitz, 2009: 1). In its strongest form, the theory suggests that decisionmakers are so constrained by the legacy of the past that they are locked into inefficient ways of working but cannot escape from them; this is an intriguing idea but the evidence for this kind of 'lock in' is not very strong.

In the history of an organisational form there are not only paths but critical moments when decisions are made that have fateful consequences. One of these is the decision by consumer co-operatives in Western Europe to give up paying a dividend on purchases and to use discount stamps instead; the consequences of this for member-involvement were drastic but unforeseen. Critical moments are more important in sectors where MOB development depends on changes in legislation or government policies. For instance, the decision by the British government in 1918 to subsidise public sector housing rather than co-partnership prevented the development of housing co-operatives until the 1960s. The decision by the Swedish government in the 1990s to open up education provision to competition from an independent sector had the opposite effect.

In the literature on co-operatives historians tend to emphasise the importance of wider processes such as nationalism, ethnic homogeneity, social equality, or high levels of literacy among the populations that were first exposed to the idea of co-operation. In this way, they describe what we might call 'fertile ground' for co-operation. They are also able to trace the relationship between economic forces and co-operative development. Consumer co-operation, for instance, followed in the wake of more general industrialisation, beginning in Britain and then spreading across Northern France and Germany, proving popular among urbanised, working class populations but not developing well in more cosmopolitan areas such as seaports or capital cities or in rural areas (Birchall, 1997). Agricultural and credit co-operation tended to follow the emergence of new markets, and appealed most to small, owner-occupier farmers rather than tenant farmers or large landlords.

However, the problem is that such high level causes are difficult to pin down, and we can always find examples that argue against the theory. For instance, ethnic and political divisions have been cited to explain the slow development of agricultural co-operation in Ireland as compared to Denmark (Cole, 1944). Yet, at the time co-operative development began, Finland also had deep divisions; between the Swedish and Finnish speaking populations and between 'social democratic' and 'neutral' political groupings. This did not seem to slow down development but produced separate but equally strong co-operative movements. The pattern of landholding has been cited to explain why farmers take to co-operation; the assumption is that small farmers need co-operatives more, and that land reform to create smallholdings is a necessary precondition for co-operative development. Yet in late 19th century German agricultural co-operation took hold among large farmers as well as small ones (Fay, 1938).

Also, it is difficult to distinguish cause from effect. For instance, the very high level of co-operative development reached in Denmark by the end of the 19th century can partly be explained by the high level of education due to the folk high school movement. Yet in Finland, while credit unions spread quickly during the early 20th century, it was only *after* they were set up that local people became educated and their levels of understanding of financial matters improved (Kuustera, 1999). We have to give up asking 'what caused what?' and realise that complex forces have been at work historically that interact as part of a systemic movement towards, or away from, co-operative development.

There is a more systematic way to create plausible explanations, through the idea of social capital; the higher the social capital the more likely co-operative development is to take place. Robert Putman illustrated this in a study of North Italy, showing that a high density of associational life (including co-operatives) is associated with high levels of social capital that go back several hundred years (1994). The idea is a simple one; it is a set of shared norms that encourage co-operation between people, what we might call a 'propensity to co-operate'. It includes a general expectation that if one co-operates others will too. It

also includes a willingness to reward co-operative behavi
approval, and to use sanctions against un-co-operative beh..
to avoid 'free-riding' by people who want the benefits of co-opt.
without contributing. There are several indicators that can be used t
measure the level of social capital: the general level of trust in others; the
level of participation in civic institutions; the density of informal networks; level of membership of formal associations, and so on (Putnam,
2000).

There are two types of social capital, bonding and bridging. Bonding
means having strong local networks with people who are like each
other, while bridging means having networks that reach beyond a local
community or class to people who are unalike but together may have
more power to affect change. In order to work well, it is said that both
types need to be present. For instance, in Finland at the end of the
19th century both were in abundance; there was a class of small farmer-
foresters who had much in common, and were convinced to co-operate
by a group of middle class intellectuals who reached out to them with
a strong message underpinned by a common sense of national identity
(Pellervo Federation, 2000). On the other hand, when there is strong
bonding social capital but a lack of bridging, there is a tendency for
MOB sectors to become defensive and unable to change to survive in
new circumstances (Svendsen and Svendsen, 2004).

What causes high levels of social capital? One cause is *associational
involvement*; participating in a club or association makes people more
prepared to reciprocate and trust others. It also equips them with
the skills they need to run organisations, and so forming and sustaining co-operatives becomes easier. In Switzerland the first producer
co-operatives built on some ancient types of association such as the
'fruitieres' for cheese-making. In Britain, the early consumer co-ops formed
part of a wider set of mutual aid associations such as friendly societies
and trade unions. Another cause is *social homogeneity*. People are more
likely to trust and have common interests with people who are like
them. This does not mean a whole nation needs to be homogeneous,
though it is said that the early co-operative movement in Finland benefitted from a strong sense of nationalism and in Denmark from a common Lutheran religious background. Communities are needed that are
high in bonding social capital. If they are self-confident enough to have
bridging social capital, their co-operatives can bridge divides. However,
it is notable that in Sweden farmers who support the Centre Party have
very little in common with urban consumers who support the Social
Democrats, and so the producer and consumer co-operatives have

remained quite separate. In Finland, similar political divides have produced two distinct consumer co-operative movements, and so on.

Another cause is *egalitarian social structures*. Societies that are low in social capital are often also strongly hierarchical and have a legacy of exploitation; Southern Italy has the Mafia, southern states of the USA have a legacy of slavery and racism, and so on. Not only do such societies score low in social capital but they actively undermine most forms of social capital (Halpern, 2005: 269–271). In such regions, there are plenty of examples of co-operatives working to heal divides and create new social capital, but it is hard going. The countries with the largest concentration in the world of co-operative businesses are Iceland, Finland, Sweden, Norway and Denmark (Birchall, 2009), and the Scandinavians are well known for egalitarian social structures that go a long way back in their history; they were among the first to come out of the old feudal system of land tenure, provide universal education, and extend voting rights. Compare their near neighbour, Scotland, which has a much more mixed history; strongly egalitarian in the industrial lowlands, but highly unequal in landholdings in the Highlands and Islands (though community land buyouts are beginning to change this pattern in favour of the crofters). During the 19th century, while a strong and successful consumer co-operative system was being founded in the towns and cities, much of the indigenous population of the rural areas were being forcibly evicted to make way for tenant sheep-farmers. It is no wonder that a producer co-operative sector took a long time to emerge, and that rural co-operative banks were not even tried.

A related cause is *economic equality*. Where people are equal, they have similar interests and can more easily agree on common goals, and there are not many examples of co-operatives that have in membership people with widely different needs and resources. In contrast, economic inequality has been found to have a close negative correlation with social capital at all levels, from the nation state to the village (Halpern, 2005). The Scandinavian countries are among the most equal in terms of income, and they have developed strong welfare states that do not just protect those who fall into poverty but also actively redistribute incomes.

Whatever its causes, social capital is remarkably persistent over time. When it is measured across different regions of the USA, the differences correspond closely to the differences in social capital in the nations from which their ancestors came. The area around Minneapolis and St Paul's – that shows up on most measures as the area of highest social capital in the USA – was populated with 'high trust Scandinavians'. As David Halpern notes 'Something has persisted over several generations'

(Halpern, 2005). Also, Scandinavian countries still show up as having the highest level of social trust in the world. While the levels of social capital in the USA, Australia and Britain are declining, they are said to be rising in Sweden. While all developed nations are becoming more individualistic, in Sweden they have managed to create a 'solidaristic individualism'. Many Swedes would disagree, arguing that their society is undergoing fundamental changes away from the kind of corporatist welfare state that used to be a benchmark for civilised society. Still, on a graph of 'national trust' compiled by the World Values Survey, Sweden and Finland (plus their neighbours, Norway, the Netherlands and Denmark) come out way ahead as 'high and rising trust' societies, with Switzerland and the UK described as 'moderate but falling trust' societies (Halpern, 2005: 217). Why should social capital be so persistent over time? Game theorists have shown that there is an 'ecology' of co-operation; over time societies reach a stable equilibrium of co-operative behaviour. Some, like our comparator countries, stabilise at a very high level of co-operation, others at a lower level. That stability then tends to persist over generations (Axelrod, 1984).

None of this explains why people's propensity to co-operate should take a particular form. To explain the rise and fall of particular co-operative sectors we need more economic explanations. Economists point to the impetus to co-operate that comes from market failure. If primary producers are cut off from emerging markets, they will tend to organise themselves in transport and marketing co-ops, as did the wheat farmers of Canada when setting up wheat pool co-operatives. If they are forced to rely on private traders for the purchase of inputs or provision of credit, or to sell to 'middlemen' who are in a monopoly position, they are likely to take action to remedy the situation; this was the main impetus behind the setting up of commodity-specific co-operatives in developing countries. Similarly, if consumers are forced to pay high prices for adulterated food, and are locked into credit-based relationships with small retailers, again they will welcome the chance to provide for themselves on terms that eliminate the 'middlemen'; this was a major stimulus to the early British consumer co-operative sector (Birchall, 1994). Private monopolies in supply have led directly to action by consumers; the earliest recorded consumer action in England was the setting up of corn mills by shipwrights of coastal towns who were suffering from high prices charged by millers. In Sweden and Finland, in the 1920s farmers and consumers took collective action against cartels that were charging them monopoly prices for a whole range of products from fertilisers to light bulbs. Market failures also include gaps in the market where an important good is not provided by anyone, and this explains the rapid growth of credit co-operatives in continental Europe in the early 20th century. It also explains why they did not develop in Britain, because here there were already alternatives such as savings banks and building societies.

Of course, even when there is market failure, people will not always organise co-operatively, and some other theory is needed to explain how they get over the 'collective action' problem. Political scientists are interested in what circumstances lead to collective action, since a 'rational actor' theory predicts that unless there are personal incentives people will not act together (Olson, 1971). There are two ways of getting round this problem. First, it seems that in most cases where successful MOB sectors have developed, leaders have emerged who do not seem to mind incurring the costs of organising. They tend to be motivated by political, religious or humanitarian convictions that seem to override the rational actor equation, and in most cases they are relatively wealthy and so can stand the costs more easily than others. In an early co-operative movement in Britain, for instance, a medical doctor William King published a newspaper, the 'Co-operator', that provided the inspiration and the information needed for the founding of around 300 societies. In Finland it was Gebhard, in Germany Raiffeisen and Schultze-Delitsch, in Canada Desjardins and Cody, in Ireland Plunkett, that drove the movement forward. These leaders were adept at using their connections to create a favourable environment through new legislation, the spread of workable business models, and the creation of a social movement.

The second way of overcoming Olson's problem is to expand the theory to include broader motivations than just personal benefit. Birchall and Simmons have compared individualistic and collectivistic motivations to participate in co-operatives, and found that people are a lot more collectivistic in their attitudes than 'rational actor' theorists will allow (2004a, 2004b). Their mutual incentives theory predicts that, when people are asked to participate in organisations that represent their interests, they will be motivated by shared values, shared goals and a sense of community, as well as by more personal incentives. The more people are motivated by these three collectivistic incentives, the more likely they are to participate.

Some useful co-operative theories

Are there other, specifically co-operative theories that might be used to explain differences between countries? The most influential may be

Attwood and Bhaviskar's theory of 'a conducive environment for co-operatives'. Developed in India in the 1980s, their work shows that co-ops tend to flourish when there is a sympathetic government, and a cultural and legal environment that supports co-operative development. The passing of co-operative laws in many countries at the turn of the 20th century, and their promotion by influential promoters explain quite a lot about the early development of co-operation (For Finland, see Kuisma et al, 1999). However, the theory is contradicted by a large study of Indian agricultural co-ops undertaken in the early 1990s by Tushaar Shah. India is a federal country, and unique in having different co-operative environments; different laws and attitudes by government, different attitudes to leadership and entrepreneurship in each regional state. What Shah found was that there were co-operative failures even in states where the environment was good and some successful co-ops even where it was bad. Where co-ops were successful they helped shape their own environment, so that government was not strong enough to take them over or interfere in their running (Shah, 1996). This is true of the early British experience; the development of the Rochdale-based consumer movement in the 19th century preceded legislation, and sympathetic politicians were merely asked to make the way clear for new developments such as limited liability and wholesaling.

Shah's explanation for co-operative success and failure looks inside a co-operative at the 'design principles' on which it is built, particularly within its governance structure. He identifies three conditions for success:

1. the purpose of the organisation is central to the members
2. the governance structure ensures patronage cohesiveness
3. the operating system finds competitive advantage in the relationship with members

Under these conditions, co-operatives will not only survive but will be replicated by people who are in similar circumstances and want to gain similar advantages for themselves. They will take the organisational design that works in one place, try it out in another place and modify it as necessary. This hints at an evolutionary theory of co-operation, in which forms that work survive and are replicated, while others – no matter how hard they are promoted by governments – will fail.

Shah's theory complements Henry Hansmann's theory of ownership. This theory predicts that business types will survive if their governance costs are lower than those of other types; the more homogeneous the interests of members the more likely the survival (Hansmann, 1996).

Hansmann uses transaction costs theory to help us understand why member-ownership is preferred in some situations and not in others. There are two propositions. First, if the costs of bringing stakeholders into ownership are lower than the transaction costs incurred in having a contractual relationship with them, then a MOB form will be chosen. This can be illustrated in cases such as life insurance, where there is a long-term contract, a potential problem of lack of trust between owners and customers, and an uncertain outcome. Here, the mutual form is chosen because the costs of keeping policyholders inside the business are lower than those of keeping them outside. The opposite also applies; where the costs of keeping customers inside the business become too high, conversion to an IOB can be predicted. Second, Hansmann brings in market failures to explain why people sometimes choose MOBs even though the costs of ownership are relatively high; it is because the alternatives – such as entering into market relations with a private monopoly – are even more costly.

Albert Hirschmann's hugely influential theory of exit, voice and loyalty has never been applied systematically to co-ops, even though he says his generalisations apply 'largely – and at times principally – to organisations that provide services to their members' (1970: 3). He predicts that the ability of a firm to avoid what he calls 'organisational slack' (under-performance and a tendency to decline) depends on the particular combination of ability to exit, willingness to exercise voice and degree of loyalty among its customers. In co-operatives and mutuals, customers who are also the owner-members tend to exercise voice rather than exit, because leaving is too costly. They also tend to become loyal and so are reluctant to leave even when the MOB is under-performing. However, if MOBs are not able to demand patronage, and their members only have a token membership share, exit is made much easier. We can expect that successful co-operatives and mutuals will demand a significant financial investment from members that they cannot easily get back, and will reward them for loyalty, as well as providing plenty of opportunities for them to exercise their 'voice'. The 'new generation' agricultural co-operatives in the Mid-West of the USA are a good example; they require members to invest capital in proportion to the amount of product they supply to the co-operative.

These theories tend to remain at the level of the primary MOB, but of course one of the strengths of MOBs is that they network together and so gain market power that they would not have otherwise. Stephen Smith has studied business clustering in co-operatives, and analysed the success of the Mondragon co-operative system in Spain. He shows how a co-operative sector grows and becomes self-sustaining through developing its own supporting institutions such as savings banks, research and development companies, training institutes and so on (Smith, 2003). Birchall and Simmons' recent study of co-operatives in Tanzania and Sri Lanka compares features of co-ops and their competitors – private traders, NGOs, government initiative – that give them comparative advantages and disadvantages (2008). It is not possible to explain the presence of MOBs without analysing their advantages when compared to those of their competitors.

The theories summarised

The approach taken here can be summed up in these four propositions:

1. no one theory is sufficient to explain success and failure in co-operatives
2. there is no substitute for gathering lots of information about a particular sector and trying to understand it from a variety of standpoints
3. sometimes one theory will work better than another
4. theories stand or fall by their plausibility in explaining what is going on, and by their usefulness in helping us to understand how to make co-operatives work better

Table 2.2 lists the theories, what they say about the conditions under which co-operatives can thrive and the kinds of outcomes they predict.

Theorising periods in the 'ecology' of member-owned businesses

Earlier, we identified seven periods in the development of MOBs: founding, growth, consolidation, decline, death, conversion and renewal. These can be applied both to individual organisations and to a whole group of organisations that share the same characteristics, in this case member-ownership. Theorising these periods depends on deductive reasoning from the kind of theories outlined above and inductive reasoning from historical accounts, case studies and other empirical studies. Putting these together, we can identify important factors that are likely to be present at each period.

First, there is a *founding period* in which a new organisation is created, is successful and enables learning to take place so that others follow.

Table 2.2   **Theories that explain why co-operatives succeed or fail**

Type of theory	*Conditions for co-operation*	*Outcomes*
Social history	Solidarity derived from nationalism or political party, high level of general education, political enfranchisement, land reform, substantial equality of condition	The ability to create solidary institutions that are well governed and command allegiance. A preference for mutual over charitable forms of organisation
Economic history	Formation of new classes (eg urban working class, small farmers). Expanding market society, dependence on money income, and need to access markets. Lack of competitors or threat of monopoly among competitors	Strong need among people in same market position to co-operate. Commitment to economic co-operation because alternatives either do not exist or are threatening to the livelihoods of people who have weak market position
Sociology	High levels of social capital, both bonding and bridging	Resources available to 'invest' in membership organisations and networks, with assurance of success and mutual benefit
Economics	Market failures – threat of monopoly, power of 'middlemen' or lack of markets. Low barriers to entry, weak competitors	The co-operative difference and co-operative advantage in business
Political science	The collective action problem is overcome, through selective incentives and sanctions against 'free riders'	Organisations are created and members recruited who have incentive to participate in governance
Mutual incentives theory (Birchall and Simmons)	People do respond to collectivistic incentives: sense of community, shared values and goals	Co-operatives achieve high levels of participation, and can develop a member participation strategy
Supportive environment theory (Attwood and Bhaviskar)	Presence of promoters, good legal and fiscal environment. Govt support but respect for autonomy of civil society	Development of co-operatives unfolds in stages, with strong, autonomous organisations created

Table 2.2   **Theories that explain why co-operatives succeed or fail**
– *continued*

Type of theory	Conditions for co-operation	Outcomes
Theory of co-operative design and evolution (Shah)	Design principles are discovered that put the member at centre of the business. These are replicated	Strong co-operative sectors emerge that command loyalty of members and maintain member focus over time
Theory of ownership (Hansmann)	A stakeholder will take ownership if this combats market failure, and/or if the costs of ownership are low. The more homogeneous the owners the lower the costs	Cooperatives are only be found in some sectors and at some times, because they need a homogeneous group of members with common interests
Theory of voice (Hirschmann)	If the cost of exit is high, members will exercise voice instead. Loyalty raises the costs of exit and promotes voice	Co-ops that foster loyalty through patronage refunds, give opportunities for voice, and demand financial commitment from members will survive

For consumer co-operatives it was the Rochdale Pioneers society in England; for rural co-operative banks it was the Anhausen society in Germany; for worker co-partnership it was Godin's iron foundry at Guise in France; for permanent building societies it was the Metropolitan Equitable in London, England and so on. These societies were not necessarily the first to be founded; for instance, the Rochdale Pioneers had been members of an earlier society that had failed. They were the first to be successful, to prove that this type of business organisation was viable and had potential. The first condition for success is that there are unmet needs that the new society is demonstrably able to meet. In Rochdale in the early 1840s, the weaving trade was in a deep depression and the opening of a store was seen as one way of alleviating terrible poverty. Similarly, the early co-operative banks in Germany were founded on the back of charitable efforts by their leaders to relieve the distress of impoverished farmers. Not all needs were so dramatic; building societies and savings and loans were founded to provide a safe haven for people's savings and a chance for middle-income people to become home owners. Another condition is that other types of business are not currently meeting the need. For instance, it was because commercial banks were uninterested in servicing the needs of low-income people and in some cases because trustee-based savings banks were seen as unsafe, that co-operative banking began.

Another condition is that potential members can draw on social capital, which consists of a propensity towards generalised trust, dense social networks through which information can flow, and a willingness to co-operate that overcomes short-termism and immediate self-interest. Accounts of these founding stages are full of references to common bonds generated by religious, politics or ethnic identities. For instance, the Rochdale Pioneers had in common multiple commitments to Owenite socialism, Unitarianism, trade unionism and Chartism (Birchall, 1995a). However, too much bonding social capital and not enough bridging can lead to sectarianism; within a few years of the Rochdale society being set up, a Conservative co-operative society was formed in the same town that had no economic rationale but was a consequence of political disagreements.

As well as favourable conditions, there have to be more specific factors that lead to the overcoming of the collective action problem. People have to be prepared to act and for this they need leaders. As we shall see in the next few chapters, the historical accounts are full of the work of leaders. They can be seen as people who can pull together a variety of resources in order to make thing happen. Some have been good at publicising the idea: for instance William King, whose magazine the Co-operator inspired an early co-operative movement that began in his home town of Brighton, England, or the journalist George Jacob Holyoake who popularised the story of the Rochdale Pioneers. Some have been good at pulling together political resources so as to pass enabling legislation: Hannes Gebhard in Finland and Edward Vansittart Neale in Britain are examples. Some have been good at running a business; it was Charles Howarth and Abraham Greenwood of the Rochdale Pioneers whose management skills helped the society to survive the early period. However, not all leaders have been so helpful. Charles Fourier in France and Robert Owen in Britain have been credited with inspiring co-operative movements, but both were keen on a utopian ideal of the self-sufficient co-operative community, and this diverted their supporters into setting up communities which failed.

Despite the contribution made by highly educated and well connected middle class and upper class leaders, for a new type of MOB to emerge it was also necessary for leadership to develop among working class people who were more typical of the members as a whole. Also, it was only when more practical leaders emerged who knew how to run a store, a workshop, a corn mill or a wholesale agency that member-owned businesses really got going (see Birchall, 1994, ch.2). They tended to be drawn from among skilled artisans and small business people rather than the 'labouring classes'. A minimum level of basic education and experience were needed, and at this time in Britain artisans were often highly self-educated and had previous experience of running other kinds of member-owned businesses such as friendly societies.

Most important at this stage is for the founding society to develop a viable business model. The Rochdale Pioneers were not the first consumer co-operative society, nor were they even the first to invent the dividend on purchases that explains much of their success. Their unique contribution was in synthesising a business model that included a set of 'co-operative principles', vertical integration into wholesaling and manufacturing, and horizontal integration into a chain of stores. Philippe Buchez did the same thing for the French worker co-operatives, and Raifffeisen for the rural co-operative banks. As Shah has shown for producer co-operatives in India, having the right model and then encouraging people to replicate it is the key to success. The right model is one that binds the members to their representatives and calls their managers to account, something that the Rochdale principles do automatically provided they are adhered to and can evolve to meet different circumstances (Shah, 1996).

Second, there is a *period of growth* during which the replication of successful societies proceeds rapidly. For this to happen there have to be several factors. Economic prosperity is important, or at least a lack of serious recessions; the steady growth of consumer co-ops in Britain during the second half of the 19th century can partly be explained by a long upturn in the economy and improvements in the living standards of the poor (Burnett, 1989). Again, social capital is important; where it can be drawn on more generally it makes democratic governance less costly, and helps ensure member-loyalty. Linked to this is a high basic level of education among the population in general; it is hard to get people to take on the responsibilities of membership when they cannot read or write, and it is no surprise that the Rochdale-based movement put a lot of emphasis on basic adult education.

Emulation continues; new groups come together to set up new societies along the same lines and so the costs of collective action are reduced and there is less reliance on leaders. However, growth brings attention and a certain respectability, and political leaders attach themselves to the cause, and they provide new legislation in order to sweep away impediments to further growth. With growth come challenges from competitors who sometimes emulate the methods used by MOBs. Here it is a great advantage to those societies that grow early so as to achieve pre-eminence in a new sector; consumer co-ops in Europe, friendly societies in many countries, farmer co-operatives all had the advantages of being first in a new market. Where MOBs were not first but were powerful enough – in wheat marketing in Canada, and dairy and bacon processing in Denmark in the late 19th century, they were able to destroy the competition and create near monopoly status. Growth also enabled them to break up cartels and see off political challenges from competitors that seek restrictive legislation.

A *period of consolidation* often follows, in which no new societies are founded and there may even be a fall in numbers through mergers between very small societies. The sector maintains or increases its market share, and because of its large size it is in an advantageous position in relation to its competitors. It may have reached pre-eminence in a particular market, or have become protected by government regulation, like agricultural co-operatives in many countries during the 1930s, or the UK building society sector in the postwar period. Inertia may be setting in as the good reputation and financial soundness of the sector lead people to take it for granted, at the same time as the competition is gaining ground. This kind of problem was reported for the British co-operative sector by the Co-operative Independent Commission (1958). There may be a loss of meaning as new generations cease to understand about the advantages of member-ownership, and managerial dominance and an oligarchic leadership may lead to neglect of good governance. These kinds of problems were pointed out in an international report on the co-operative sector written by a Canadian co-operative leader, Alex Laidlaw (1980).

There may follow a *period of decline* as MOBs are unable to compete effectively, leading to a vicious circle of poor reputation, indifferent leadership, and inability to attract good managers. The decline of profitability may lead to a loss of interest by members, which may be exacerbated as societies abandon practices that reward members such as the well-known co-operative 'dividend'. There may be deep social changes that lead to the decoupling from social movements or geographical communities that used to supply social capital. Isomorphism may set in, as the attempt to become more like one's competitors; this may lead to a loss of loyalty among members, and a lack of distinctivenesss in the market. Poor governance may lead to what economists call, rather delicately, 'rent-seeking' among leaders and managers; at best a society may in fact be converted into a kind of non-profit led by its managers, while at worst there may be corruption and fraud.

Just like any other business, an MOB can enter a *period of terminal decline*, ending in bankruptcy. This is quite rare, because more often MOB federations will ensure that ailing societies are taken over by a healthier society. Sometimes, as in the Co-operative Retail Services in the UK, a special society is created just to rescue ailing societies and sell off the loss-making parts of their business. Sometimes this results in the gradual consolidation of a diverse sector into one or two large businesses, as in some large agricultural co-operatives in the USA and Finland, or consumer co-ops in Austria. However, mergers from weakness carry grave dangers, and sometimes when the resulting national society goes bankrupt a whole sector disappears; this happened to the national consumer co-operative, Consum Austria.

At some times in history, the state has been an enemy of co-operation. Communist states tended to take over existing co-operatives and turned them into public bodies under political direction; in 1935, for instance, Stalin abolished all urban consumer co-operatives, confiscating their assets without compensation to their members (Birchall, 1997: 52). More subtly, they would leave the co-operatives in place but take them over politically; during the cold war period, the International Co-operative Alliance had a difficult task deciding which of the communist consumer co-ops to allow into membership; East Germany was found to be too state-controlled but Centrosoyus of the Soviet Union was allowed in even though it was no more independent (Rhodes, 1995). Fascist states set about attacking co-operatives and murdering their leaders, and then incorporated them into the state; Mussolini did this in 1925, Hitler in 1933. There was one upside to this dismal story; Spanish and Italian co-operators who were forced into exile went on to set up successful member-owned business sectors in Latin America.

It is not just in fascist and communist countries that MOBs have been damaged by government action. In the 1930s there was a lot of protectionism and some democratic governments decided to replace agricultural marketing co-ops with state marketing boards. At the time it did not seem to be a significant line to cross, but looking back we can see that the decision was a critical one that privileged marketing co-ops in some countries and killed them off in others. This helps explain why, for instance, there is a large and old-established farmer-owned business sector in Finland but a small, more recently established one in Scotland (Birchall, 2009).

For MOBs that have lost touch with their members and whose boards of directors have been acting more like trustees than representatives, *conversion* to an investor-owned form is attractive. The catalyst for this seems to be new legislation and liberalisation of regulatory environments. First, they may allow conversion for the first time, as in the UK building society sector in 1986. Second, they may intensify competition and lead managers to see comparative advantages in becoming an IOB, as in the savings and loan and savings bank sectors in the USA in the early 1980s. The causes of demutualisation are well discussed in the literature. There are two dominant narratives, one positive and one negative. The positive one emphasises the need to raise capital in money markets and achieve the advantages gained by being an IOB, while the negative one emphasises self-interest and greed among managers and short-termism and lack of understanding of the idea of mutuality among members. Since the demise of savings and loans in the USA and former building societies in the UK, the second of these is gaining ground. Lastly, conversions may occur through weakness. Mistakes made by two very large UK life insurance companies led recently to their demutualisation, because they needed to be bailed out by new investor-owners (see Birchall, 2001). Less dramatically, life cycle effects in some types of co-operative can lead to sudden calls on the society's capital; in the 1990s Canadian wheat pools had to open up to investor-ownership because they could not meet increased commitments to members who were retiring.

Instead of death or conversion there can, of course, be a new lease of life. A *period of renewal* can occur in the oldest of businesses. First, new leaders may be appointed who see the potential. For instance, the UK Co-operative Bank became the world's leading ethical bank and a major innovator in the UK market after a new chief executive arrived in the 1980s (Birchall, 2005). It helped that he had a sympathetic board that, linked to the economic power of the largest co-operative retailer, were able to do without profits for several years while the Bank grew. Second, consolidation of societies in one national body can turn a business round as new expertise is hired and primary societies are offered new business services; this has happened in several co-operative banking federations such as Rabobank in the Netherlands. Third, links to a new social movement may revivify an MOB sector, particularly if it also involves an influx of new leaders. For instance, the fair trade movement has recently led to a renewed interest in consumer co-operatives in the UK and Italy. Fourth, occasionally, a bold step can be taken to take an MOB out of a sector in which it is not competing effectively and concentrating it somewhere else; in the 1990s, the UK Co-operative Group gave up trying to compete with superstore chains and concentrated on small supermarkets and convenience trading, where it quickly gained pre-eminence.

Table 2.3   Some periods in the life of a MOB sector

Periods	Main features	Challenges faced
Founding period	• Unmet needs, not met by other forms of business • Specific social capital: common bonds and networks • Leadership with a wide range of skills and experience • A viable business model	To overcome the collective action problem
Period of growth	• A replicable business model that can be emulated • Economic prosperity • Long-term social capital and widespread basic education • Supportive political leadership • Being first in the market • Ability to break up cartels, defend v political opposition	To replicate the business model as far as it will go
Period of consolidation	• Favourable government legislation and regulation • Inertia setting in, with problems of poor and oligarchic governance • Growth falling off, but market share rising	To avoid inertia and complacency
Period of decline	• Inheritance of an outdated asset base and technology • Inability to compete with the competitors, or attract good managers • Loss of market share and sale of assets to cover losses • merger of weak societies • Isomorphism, loss of rewards to members • Defensive boards, manager takeover, corruption • Loss of social capital	To refocus the business and redeploy assets, reconnect with members

Table 2.3   **Some periods in the life of a MOB sector** – *continued*

Periods	Main features	Challenges faced
Death of the sector	• Societies are sold off or go bankrupt and the federal is unable to prevent this, or • Whole sector reorganises as one unit, then goes bankrupt or • The state nationalises or destroys it	Too late
Demutualisation	• Negative narrative: attempt to asset strip and pursue self-interested short term gain • Positive narrative: attempt to gain comparative advantage • Conversion as a strategy to avoid bankrupcy	To see the best business case without short-term self interest and to defend viable mutuals
Renewal	• New leaders who see the potential comparative advantages renew the norms, values, traditions of the past • New ways are found to reward member loyalty eg bringing back the dividend • New ways found to connect members with social issues • Alignment with social movements brings influx of new leaders and members • Consolidation/reorganising of the asset base leads to ability to hire good managers and invest in new products, markets • Concentration on markets where there is an OCA increases market share	To find a mutual comparative advantage, align the sector with social movements

Finally, in the largest and most powerful MOBs a new *period of internationalisation* is being entered into as they attempt to compete with their competitors in regional and global markets. This calls for radical changes that may involve setting up subsidiaries that are not member-owned, or the setting up of an investor-owned holding company. We will be discussing this in more depth in Chapter 11 when we discuss the impact of globalisation. Table 2.3 is a summary of some of the main features of each of the seven periods.

Where to begin

This chapter has identified some general theories that explain why MOB sectors are more or less successful. It has identified more specific co-operative theories that can make the explanation more complete. It has considered the background conditions and foreground factors that affect MOBs at different periods in their life cycle. We should now be able to get on and begin to provide a detailed description and analysis of each of the MOB sectors in turn. However, there is one more question to be asked first. Where, in time, do we begin? The idea of membership is as old as the human species (even older if we acknowledge the similarities between the behaviour of humans and that of our cousins, other higher primates). Accounts of the early history of some types of MOB go right back in time, for instance citing the similarities between friendly societies and medieval guilds or Masonic lodges. However, more credible accounts start with the impact of the industrial revolution; for instance, the spread of consumer co-operatives seems to have mirrored the spread of industrial systems of production from Britain in the early 19th century, expanding through continental Europe to Russia and Japan at roughly the same time as industrialisation was spreading (Birchall, 1997). Accounts of the origins of farmer co-operatives start with the development of wider markets for farm produce that began in the mid-19th century in the USA, Germany and then Denmark (Fay, 1938).

The common element here is the development of a market society. As Polanyi describes it, 'the change from regulated to self-regulating markets at the end of the 18th century represented a complete transformation in the structure of society' (1957: 71). The economic order ceased to be embedded in the social, but became free to run under its own logic, with labour, land and money becoming commodities. The protection of cultural institutions that had guaranteed subsistence was swept away and people were exposed to the market in a way they had not been before. Consequently, they had to invent new methods of protecting themselves, of learning to deal in the market to survive. Not surprisingly, people who were disadvantaged under the new system – wage labourers, artisans, farmers – learned that their strength was in numbers. They could only survive and adapt if they invented new ways of co-operating together.

Historical accounts tend to begin with simple acts of collective provision: consumers buying a sack of flour and dividing it up; wage-labourers pooling small sums from which to insure members against illness or death; farmers collectively buying seeds or fertiliser; retailers dividing up a cartload of soap to sell on to their customers; building workers pooling money to buy land and build houses. These acts lead to more self-conscious acts of mutual aid that become codified in business laws. The point at which the history of member-owned businesses really takes off is when their organisations become legal persons and they achieve limited liability. Their businesses can then take on a life of their own; the membership changes but the business remains more or less constant. Most of the types of member-owned business we are now going to describe achieved this status in their countries of origin at some time during the second half of the 19th century. One important moment is the recognition of friendly societies in England in an Act of 1793. This is probably the earliest legislation that we should consider as material to the 'modern' member-owned business sector. Another important moment is the passing of the first Industrial and Provident Society Act in Britain in 1852 that allowed consumer co-operatives to be recognised and another in 1862 that gave them limited liability. It is interesting to note that joint stock companies did not get limited liability until 1862. Though from a historical viewpoint, member-ownership is a modern invention, it is at least as old as the now dominant form, the investor-owned business. Both were 'invented' during the same period of rapid social and economic change that led to what we now call modern society.

In the next six chapters we provide an account of all the main types of MOB, using the theoretical framework sketched out above to try not just to describe what happened, where and when, but also to explain why it happened at those particular times and in those particular places. We begin with probably the best known member-owned business, consumer co-operatives in retailing.

3
Consumer-owned Retail Businesses

Consumer co-operatives are probably the best known MOBs, and their history is well documented, not least by this author! The idea that consumers might organise to meet their own consumption needs reaches back to the earliest stages of the industrial revolution. However, it presupposes that people see themselves as consumers and have enough income to support the business. It also relies on their ability to find a method of governance that will ensure the business runs in the interests of the members, and a method of distributing surpluses in a way that is fair and provides an incentive to do business with the 'co-op' rather than with its competitors. Although the earliest experiments date back to the 1760s, this is why the official history of the consumer co-operative begins with the Rochdale Pioneers in 1844.

The founding period

Before this type of MOB became viable there were two distinct beginnings and a failed movement. The first beginning was in 1760 when the shipwrights who worked in the British Navy's dockyards at Chatham and Woolwich acquired their own flour mills. We do not have to look far for their motives. At that time, the price of bread was the most important factor in the daily life of the 'labouring classes', as they had not yet begun to depend on potatoes for their staple diet (Burnett, 1989). Mills relied on water power and so the industry was highly location-specific and this, combined with slow and poor communications, meant that natural monopolies grew up. This was a simple case of market failure; they were suffering from local monopolies of millers and bakers which resulted in high prices and adulteration of the flour (Potter, 1899). The idea spread slowly, but it was given an economic impetus from the 1790s onwards by the rise in the price of bread due to a war with France. It spread North along the coast to ports such as Hull (in 1795) and Whitby (in 1812). Further south, skilled artisans rebelled against millers who were adulterating flour with china clay, and they formed a baking society at Sheerness (in 1815) and another corn mill at Devonport. It was a short step from milling to baking, but it took until 1816 before the Sheerness Economical Society got round to opening a store (Cole, 1944).

We know these early experiments were successful because they provoked serious opposition; the Woolwich mill was burnt down and local bakers were accused of arson, while the Hull mill was taken to court as a 'nuisance' by the local millers. The jury found the co-operators not guilty, finding (as Beatrice Potter puts it) 'poverty a still greater nuisance' (Potter, 1899). It is not difficult to understand why this early form of consumer action was successful; it was undertaken by a homogeneous group of skilled workers who would have had a lot of social capital and enough financial capital to be able to afford to subscribe. Being highly self-educated, their leaders would have had the requisite skills. We do not know what their business model was, but it must have been simple enough to be easily replicated.

The second beginning was at the industrial village of Fenwick in Scotland. Here, in 1761 a group of weavers set up a trade association which in 1769 began collective purchasing of food and books. At that time, the weaving trade was much more prosperous than it would be during the next century. We know little about these pioneers, but there would have been committed leaders, a strong sense of both geographical and occupational community, and an association that would move naturally from meeting one need to another. They combined in the same organisation a mix of charitable and mutual motivations that reminds us of the medieval guild. The Fenwick association led to a scattering of experiments around Scotland in storekeeping, at least one of which (at Lennoxtown) is said to have discovered the idea of paying a dividend on purchases (Cole, 1944). They did not grow into a movement though, probably because they had not yet distilled the principles needed to keep a store society both democratic and economically strong; the dividend principle was tried alongside others such as equal distribution or distribution by shareholding.

The first real movement began in the unlikely setting of the Southern English seaside resort of Brighton. Here, skilled workers such as shoe-makers, tailors, printers and cabinet-makers were suffering from what we would call a 'deskilling' of labour, due to the new factory system and the outsourcing of work to unskilled workers. A slump of 1826 made the situation even more urgent. They possessed a great deal of what we would call social capital: local trades were well organised in friendly associations and they were able to study their problems at a local mechanics' institute. Their leader, William Bryan, had been elected in 1825 as chair of a Committee of Brighton Trades. Their aims were ambitious; to make enough profit to invest in workshops that would provide work for their members, and to buy land with which to put unemployed members to work growing food (Birchall, 1994). Storekeeping appealed because it was relatively easy to get into, requiring little capital or expertise. Also, it enabled them to meet more immediate goals of decreasing their living expenses through joint purchasing, and finding an outlet for their finished goods.

The Brighton Co-operative Trading Association started with only £5 in capital, and during the first year they raised their weekly sales to £40, soon accumulating enough capital to lease a 28 acre plot on which unemployed members were put to work. They were helped by a local medical doctor, William King, who publicised the idea in a series of monthly pamphlets that both provided strong arguments for co-operation and showed people how to do it. He was one of those dedicated leaders who are prepared to incur costs out of all proportion to the benefits they derive as individuals, and so he was able to overcome the 'collective action' problem. He published a monthly magazine, *the Co-operator*, which, according to the poet Southey, reached a circulation of 12,000 copies. His systematic exposition of the co-operative philosophy and shrewd advice about how to run a shop ran to 28 editions over three years. His arguments persuaded his readers, while the information he conveyed enabled them to emulate the Brighton society. It seems that in every town the paper reached a co-operative society was formed (Mercer, 1947). Within three years 300 co-operative stores had been set up all over the British Isles, as far apart as Dublin, Belfast and Aberdeen, in every industrial area apart from South Wales, and in nearly every large town. Its supporters founded a British Association for the Promotion of Co-operative Knowledge, and from 1831 twice-yearly congresses began to be held. By 1832 the number of societies was estimated to be around 500 (Cole, 1944). Unlike the earlier experiments it was a self-conscious co-operative movement, aiming to replace the emerging 'capitalist' society with a co-operative economy. Sadly, by 1834 it had almost collapsed, with only a few societies hanging on to be rediscovered by a second co-operative movement that began in Rochdale in 1844.

The reasons for the collapse were partly external. In 1832 a Reform Act denied working class people the vote, then in 1834 a New Poor

Law threatened them with the 'workhouse' if they became destitute. Many people turned to political action through the Chartist movement, while others turned to more militant trade unionism, or were diverted into Robert Owen's labour exchanges that seemed for a time to offer an alternative to the stores (Potter, 1899). Then in 1834 the government became much more repressive and this also affected the movement (Cole, 1944). However, none of these reasons is totally convincing; a decade later, some of the Rochdale Pioneers were Chartists, trade unionists or Owenite socialists, and none of them saw any contradiction in also opening a co-operative store.

Internal weakness may have been even more important. First, the co-ops had no legal status and so there was no remedy against fraud. This would only account for a few failures though, and as we shall see, under similar circumstances other movements quickly gained political support for legislation. Second, there was said to be a lack of loyalty to the store (Potter, 1899: 53), which is understandable as at that time many people were indebted to private traders and so were not able to choose where they shopped. Third, since William King insisted on accurate weekly bookkeeping, we can infer that some societies lacked commercial experience. Fourth, those that did eventually employ their own members had to try to sell their goods through the store and so may have become overstocked (Potter, 1899: 54). Fifth, faced with economic depression and poverty among their members, they sometimes abandoned the principle of cash payment and became, as the contemporary historian Holyoake put it, 'stranded by credit' (1857). However, the most important reason for failure may be a fundamental design fault. The aim of the societies was to accumulate capital so as to employ all their members in manufacturing goods they could then sell through the store. Yet to keep their members interested they needed to find a way of distributing at least some of the trading surpluses so as to reward them for their loyalty. The only way to get at the accumulated capital was for members to terminate the society and divide it up. This is how the Brighton society failed, when some members wanted to cash in their shares and buy a fishing boat (Mercer, 1947).

The Rochdale Pioneers had also run a society at this time and it had failed through giving too much credit. They were prepared to learn by their mistakes and try again, this time with a viable business model that would succeed and be copied all round the world. Again there was a pressing need for some kind of action that would meet people's basic needs. During the 18th century, weaving had been a proud trade, decentralised in well-built industrial villages such as can still be seen in rural Lancashire and the Cotswolds, and employing whole families in a mixture of self-employed weaving and small farming (Thompson, 1968). Within two generations they had been reduced to destitution. The first blow was a supply chain monopoly; small masters gave way to large merchants who cornered the market in supply and marketing of cloth and were able to use their monopoly power to force the earnings of the weavers down. The second blow was the growth of a factory system with its mass production, its extreme division of labour, and a deskilled workforce. In the cotton industry, there had been a big expansion of weaving but the boom disguised a fundamental loss of status among the workers; they had become dependent on the spinning mills and had also seen their wages reduced again and again. As in Brighton, the old apprentice system had collapsed and new entrants to the market such as Irish immigrants and returning soldiers were able to undercut them. Combined with this loss of status and income came rapid urban-isation and serious public health problems and epidemics; in 1848, when the Pioneers' store was just beginning to establish itself, the average life expectancy in the town was just 21 years. Reports from the poor law commissioners of the time describe how, in the recession of 1841–2, 60% of workers were unemployed. The irony was not lost on the commissioners that blanket weavers had had to sell their own blankets and sleep on straw (Thompson, 1968).

Twenty-eight men met together to see what could be done, and they considered several options. They had been attracted by Robert Owen's utopian schemes for co-operative communities that would opt out of modern society altogether, but several had lost money on the last of his communities at Queenwood and it had become clear that there would be no opting out. They considered political action, but a mass movement to press for the vote had ended in repression, and agitation to limit the number of hours worked in the factories had got nowhere. They considered trade union action but a long strike by the weavers for higher pay had just collapsed. A measure of their desperation is that they considered setting up a society to help people to emigrate.

Having failed with storekeeping in 1835, in 1844 they turned to the same solution again, but this time with a clear idea of the business principles on which it might succeed. They were helped by the under-developed nature of the trade at the time. A revolution in industry and urban living had not yet been matched by a revolution in distribution, and town dwellers were dependent mainly on weekly markets. High class grocery was a skilled trade, but working class people relied more on family-owned general stores that were few in number, poorly stocked and charged high prices to offset the risk they ran from giving credit (Davis, 1966). Wholesaling was not very well organised. A new working class was taking shape whose demands were simple and easy to estimate, but the industry was inefficient and in need of new methods of organisation (Jeffreys, 1954). The Pioneers virtually invented retail management via branch stores, and through co-operative wholesaling and manufacturing were able to organise distribution much more effectively than their competitors (Birchall, 1994). They were underpinned by a great deal of bonding social capital; their leaders had multiple affiliations locally to causes such as Owenism, Chartism, Unitarian Methodism, teetotalism and so on. Some of them were well travelled and could bring bridging social capital too, while others had a flair for business management. A journalist, George Jacob Holyoake, got to know them well and wrote with brilliance and humour of their attempts to get the business started (1857).

Above all, they had a viable business model. They laid down some basic principles that would ensure both business success and democratic control by consumers. There was the 'dividend principle' by which surpluses were distributed regularly to members in proportion to their purchases. There was a principle of giving no more than a fixed and limited return on shares. Together these principles meant that there was a sound economic reason for being a member and shopping as much as possible at the 'Co-op', and that the organisation could not deform into an IOB. The low cost of entry, combined with an open membership principle, meant that all but the poorest could afford to join. There was an incentive to encourage others to join, because, other things being equal, the larger the membership the lower would be the expenses and the higher the dividend. There was the principle of one member having one vote regardless of the size of shareholding, an education principle that encouraged societies to spend part of their surpluses on educating their members, and a principle of political and religious neutrality. All of these contributed towards a high quality of member participation in decision-making. There was a prudent principle of cash trading which, though it had the effect of excluding the very poor who relied on weekly credit from small shopkeepers, ensured that the business would survive in bad times. Finally, there was a principle of supplying only good quality products, which meant that at a time of almost universal adulteration and short measures the co-operatives could be trusted to work whole-heartedly in the interests of consumers (Holyoake, 1907).

Because their work was so influential, the Pioneers have been the subject of some attention from historians and we know quite a lot about them (e.g. Birchall, 1995a). Out of the 28 men who attended the first meeting only eight were flannel weavers, though half were associated with the trade. The rest were skilled artisans and small business people, and so they were not the poorest; as one historian described it, they were moved more by idealism than by hunger (Bonner, 1970). This is understandable, since poverty leaves little energy left for institution-building. It is a pattern we will meet again, people on middle incomes setting up a society that will benefit the poor, not as a matter of charity but of mutual aid. They were also committed reformers. At least half classed themselves as 'Owenites', followers of Robert Owen who, despite many setbacks, was still trying to find a way of setting up co-operative communities. Some were teetotallers, some Unitarian Methodists, some Chartists, some campaigners for the 'ten hours' act, and several had overlapping memberships in these movements. It is their unusual com-bination of idealism and pragmatism that we have to thank for the founding of the consumer co-operative movement.

The rules of the Society were adapted from those of an existing friendly society and it was registered officially with the Registrar (it would be another eight years before they got full legal status). They raised £28 (from the minimum shareholding of £1 each), rented the ground floor of a small warehouse and began to stock basic goods such as flour, oatmeal, candles, butter and sugar. At the end of the first year their membership had grown to 74, their takings were a modest £710 and their capital £181. They had made a surplus of £22. A trade depression of 1847–8 nearly finished them off, but they had a stroke of luck; in 1849 the Rochdale Savings Bank collapsed, and many people rushed to join the Co-op which was the only safe haven for their money. Membership grew to 390, trade to £6612, capital to £1194 and surplus to a remarkable £561 (Holyoake, 1857). We ought to add luck to our list of factors ensuring success in the founding period of a member-owned business!

A period of growth

To understand the pattern of growth of the movement, we need to look first at the Rochdale society, then at the wider situation in Britain, then at the growth of this type of MOB around the world. They are all inter-connected; without the continued success of the Rochdale society growth within Britain would probably have faltered, and without the success in Britain the growth in Europe and then the rest of the world may not have happened. On the other hand, around the time the Rochdale Pioneers were setting up similar experiments were being made in several other countries. We can hazard a guess that without Rochdale there would have been 'store movements' in other countries, but they may not have had such a unified set of business principles, and would have taken longer to discover how to make co-operative retailing work.

In Rochdale, from the 1850s onwards growth was steady and almost uninterrupted. Food was becoming cheaper because tariffs had been abolished, and working class people were becoming steadily better off. By 1880 there were well over 10,000 members. During economic depressions members tended to withdraw savings to live on, but the impetus to growth rarely faltered. Trade grew in three ways. First, new lines would be stocked and when established would become separate departments; butchery, drapery, boot-making, and tailoring were added to basic food shopping. The Toad Lane store spilled over into neighbouring buildings until, in 1867, a central store was opened. Second, from 1856 onwards the Society began to respond to pressure from members in other areas to set up branch stores, and in this way they invented modern chain store retailing. Third, in 1850 they began wholesaling, supplying other new societies and then in 1864 setting up a Co-operative Wholesale Society that would be an engine of growth for the whole movement.

The movement grew rapidly. By 1881 there were 547,000 members in 971 societies with sales of nearly £15.5 million. By the end of the 19th century there were over 1.7 million members in 1439 co-operative societies, with a turnover of more than £50 million a year. By 1914 there were over three million members in 1385 societies (some smaller ones had amalgamated), with a turnover of £88 million which 'in those days was an awesome amount of money' (Birchall, 1994: 65). The co-operators had also expanded their business vertically into the wholesaling and production of the goods they needed. Starting from nothing in 1863, the Co-operative Wholesale Society had by 1914 become a massive business in its own right, with a turnover of £35 million with retail societies, productions worth £9 million a year and a workforce of over 22,000 people (Redfern, 1938). The Scottish CWS had grown along similar lines and had by 1914 sales of £9.5 million. As well as being one of the largest wholesalers in the world, CWS and SCWS had become major growers, manufacturers and importers, bringing to the British consumer the benefits of cheap food from abroad and cutting out the 'middle man' throughout the supply chain.

There were several background conditions that help explain this success. Until retail chains and department stores began there was a lack of real competitors; the chains only began in the 1870s and the department stores in the 1890s, giving the co-operatives 'early mover' advantage (Jeffreys, 1954). Demand was growing. There were more and more customers (population doubled between 1851 and 1914), and wages were more than keeping pace with prices, growing by 35% by the end of the century. A revolution in railway transport coincided with the growth period, making it possible to supply towns and villages cheaply and reliably, while the development of steam ships led to import of cheap food (Burnett, 1989). It has been estimated that in the ten years from 1877 the price of food in a typical working class family dropped by 30% (Redfern, 1938).

There are more specific reasons for this period of growth. The invention of the branch store led to horizontal integration, and that of the wholesale society led to vertical integration. The needs of co-op members were easy to estimate and so plans could be laid that seemed ambitious but were based solidly on a guaranteed market. The soundness of the Pioneer society as an institution was demonstrated when other societies began to adopt the Rochdale model. Redemption societies that had been saving their profits to fund Owenite communities began to give dividend on purchases. In Scotland, old societies that had formed as joint stock companies giving dividend on capital were persuaded by a co-operative 'missionary', Alexander Campbell, to adopt the Rochdale principles. Influential supporters of the movement such as EV Neale created enabling legislation that kept up with the needs of an outstandingly innovative movement. Journalists such as George Holyoake in his book on the Pioneers, and Samuel Bamford who edited Co-operative News, gave it publicity. In 1870 Neale helped found a national federation, the Co-operative Union that would become another key institution that would be copied all over Europe.

At around the same time as the Rochdale Pioneers were opening their store, similar experiments were being carried out in other countries, but it was only when promoters in each country discovered the Rochdale 'system' with its dividend on purchases that their own movements began to take off. In Switzerland, existing societies converted and by 1904 there were 204 of them, with their own wholesale society and national union. In France, by 1907 there were 2166 societies, with over 600,000 members. The Belgian movement was inhibited by religious and political divisions, but even so by 1905 there were 168 societies with a national federation. In Italy, by 1904 there were 1448 registered societies, with around a third as many again unregistered. In Germany, early development was mainly of rural and urban credit banks, but by 1905 a central union of consumer co-operatives had 787 societies in membership, along with 260 attached to the credit banks; their wholesale society was explicitly modelled on the English CWS. In Russia, by the 1905 revolution there were nearly a thousand societies with 300,000 members. After this, a more liberal political climate led to rapid growth, so that by the time of the Bolshevik revolution they had become a vital part of the supply chain. Other central and eastern European countries also established small, but nationally federated co-operative sectors, and some can boast co-operative-type stores as old as that of the Rochdale Pioneers. In Japan, co-operatives began in Tokyo and Osaka in 1879 (Kurimoto, 2010), and by 1907 there was a society 'in every town of any importance' (Vacek, 1989: 1033). However, their expansion was checked by a government suspicious of independent associations. By the time of the First World War all the countries of Western Europe and Scandinavia, Russia and several countries in Central and Eastern Europe had well developed consumer co-operative sectors. The largest was still the British movement with three million members, but the Germans, with 1.7 million members, were not far behind.

A period of consolidation

It has been a curious but understandable feature of consumer co-operative history that, except in countries where they have been suppressed, they have tended to prosper during wartime. Governments come to need co-operative distribution systems to meet basic needs, and the populace comes to a new understanding of the fairness and integrity of retailers who believe in putting the consumer first. For instance, during the First World War the 'Co-op' in Britain distinguished itself by refusing to profiteer and introducing voluntary rationing even before the state intervened. The movement grew steadily during the interwar period., and by the start of the Second World War, it consisted of 1100 societies, controlling 24,000 stores, and having 40% of the market in butter, 26% of milk, 23% of grocery and provisions, 20% of tea, sugar and cheese. When rationing was introduced, 28% of the population – 13.5 million people – registered with the Co-op (Birchall, 1994, ch.8). It employed a quarter of a million people in retailing and another hundred thousand in manufacturing and distribution. With 155 factories, the CWS was one of the biggest businesses in the world.

In all countries with established co-operative movements, this was also a time of steady expansion. Because they were dealing in basic commodities, co-operatives tended to stand up to the shocks of economic depression and mass unemployment. In times of trouble, member loyalty tended to increase, even if for a while their total spending went down.

In most countries the rise of big city societies and powerful national wholesale societies enabled the building up of very large, modern businesses. There were structural weaknesses: the Co-op tended to deal in a narrow range of staple food products, there were too many small societies and they were concentrated mainly in industrial working class areas. The movement was tending to grow organically, along lines of least resistance rather than by planned development (Birchall, 1997). However, these weaknesses did not become noticeable until after the Second World War.

During the interwar period the idea reached North America. In Canada, it took root most firmly among the mining communities of the Atlantic Provinces. Here, for similar reasons as in mining villages in Western Europe, people co-operated to overcome the 'truck system' by which mine-owners supplied goods needed by their workforces in company stores. In Nova Scotia, they were aided by an adult education system developed by the Antigonish movement that stressed the importance of co-operatives to the local economy (Fay, 1938). Growth was checked, though, in countries taken over by Fascist or communist governments; autonomous consumer-owned businesses and totalitarianism did not mix. In Italy, Germany, Austria, Japan and Spain the movement was destroyed as an independent force. The threat from communism was more subtle. In Russia, by 1918 there were 26,000 societies with nine million members. The Bolsheviks extended them so that they became an almost universal provider, though in the process they killed off the voluntary nature of membership. Lenin realised he had made a mistake and in 1924 tried to restore their autonomy. However, once lost it proved impossible to restore, and in 1935 Stalin then completed the process by abolishing all the urban consumer co-operatives and confiscating their assets without compensation to their 10 million members (We have to add to our understanding of the reasons for MOBs dying out their deliberate destruction by totalitarian governments). Despite these setbacks, by 1937 the International Co-operative Alliance had in membership 50,000 consumer co-ops with nearly 60 million members.

Expansion into more specialist areas of retailing occurred naturally, as a reaction to demands by members that their Co-op meet other needs than could be provided by a general store. Milk and coal deliveries, department stores, funeral services, pharmacies, travel, petrol sales, car sales, banking and insurance, restaurants and hotels were added to the business at various times and places. Usually this was stimulated by a solid and loyal customer-base, but the emphasis was still on basic goods and services that low- to middle-income customers could afford. Co-operatives were not good at developing more upmarket products, and in several countries excursions into department stores were not successful.

After the War, the movement in the UK continued to expand. It was at the forefront of innovations such as self-service and supermarkets, but these hid underlying structural problems. With over 1000 societies, a range of different-sized shops, many of which were too small, and with a lack of integration between societies and their wholesalers, the movement was losing ground to the multiple chains. By the late 1950s, the Co-op had 11% of the retail trade, the multiples 22%, but it stopped growing and then began a long decline.

A period of decline

In the postwar period, at first consumer co-operatives were ahead of the field, opening self-service stores and supermarkets, but then they become seriously challenged by the competition. A fatal weakness occurred when, in several European countries, falling profit margins led them to give up paying dividend to members and shift to giving all customers a discount, usually in the form of bonus stamps. In this way they undermined the relationship between membership and governance and, as they began to merge and form larger, regional units, they become more and more remote from their members (Brazda and Schediwy, 1989). There then began a long and often dismal struggle to persuade local societies to merge and form regional societies or even one national society, to divest themselves of their wholesaling and manufacturing businesses which by now had become a liability, and to reshape themselves along similar lines to the multiples, who did not go further back in the distribution chain but used their buying power to gain advantages over manufacturers.

In Britain, what had been the movement's strengths – local loyalties, the cherished independence of each society, a prejudice in favour of letting managers emerge 'from the ranks' and against those who were university educated – all these began to work against the consumer co-operative. There was no lack of detailed analysis of what was wrong (see Co-operative Independent Commission, 1958 for UK), but there was weak central direction and a determination among societies to continue trading until they had to merge in order to survive. By the end of the 20th century, in Britain mergers had reduced the original 1000 societies to around 40, and faced with some of the most effective and efficient multiple retailers in the world the movement's market share had declined to just 3%.

The German movement was reconstituted after the War, and by 1953 had nearly two million members. However, as in the UK, it faced stiff competition. Though the Co-op continued to grow it lost market share; by 1965 it had just 8.6% of the market (Brazda, 1989). The response was also similar. Instead of paying dividend to members, co-ops began to offer rebates to all customers, thus weakening the vital connection between membership and economic returns. Similar too were the structural weaknesses of the sector; attempts to organise mergers were hampered by weak central direction and the resistance of small societies determined to keep their autonomy even at the risk of extinction. As in Britain, a plan for regionalisation took shape slowly and mergers took place out of weakness rather than in a planned way. In the early 1970s, in response to mounting debts, societies began to convert to a conventional limited company form, and amalgamated in one central organisation, Co-op Zentrale AG which by 1980 was back in profit. However, weak accountability structures and fraudulent management led to further drastic reorganisation until by 1989 the movement had only 37 societies with 650,000 members. Some of the healthiest societies, such as Co-op Dortmund, resisted the conversion to a joint stock company. This society, by continuing to pay attention to member-relations and pay a traditional dividend, remained highly successful (Brazda, 1989). By 1988, it had nearly half a million members and over 14% of local retail trade. However, stagnating retail trade and intensified competition led to a withdrawal of shares by members, the sale of stores, and the society's eventual dissolution (Kurimoto, 1999).

A similar story can be told in other Western European countries. In Austria, a too rapid expansion in the 1970s led societies into a serious debt burden, and eventual amalgamation into one Konsum Austria. It is interesting to note that in the UK some co-operative revivalists have promoted the idea of one national society; in this case stagnation and the concealing of the crisis from consumer-members led, in 1995, to the national society's – and therefore the whole movement's-bankruptcy (Schediwy, 1996). In the Netherlands, in 1973 the movement had to be sold off to the private sector. In France, in 1985 around 40% of the movement was sold off, and now only a few small societies remain (Schediwy, 1989).

Consumer co-operators in the Scandinavian countries also faced strong competition and the need to rationalise the number of societies. They made a better job of it than their southern counterparts. In Finland, until recently there were two distinct movements, the politically neutral SOK and the social democratic E-movement, and one large independent society Elanto based in Helsinki. In the 1960s, SOK branched out into hotels and department stores and successfully streamlined its structure, but by 1967 it was still in deficit; like other movements across Europe, it was held back by a social conscience, keeping open loss-making shops in rural areas. From 1970 onwards it began to subsidise ailing co-ops, using the massive reserves it had built up in the good times. The numbers reduced from 178 to 32 regional societies, plus 45 small societies that refused to join. By the late 1980s, only two of the regionals were in a satisfactory state, and reserves were ebbing away and real estate being sold to hide the losses. Meanwhile, the E-Movement also embarked on a drastic strategy of modernisation and shop closures, but its wholesaler, OTK, failed in an initiative to promote department stores. By the mid-1960s, it was the familiar story: some societies running at a loss, parochial rivalries preventing mergers, exacerbated by the split between Swedish and Finnish speaking societies. The political ties of the E-movement were an obstacle to closer ties between the two sectors, preventing a sensible merger between the two wholesalers, SOK and OTK. In 1983, 39 regional co-ops joined OTK to form Co-op Finland (EKA), which instantly became the third biggest company group in Finland. By 1997 it had 23% of the retail market, and by 1998, the two groups still had a 35% market share between them, plus Elanto that remained independent (Birchall, 2009).

In Sweden, the situation was simpler, with one consumer co-operative sector, represented by its federation, KF, founded in 1899. It benefitted from not having been destroyed or weakened by the Second World War, and so from the 1950s it became the most dynamic and innovative of all the European sectors, introducing self-service, supermarkets and frozen foods and beginning structural reorganisation. By 1970 the number of societies had fallen from 637 to 232, the number of shops reduced from 7400 to 2700. As a result, the market share increased to 18% and membership to over 1.6 million households. Yet the mid-1970s were a time of crisis, with a costly expansion into town centre department stores that did not work, and a stagnating market share. The aim of getting down to 20 societies was not being achieved. By the mid-1980s it was still among the top ten companies in Sweden but the worst performing. In 1986 of the 142 co-op societies 40% were in deficit; as in other countries, it was a cushioned decline, based on the use of built-up reserves.

Two success stories are the movements in Italy and Switzerland. In Italy, we might have expected the gradual decline seen in other countries, but because of the relative backwardness of the retail trade during the 1980s the co-ops experienced 'expansion and growing social recognition' (Setzer, 1989: 853), though with only a small share of a fragmented retail trade. The consumer co-operative sector in Switzerland faced similar challenges to that in the UK, with a move to regional warehousing, closure of 500 small shops, resistance to mergers and a switch to discount stamps and a low price policy. However, the national Union of Swiss Consumer Co-operatives (USC) took a tougher line than did the UK Co-operative Union, threatening weaker societies with expulsion from the Union and the wholesale society if they did not merge: by 1983 it had succeeded in its aim of reducing the number from over 400 down to 40. Also in contrast to the UK the group was disciplined, as early as 1960 adopting a single logo, placing its members' stores under the Coop brand and using television advertising campaigns. From the mid-1970s, in contrast to other countries, it began a period of strong growth, increasing its market share from 9% to 12%. Like CWS it was a pioneer of honest labelling and stopped promoting tobacco, and it kept open loss-making shops in remote areas. The Union continued to reorganise its distribution and purchasing operations into a centralized structure, and changed its name to Coop Schweiz (in French-speaking areas, Coop Suisse). It began to acquire a wide range of new businesses and then to launch its own organic and fair trade products.

Its strong performance can be accounted for partly by the need to compete with another consumer co-op, Migros. This was started in 1925 by a complex character called Gottlieb Duttweiler, whose father had been a co-op manager and who, despite being a talented entrepreneur, admired co-operative values. At first he sold only coffee, rice, sugar, noodles, coconut oil and soap from trucks that went from one village to another, then he moved into more conventional retailing, but still with low prices being his main strategy. He built a large retail chain then turned it into a non-profit, and then in 1940 into 12 regional co-ops grouped into a federation. Unencumbered by the decentralised structure of USC, it was able to expand rapidly, by 1952 having 120 self-service shops and opening its first supermarket. He continued to campaign for low prices, and by the 1960s Migros had become a massive conglomerate, with own production, a bank, and an insurance company. Although it did not give the traditional co-op dividend, it specialised in low prices through its M-Budget range, and gave back profits through extensive adult education activities. Unlike consumer co-operatives in other countries that were struggling with the need to restructure from a decentralised system to a unified retailer, Migros simply continued to grow; it diversified into hotels, fitness centres, garden centres, and a range of other kinds of retailing.

The best example of a successful consumer co-operative sector in the postwar period is, undoubtedly, Japan. Here, there were three waves of development and it was only by the 1960s that a viable model evolved, but when it did so its success was remarkable. First, around 6500 local bulk buying clubs were set up seeking to provide their members with food; these collapsed after rationing was introduced. Second, in the 1950s a co-operative sector was sponsored by trade unions. After a brief success, it succumbed to intense competition from retailers; it was lacking in management expertise and neglected member education (Kurimoto, 2010). It was the consumer movement of the 1960s that really established a sustainable co-operative sector. It was a large-scale citizens' movement that arose in response to widespread food adulteration, misleading labelling and environmental pollution. They were held back by opposition from retailers, who obtained laws restricting the co-operatives' growth: they had to deal only with members, were not allowed to form wholesale societies, to grow beyond prefectural boundaries or to have their own bank. Until 1998 the size of stores was strictly controlled so they were only able to operate small stores. Yet, despite these restrictions, the movement experienced sustained and rapid growth. Membership grew from two million in 1970 to 14 million in 1990, while turnover grew ten times. Some reasons for success were the active participation of housewives as members, a home delivery system organised through small 'han' groups of consumers, and a strong social movement dimension ranging from consumerism through to pacifism. Also, co-operative leadership and management were revitalised by an influx of educated people who had experienced the very successful university co-operative movement, and they gave the movement new direction and expertise. They managed to succeed in doing what other movements had thought was impossible; to make large-scale organisation compatible with member-democracy and with organisational efficiency.

A period of recovery and new growth

In the second half of the 20th century, the co-operative sector in Britain was fighting for survival. In the first decade of the 21st century it has begun a noticeable revival. Specialising in small to medium-sized supermarkets , it has begun to capitalise on its strengths rather than copying the competition (Birchall, 1987). It has brought back the dividend (using an electronic card), and is trying to revitalise the idea of membership. The UK Co-operative Group is probably the largest consumer co-operative in the world, with 5.5 million members, 120,000 employees and 4800 retail outlets and sales in 2009 of over £13.7 million. It is a cluster of businesses that include food retail, pharmacy, funerals, travel, farming, banking and insurance. It is the fifth largest food retailer in UK, with over 3000 food outlets. In pharmacy, it is the third largest in the UK with over 800 outlets and the dispensing of 53 million prescriptions per year. In funeral services it is the number one provider with more than 800 funeral homes. In travel, it is the largest independent agency with over 400 high street agencies plus call centres and online services. It is the largest farmer in Britain, farming over 70,000 acres in England and Scotland. It has strong market positions in banking and insurance and it is growing quickly, having recently bought the Somerfield chain and agreed a merger with a regional society, Plymouth and South West. The Group also provides essential services to other co-operative societies, running a joint-buying group (Co-operative Retail Trading Group) that supplies nearly all consumer co-operatives in the UK, which increases their buying power considerably. Its rebranding of stores into the 'Co-operative' brand is offered to these societies, as is its dividend card; independent societies just choose how much dividend to give to their own customers. With the strong performance of the Group and of some regional societies, market share has leapt to more than 8% of UK retail trade.

In Finland a dramatic reconstruction of the sector has led to renewed growth. In 2005, the OTK-group (now known as Tradeka Corporation) formed a limited company of all retail stores and then sold over 80% of the shares to a Swedish investment company, leasing the stores back. However, it remains a co-operative with 370,000 customer-members, owning a large number of hotels and restaurants and giving bonuses through its E-card in the retail stores. In 2002 Elanto merged with the 'S-Group'. Altogether, the new unified group has retail sales of nearly Eur10 billion, including Eur8 billion retail sales of the co-op enterprises. Sixteen local and 22 regional co-operatives are included, and at the end of 2006 they had 1.6 million members and 34,000 employees. In 2006 it paid Eur232 million to consumers in bonuses, and had a 40% share of the grocery market in Finland. What is the secret of its success? One element is the S-Etukirtti card, which is not a loyalty card but a genuine membership card that covers S Group's whole range of services and acts as an umbrella brand. It is a bonus card and also a debit card, and it earns bonuses not just with the Group but with partner organisations who want to gain access to its (now) 1.7 million customer-members. The extent of the business is very wide; it includes substantial subsidiaries in farm inputs, car sales, hardware, restaurants, hotels, department and speciality stores, and in 2007 it opened its own bank. In its core business of the supermarket trade, S Group is now the market leader.

In Sweden, during the 1990s the national federation, KF, took most of the primary societies into a new Co-operative Retail Group, which resulted in a more disciplined business organisation. By the end of 1993, it still had 102 societies but the discipline had worked; its market share had begun to rise. It now has around 50 co-ops in membership, with a combined membership of over three million, and a 21% market share. Like other co-operative consortia, it has a complex structure, with a retailing arm, Co-op Sverige running the supermarket chain, and several subsidiaries in real estate, bookshops, home entertainment, environmental engineering and so on. Like the Finnish S-Group, it has a bank whose membership card is crucial for maintaining the relationship with members and delivering an extensive reward scheme. In 2007 for example, members received 7.7 million reward vouchers with a redemption value in discounts of around SEK 465 million (Birchall, 2009).

In Italy, nine regional societies are now integrated in one group, Co-op Italia, which has become the largest supermarket chain with a market share of nearly 18% of retailing and 30% of food retail. As of 2007, 'Coop' operates 1,394 stores and employs almost 55,700 people, with 6,700,000 members, which equates to one in five households. With a turnover of Eur12.1 billion it is close to the UK Co-operative Group in size. In France, where consumer co-ops almost disappeared, the few that survived are doing surprisingly well. Cooperateurs d'Alsace is the biggest of them, with 150,000 members, and 17% of the market in Alsace, where it is the largest independent retailer. Interestingly, it has formed an alliance with the retailer-owned wholesaler, Leclerc, as its wholesaler. In Switzerland, Co-op Schweiz has succeeded in merging the remaining 14 regional societies into one, completely transforming itself from a decentralised, local society-based union into a unified national retailer. With over two million members, and a market share of around 17%, it is one of the top three or four consumer co-ops in Europe. Its rival, Migros, now has over two million members, over 80,000 employees, and a market share in retailing of 32%. It also has Switzerland's fifth largest bank. In 2007, it acquired a majority stake in a discount chain, which meant the merger of the largest and third largest food retail chains in Switzerland. Now the two co-operative groups have a combined market share of around 50% and are facing pressures from European competition laws inhibiting further expansion (Birchall, 2009).

In Canada, consumer co-operatives have also faced difficult times. However, there are still strong sectors in Western Canada and the

Atlantic region that have retained the traditional structure of local primary societies backed up by strong wholesale arms. In Western Canada, they have more than 1.3 million members in 500 communities, and the largest primary society, Calgary Co-op, is still one of the largest retail co-operatives in North America (with 425,350 members, 4000 employees, and annual sales approaching $1 billion). Federated Co-operatives provides manufacturing, wholesaling and distribution to 270 retail co-ops. It has its own oil refinery, and a wholesale company supplying 300 independent retailers. In the Atlantic region, there are 128 co-ops supplied by Co-op Atlantic, one of the largest agri-food wholesalers.

In Japan the long economic recession, changing lifestyles, and stiff competition from retail chains have meant that the co-operative sector has ceased to grow. Here, the market is still dominated numerically by small retailers, with complicated distribution channels, market domination by major manufacturers and government protectionist policies in favour of small retailers. Since the mid-1990s membership has continued to increase but turnover has stagnated, the number of store outlets has decreased by 22%, and the stores have been unable to make a surplus; if it were not for home delivery this sector would be in trouble. With a steady increase in the proportions of women in paid employment and a change to a more individualistic lifestyle, the mainstay of the co-operative strategy, joint buying, has become less popular. However, non-store retailing is still sustainable because of a switch from joint buying to individual home delivery. The legal restrictions mean the system has remained decentralised; regional consortiums have succeeded in maintaining overall turnover, but still only 17% of purchases are centralised. On the other hand, their decentralised structure means they have entered into agreements with producer co-ops to guarantee pure products that are locally produced. In this respect they are still way ahead of their competitors (Kurimoto, 2010).

We noted how, before communist regimes turned them into parastatals or abolished them altogether, consumer co-operatives were strong in Russia and Eastern Europe. In the transition to market societies in the 1990s, many were privatised or failed. In Poland, for instance, between 1987 and 1991 retail turnover declined to a third of what it had been, and membership was cut by half. Yet in other countries intervention by the International Co-operative Alliance and the Co-operative Branch of the International Labour Organisation enabled co-operatives to avoid dissolution and create a real membership; by the mid-1990s, they still had around 20–30% market share in most central and eastern European countries and in Russia and Armenia they are growing strongly (Birchall, 2003). However, it would be a mistake to generalise from this that it is always the withdrawal of governments that provides the conditions for a new sector to emerge. In Singapore, it was the strong support of government for a trade union-led consumer co-operative that led to NTUC Fair Price becoming the market leader in that country. Its origins are in a 1970s initiative to control inflation and safeguard citizens' living standards, and partly as a result of strong government support in securing prime locations. It now has over 400,000 members (more than one in ten of the population), and 57% of the grocery market (Davies, 2005). It seems that, when it comes to explaining the growth, decline and recovery of consumer co-operatives we do have to consider carefully the conditions in each country.

Future prospects

Will this modest renaissance of consumer co-operatives continue? Those that have survived do seem able to compete against fierce competition, but they are continually challenged by competitors such as Tesco and Wal-Mart that are among the most efficient businesses in the world. What will be the effects of globalisation? Strangely for such a dynamic sector, retailing has not yet seen significant transnational developments. Retailers do not seem to be able easily to enter the market in another country and compete, unless the local competition is weak. There is a premium on local knowledge that is not easily matched by even the most professional incomer, and what works at home cannot always be replicated (Davies and Burt, 2006). For instance, in Japan Carrefour retreated after eight years, while Wal Mart is struggling to turn round the loss-making Seiyu chain (Kurimoti, 2010). However, further up the supply chain there is much to be gained from transnational co-ordination in buying groups, and this is the level at which consumer co-operatives have had most success in the past: As far back as 1918 a joint-purchasing body was set up by the Scandinavians, while from the 1960s onwards Euroco-op in Western Europe and Interco-op in Asia began to do modest interco-operative business. When they have tried to enter another country as retailers they have been much less successful. Co-op Norden began in 2001 as a joint venture by the Swedish, Norwegian and Danish co-operative sectors, but it was not a success and was wound up in 2007. Migros in Switzerland, NTUC Fair Price in Singapore, SOK in Finland, Eroski in Spain have all tried it and only the last has succeeded so far, and then only with an excursion into

France in partnership with a retailer-owned chain, Leclerc (Davies, 2005). In addition to the common logistical problems faced by all retailers, co-operatives face the problem of behaving like an MOB in the home country and like an IOB abroad. It is much easier, and ethically more comfortable, for them to advise and assist existing co-operatives in other countries, and to enter into joint partnerships.

Are consumer co-operatives likely to be a target of demutualisation? There has been one serious attempt to target a co-operative when a 'carpetbagger' who had previously targeted building societies saw the chance to convert CWS (now the Co-operative Group) (see Birchall, 2000). His approach to the Board was rejected, not least because illegal methods were used to obtain commercial information and two co-operative managers ended up in prison. Retail co-operatives are not such an attractive target, as they tend to be highly geared and have fixed assets rather than reserves that can be shared out; the real target of the demutualiser was the wholly-owned subsidiary of CWS, the Co-operative Bank. One beneficial outcome was a recognition by co-operatives in the UK that they needed to value their members and communicate with them more effectively.

Recently there have been signs of a growing confidence in the comparative business advantages of consumer-ownership (Co-operative Commission, 2000). There are four distinct advantages that are all about revitalising the idea of membership. First, an electronic dividend card can be issued that restores the link between membership and purchases. This has been developed independently in both Finland and the UK and has led to a huge increase in membership. The idea of a half-yearly dividend based on real surpluses made by the business has strong appeal to customer-members, and provides an economic rationale for membership that has for a long time been missing.

Second, membership strategies can be employed to differentiate between types of member and to encourage those who are most interested to get involved in governance; the UK regional societies and the national Co-operative Group are doing this. They simply ask new members if they want to receive regular information, and then build on this passive but interested layer of members to identify and nurture those who wish to become active. Through using the internet they cut down on the costs of organising and the costs to the members of participating, and enable a wide range of interests to be catered for. There is no way they can recover the old, working class community based on a strong commitment to place, but communities of interest can be formed that are a kind of substitute. At least, they provide another avenue through which active members can get involved in governance. Again, there is no way that the old structures can be recovered which offered a place in the governance structure to large numbers of people; every merger between co-ops that took place in the 1970s and '80s has closed down opportunities to participate. However, new types of governance can be created through special interest groups and local store-based committees.

Third, links to social issues can be fostered that bring in new members and refresh the idea of consumer-ownership. Issues that people care about are a strong incentive to participation (Birchall and Simmons, 2004a/b). In the 1980s, co-operatives in the UK, Japan and other countries gained a good reputation for purity of own-brand products and honest labelling. The UK Co-operative Bank became well known for its commitment to free banking and its ethical investment strategy (Birchall, 2005). Since then, they have tapped into a commitment to other ethical issues such as fair trade, environmental concern and local food sourcing. Co-ops in the UK and Italy are leading the field in fair trade (with co-ops in Spain, Finland and other countries close behind), collaborating with producer co-operatives in developing countries and using their considerable marketing and branding skills to increase the numbers of fair trade products on the shelves (Lacey, 2009). It is true that the investor-owned retail chains are also doing fair trade, but they tend to choose less stringent criteria for fairness and do not have the advantages of active members pushing the idea at the local level. Commitment to the environment is an issue where it is more difficult to differentiate oneself from the competition, but this issue is rising up the agenda; in the UK the Co-operative Group has, rather dramatically, built a wind farm on one of its estates. Local food sourcing is also becoming a major issue in which the neighbourhood or village co-operative store is seen as a crucial resource, and its members a potential lobby group for the idea (Burgan, 2010).

The renaissance of the co-operatives is partly explained by the drastic restructuring of the last 50 years that has enabled them to compete through gaining economies of scale and being able to hire good managers. At first, this led to a democratic governance deficit and a sense that, though the co-operatives could compete, they did not serve a clear purpose. Now, a new generation of managers and directors have emerged who can see the potential of consumer-ownership as a business advantage and are keen to reconnect with members. If they find ways of doing this cost-effectively, this type of MOB will continue to prosper and find a distinctive place in the retail market.

4
Consumer-owned Insurance Providers

Life is a risky business. Anything that can go wrong will go wrong somewhere, sometime, to somebody. Life is riskier for people on low incomes because they have so little to lose before they fall into poverty. However, people on middle incomes also face risks particularly from illness, and one has to be very rich to avoid the costs of long-term ill health, losing one's home to a fire, or just growing older. This is why most people in developed economies support some kind of welfare state to insure them collectively against the most common risks of unemployment, ill health, disability, dependency in childhood and old age. Even then, there are risks that are not covered; welfare states vary considerably in the extent to which they provide social insurance and affordable health care, and in every country in the developed world there is a large private insurance sector providing assurance against accidents, fires and floods, as well as health and life insurance. Also, governments need help in delivering benefits and services and often choose to do so in partnership with member-owned insurance providers. In this chapter we explore the historical development of three distinct types of insurance mutual: friendly societies, mutual insurance companies and insurers set up as secondary co-operatives.

Type 1: Friendly societies

People have to find ways of insuring themselves against common risks such as ill health, unemployment, old age and death. They do this in one of three ways: through state-sponsored social insurance schemes, through buying insurance products from commercial insurance companies, or through mutual aid. We will be exploring the third option, mutual aid through organisations known variously as friendly societies, fraternal societies or mutual insurers. The need for such insurance is so common that ways of providing it can be found in most societies. We will be focusing on Britain and France and other countries that have been influenced by them, but this does not imply that the mutual aid systems of other countries are less important, just that there is not enough space here to do them justice. Also, unlike the other people-centred businesses that we are looking at, friendly societies were not invented during the industrial revolution but go back much further in time. They have taken a modern form, but with an unbroken tradition going back probably to the medieval guilds. Again, we have to compromise by focusing on their more recent history.

The founding period

In Britain, they began in the simplest way, with a group of members, an alehouse and a money box. The members deposited a small amount of money each week in the box, and agreed to pay out of it an allowance to any member who became ill, the cost of being attended by a medical doctor, and a death benefit to the family of any member who died; in modern terms, they provided sickness insurance, health insurance and life insurance. To prevent theft the box was administered by three key holders, with officers decided by rotation. The whole society was overseen by the members at a monthly meeting in the pub at which some of the funds were used to buy ale. There are records of societies in Scottish ports in the 17th century; a society with the grand title of the United General Sea Box of Borrowstounness Friendly Society was set up in 1634, and a Sea Box Society of St Andrews in 1643 (Gosden, 1973). An Incorporation of Carters in Leith and a Fraternity of Dyers in Linlithgow followed. By the end of the century, the novelist Daniel Defoe could describe them as being quite common throughout Britain. They were closely related to savings societies that worked in the same way, enabling people to save to buy specific items such as clothing, boots and shoes. Huguenot refugees formed societies in East London in the early 18th century, and by the end of the century there were several thousand box clubs and friendly societies. An act of parliament, called 'Rose's Act' was passed in 1793 to attempt to regulate them through registration with a magistrate.

It is easy to account for this type of MOB. There were unmet needs that could not be met by anything other than mutual aid, there were the common bonds provided by working in the same industry and in the same locality, and there was a simple, replicable business model. What is absent from the historical accounts is leaders. We can theorise that the collective action problem here was not great; it did not cost much to get started, the members had all the skills they needed, and so there was no need for help from wealthy or well-connected supporters.

In France, mutual aid societies also trace their origins to the medieval guilds, and to workers' associations called 'compagnonnages'. As in Britain, there was a time lag between the founding of mutual aid societies and legal recognition; the law did not catch up with these associations until 1850, and it was not until 1898 that legislation was enacted that encouraged their growth. As in Britain, many societies remained unregistered. Like the British friendly societies, the movement was self-generating. A historian comments 'neither the legislators, nor the philosophers, nor the learned have exercised any notable influence on their development' (Mabilleau, quoted Aubrun, 1915: 7). It was the people's needs, their co-ordinated efforts and the publicity given by sympathetic supporters that caused the movement to grow.

The period of growth

For the entire 19th century, growth in Britain was rapid and sustained, and it was accompanied by a remarkable development of new types of society that were designed to meet a wide range of needs. By 1801, it was estimated there were 7200 societies with 648,000 members out of a total working population of nine million (Gosden, 1973). By 1815, the overseers of the poor gave a higher estimate of 9672 societies with 925,000 members. The average society had around 100 members, which meant that 8.5% of the population were members, though like the consumer co-operatives they were predominantly in industrial areas, and particularly strong in Lancashire and the West Riding of Yorkshire (Hopkins, 1995). Working in industry meant greater risk, but workers earned higher wages so were better able to afford the cost. In rural counties, less than 5% of the population were members, and attempts by the gentry to set up county societies for rural workers were not very successful, because the spirit of self-help was missing.

At this time, friendly societies were purely local, completely independent, and hard to regulate. They had rules that limited their liability, but there was a high failure rate; they could easily become financially exhausted and collapse. The problem was that actuarial knowledge was undeveloped and statistical tables for calculating risk were unreliable. The societies charged a flat rate contribution regardless of age, and as their members grew older and so liabilities grew over time, they found it difficult to attract younger members; younger men would simply form a new club so as to avoid the liability. The widespread use of funds for drink provoked stern condemnation, but the conviviality of the club night was important in generating the bonding social capital needed to keep the society together. It was also useful in preventing what economists call 'moral hazard' – members claiming more than they were entitled to in benefits. The sense of mutual obligation, combined with detailed knowledge of each other's situation, meant that members tended to limit their claims against the society.

The friendly society movement benefitted from the same background conditions that helped the consumer co-ops: the increase in population, the growth of towns, the railway boom, a rise in real wages, and in particular the effects of a Poor Law Amendment Act of 1834 that threatened people who did not insure themselves with the 'workhouse'. More specifically, from the late 1830s onwards it benefitted from the invention of regionally-based societies called 'orders'. These had a federal structure, with the order providing economies of scale and groups called 'lodges' preserving some local independence; the Independent Order of Oddfellows, the Manchester Unity, and the Ancient Order of Foresters were, according to one historian, the best organised of all societies invented by working men to meet their needs (Gosden, 1973: 39). There were a few societies for women, but the patriarchal nature of the wider society and the high costs and risks attached to maternity meant they tended to be excluded. By 1872 there were 34 societies with more than 1000 members each. There were 1,282,000 members in the orders, two thirds of whom were in the Manchester Unity of Oddfellows and Ancient Order of Foresters that had grown into national societies. Despite their growth they remained convivial, with monthly club meetings, Whit walks and annual feast days.

The societies went through three stages in their financial development. In the first half of the 19th century they operated a system of equal contributions and locally-determined benefits that took no account of risk and needed a steady influx of younger members to counteract the risks related to age. Then, from the second half of the century onwards they began to use actuarial tables to calculate risk and set contributions and benefits to cover the anticipated liabilities. Finally, towards the end of the century the affiliated orders began to fix contributions and benefits centrally in order to reduce the risks of lodges becoming financially exhausted. Gradually, they were discovering the principles of modern insurance.

As members of societies emigrated to Australia, the USA, New Zealand, South Africa and the West Indies they took the idea with them. Returning emigrants also took the idea back into continental Europe. The Order of Oddfellows in particular became an international institution. It arrived in the USA in 1819 (when a subordinate lodge of the Oddfellows opened in

Baltimore – Emery, 2010), and it arrived in Canada in 1852 (Siddeley, 1992). Australia proved to be fruitful ground for the idea, as the early colonists suffered great hardships and inadequate medical care. The first society was set up in 1830 in New South Wales when there were only 37,000 colonists, over 40% of whom were convicts! Branches of the British affiliated orders began to be formed, and colonists could simply transfer their membership from the home country. Within a few years of settlement each of the states had friendly societies, its own legislation and a registrar. By the 1860s they were a major presence in every town, providing medical services, medicines, sick pay, and help in hard times, and as in Britain, they also emphasised conviviality. By the beginning of 20th century they were serving 30% of the population (Green and Cromwell, 1984).

The idea also spread all round Europe, with societies being founded in most European countries, though nowhere did the coverage reach the scale of that achieved in Britain. They also had to learn the hard lessons of how to run an inherently risky business; how to avoid the trap of what they called 'old men's societies', and how to set contributions and benefits to keep pace with calculable risks.

In France, after its recognition in law in 1852 the movement grew rapidly, increasing from around 2000 societies with 100,000 members in 1850 to 13,000 with 2.1 million members by the end of the century. It was more broadly based than the British movement, branching out from its basic insurance function to include provision of doctors, pharmacies, maternal and child welfare health centres, employment services, training courses, public baths, soup kitchens and other programmes (Wisconsin, 2010).

A period of consolidation

In Britain, we can label the period from 1875 onwards one of consolidation. A Royal Commission that reported in 1874 found great diversity. There were 17 types of society, including the affiliated orders, independent local societies, dividing societies, and deposit societies that combined an element of saving along with insurance. The Commission led to a law of 1875 that allowed affiliated societies to be registered, and required all registered societies to submit audited annual accounts, annual returns of membership, and five yearly returns of sickness and mortality. Actuarial staff were appointed to the Registrar's office. We can see how from then on the societies became real insurance mutuals. The affiliated orders continued to have the largest numbers of members and their growth continued, but at a slower pace. The character of the societies became more business-like, with fewer meetings, graduated contributions, better management, and less money to spare for beer; it was significant that the societies that grew the most from then on were the Rechabites who were teetotallers. Gradually, a three-tier structure was emerging of branch, district and national societies, with each affiliated order having annual or biennial assemblies. By 1904 the movement had reached its peak. There were 5.6 million members in registered societies, plus an unknown number in small, unregistered societies. Out of a total of seven million working men, nearly all were members of friendly societies.

A new form of society grew up, called a 'collecting society'. This was a much more commercial undertaking that concentrated on selling life insurance policies through local agents who collected weekly premiums. By 1903 there were 43 of these with nearly seven million members. The Royal Liver, founded in 1850, was the best of them, but others took advantage of their remoteness from members to neglect governance and charge high management fees. The United Assurance Company was the worst; there were problems of mismanagement and extravagance, culminating in 1883 in its collapse. In this type of society, members were almost excluded from governance. Even in the supposedly well-run Royal Liver, in 1884 a petition from 500 members led to an investigation that found extravagance, high management costs, and inflated salaries and commissions. It turned out that the annual meetings had been packed with members of staff and their relatives, so that managers and directors were able to engage in what economists call, rather coyly, 'rent seeking'. On the other hand, they had one big advantage; as one historian points out, they 'catered for the needs of the very poorest' in a way that the affiliated orders could not (Hopkins, 1995: 59).

The friendly society movement also faced a growing challenge from commercial competitors. The Prudential Insurance Company had begun business in 1854, and by the end of the century 'industrial insurance' companies had grown into a gigantic industry with over 30 million funeral benefit policies outstanding, and a workforce of 100,000 to administer them. Like the collecting societies they gave very poor value for money but they had a lot of political power; the 'Pru' had grown into the largest private owner of freehold property in the country. Friendly societies were also coming up against other limitations. Longer life expectancy among working class people, coupled with a lack of rules about retirement, meant funds were being drained as sickness benefits became de facto pensions. The Manchester Unity and the Foresters introduced pension schemes, but few could afford them. In 1908 a Liberal government introduced non-contributory pensions that took some of the strain.

The limitations of self-help were being made clear. The friendly societies opposed government intervention but were unable to show how they would make up for the deficiencies in coverage, and so the introduction of state-funded social insurance was seen by many as being inevitable.

In the USA friendly societies came to be called 'fraternal societies'. Before the great depression of the 1930s, they were the leading providers of social welfare apart from the churches (Beito, 1990). Like the British societies, they mainly provided sickness benefits, death benefits and medical care through society doctors. By 1920, their National Fraternal Congress had 200 member-societies with 120,000 lodges that were insuring nine million members. However, this was the tip of the iceberg, because most societies were local and not affiliated to the national congress; in Chicago alone there were known to be 313 fraternal organisations providing insurance (Siddeley, 1992). One historian estimates that altogether, 18 million people or nearly 30% of all adults over 20 belonged to such societies, though the insurance-based societies overlapped with secretive Masonic societies that provided more informal mutual aid, and only 40% of members subscribed to a sickness fund. They dominated the health insurance market, helped resettle vast immigrant populations, and were particularly popular among African Americans (Beito, 1990). Because they could micro-manage the administration of sickness benefits so as to avoid moral hazard, they 'provided an efficient delivery of working class sickness insurance that commercial insurers could not match' (Emery, 2010: 5). They also, like the collecting societies in Britain, began to specialise in selling life insurance. They began to convert from weekly flat-rate payments to the mutual practice of annual premiums assessed on age. By 1905 there were 600 fraternal societies providing life insurance, with over six million members (Murphy, 2010).

They had also become popular in Canada. Here growth had been held back by a lack of awareness of sound actuarial principles, but by 1931 there were eight registered societies, plus 24 that had come in with immigrants from the USA. In Australia, by 1914 46% of all Australians were benefitting from them. Membership dipped during the depression and by 1938 it had fallen to 29%, but the movement continued to provide a wide range of services including home loans, life, accident and fire insurance.

In France, by 1915 there were nearly seven million members in 25,000 societies for mutual aid that had sickness benefits as their main activity (Aubrun, 1915). They also provided doctors' fee and medicines. Some societies also paid pensions; they were funded out of the interest on a society's reserves, and they were not very generous, though Aubrun says that in 1911 5000 approved societies paid out 100,000 pensions. In contrast to Britain, most of the French mutuals encouraged women members and provided maternity benefits. As in Britain, societies were facing strong competition from large insurance companies that used actuarial tables to set their rates, and they were beginning to become more business-like in response. However, as in Britain there was little taste for providing life insurance beyond the usual death benefits that covered funeral expenses. It seems that for life insurance to be made to work it required large numbers of members and good actuarial skills. In 1903 Felix Raison, head of the Mutual Aid Department at the Musee Social in Paris, founded a union of 125 societies uniting 20,000 members, with a central reserve fund to even out demand. This was big enough to compete with the commercial insurers.

One feature that distinguishes the French movement from the British was its capacity to form superstructures beyond the individual society. As early as 1821, a grand council brought together 34 Marseille societies and then went on to set up many more. In 1883 the first national congress was held and in 1902 a national federation was set up by 52 unions, along with 17 pension funds and eight medical and pharmaceutical unions. By then there was the three-tier system (familiar to many other co-operative sectors) of primary societies, regional unions and a national federation. This enabled them to provide further services such as reinsurance, hospital and pharmacy services and sanatoria.

A period of state intervention

Given the importance of insurance against such basic risks as sickness, it would be surprising if the state had not intervened to make coverage more generous and comprehensive. Voluntary insurance can never cover everyone, and there is an argument that it should not do so because mutual insurance is character-building (Beito, 1990). There is also a counter-argument that if it does not cover women or people on low incomes it fails a more important test based on criteria of equality of condition and social justice. Some mutualists believed that eventually mutual societies would evolve to cover all of people's risks. In 1915, Rene-Georges Aubrun confidently saw an evolution from sickness services through old age pensions to life insurance, orphanages, maternity services, and insurance against invalidity. However, he had no proof that mutual aid societies could do this on a large scale, and others were beginning to see that the limits of mutuality may already have been reached.

When the state begins to take an interest there are really only four options. The state can use mutual and investor-owned insurers to deliver a statutory service, it can take over completely, it can provide comprehensive cover for part of the cost letting mutual or investor-owned insurers top it up, or allow a private market and provide residual cover to those who cannot afford any private provision. The first option occurred in Britain and France in the period from 1911 to the 1940s, the second in Germany in the 1880s and Britain in the 1940s, the third in France and some other European countries in the postwar period, and the fourth in the USA. In Australia, an attempt was made to set up a compulsory social insurance scheme in 1928, for which the friendly societies agreed to be the agents. However, it was abandoned through opposition of the medical doctors' association, and after the Second World War the societies agreed to become health insurance funds under a government national health scheme. Thus it came about that the future of friendly societies in each country was decided by politicians, influenced by the medical profession, and in the resulting health care settlement they were either incorporated or completely shut out.

1. Mutual delivery of a statutory social insurance system

In 1911 the British government introduced national insurance, with employees, employers and the state each paying part of the cost of sickness benefits and free medical treatment. It was to be administered by 'approved societies' that included both friendly societies and commercial insurance companies. Hopkins says 'It constituted a substantial and irreversible setback for the friendly societies' (1995: 69), with the government placating the industrial insurance companies and the more commercial collecting societies. However, the friendly societies got off to a good start; 6.6 million of those to whom the Act applied were already members of registered societies, and many more of unregistered; one estimate is that of the 12 million covered under the 1911 Act, nine million were already covered by friendly societies (Green, 1993). To be approved a society had to be non-profit and under member-control, and so the commercial companies had to establish a separate branch that was also non profit and member-controlled. Surplus income could be used for extra benefits (if approved by Ministry of Health), and so a well-run mutual could foster member loyalty. However, the financial health of each society varied with the risk characteristics of its members, and the rate of subsidy was cut over time, so in effect the government raided the reserves of the more successful societies. Nor did member-ownership really make a difference, since the powers of government to intervene gradually increased (Mabbett, 2001).

Friendly societies had the advantage of being able to guard against moral hazard; through the lodge system members knew each other and visited those who were sick. However, the commercial companies and collecting societies could keep down their costs by using the scheme to press the sale of life insurance and, because it was underwritten by the government, moral hazard in benefit claims was not their problem. The friendly society movement began to stagnate, and the new compulsory members had no interest in their fraternal aspects. By 1938 they had experienced a net loss of nearly 5% of members, and 'The heyday of the friendly societies was over' (Hopkins, 1995: 70). In the postwar setting up of the welfare state, the societies were completely sidelined and cut out of the system.

In France, a law of 1910 provided state pensions, with societies in partnership as collecting agents; by 1912 societies had established 27 working funds, and over 3000 societies were authorised to collect contributions (Aubrun, 1915). They were seen as the natural instruments of social insurance, but as in Britain other collectors were admitted to the pension scheme as well. In 1930 a national social insurance system was introduced that made health insurance compulsory for all employees. Mutuals were given management of 500 health insurance funds covering 40% of insured persons, and 63 pension plans covering 60% of those insured. By 1938 there were 22,000 mutuals with 9.8 million members (Wisconsin, 2010). However, the partnership with the state did not seem to damage the movement in the same way as in Britain and the mutuals came into the postwar period with their reputation intact.

2. Takeover by the state

It is worth recounting the arguments that led to the sidelining of friendly societies in Britain from 1948, as these show the strengths and weaknesses of the friendly societies compared to their commercial competitors. In his famous report published in 1942, William Beveridge argued that the incentives of the MOBs were compatible with the aims of the government but those of the IOBs were not. IOBs were interested because they could bundle additional products in with the scheme, and they had the advantage of vigorous sales through agents. However, they did not discriminate against people who were bad risks; they wanted to sell to the poor, because life policies would often lapse and they would profit. The MOBs guarded against adverse selection through restrictive recruitment policies, and so it was they who were guilty of what economists call 'cream skimming', selection of members with lower risks. The societies' offer of additional benefits was criticised as it came from cream skimming as well as from good management. Beveridge was against the IOBs because they had no local structure for scrutinising claims, and they sold life policies (which he saw as a form of gambling) rather than real insurable losses. However, the Labour government that came in after the War decided to set up a state-delivered social insurance scheme and a national health service that was free at the point of use. From then on, friendly societies had no role at all other than as private providers of various kinds of voluntary insurance and savings. We have to add to our understanding of the causes of decline of an MOB sector competition from governments as well as from IOB competitors.

3. Comprehensive cover but for part of the cost

In France, after the Second World War the government decided on a mixed funding system. The mutuals continued to play an important role as an acknowledged partner, with the supplementary role of topping up payments by the state (Sandler et al, 2004). Three statutory schemes were set up that covered around 70% of health care costs, the rest being insurable through complementary insurance. Now, around 87% of households are covered for the supplementary costs by medical insurance from three types of insurer: mutuals, commercial companies and provident societies run by employers and employees. Forty-three per cent of complementary insurance is purchased individually, the rest through employers with collective group contracts, and it accounts for 12% of total health spending. Among OECD countries, the share of health care financed by private insurance is higher only in the US, where private insurance is the predominant source of coverage, and the Netherlands, where private insurance represents the primary payer for 36% of the population (Buchmueller and Couffinhal, 2004).

The mutual insurance associations have played a dominant role from the start. In 1990 there were around 6000 of them, with 12.5 million members and a total of 25 million people covered. By 1995 the numbers covered had grown to 27 million, half the French population (Wisconsin, 2010). Now, the numbers of societies has dropped considerably to 823, but they are covering even more people; 38 million (Federation Nationale de Mutualite Francaise, 2010). Many societies are organised along occupational lines, the largest covering public sector employees such as teachers or postal workers, while others draw their membership from individuals living in a particular *departement*. Their market share has remained fairly constant at around 60%; in 2000, they were providing 59% of all complementary health insurance contracts and financing 7.5% of total health care expenditure while private insurance companies account for 21% and 2.8%, and the provident institutions for 16% and 2.1%, respectively.

Some of the mutuals are also involved in health provision; 62% of hospitals are publicly owned, 18% non profit, and 18% for profit, and some of the non-profits are mutuals. They have a long tradition of direct service provision through dental clinics, optical centres, medical centres, pharmacies and hospitals. They have 105 hospitals, 64 health centres, 441 Dental Centers, 290 Hearing Centers, 670 optical centers and 61 Pharmacies. They also provide a wide range of social care services, in 150 centres for people with disabilities, 172 for young children, 329 for older people and 110 outreach centres. They also have a range of other insurance products such as death benefits, insurance against loss of income through incapacity, and savings plans.

How have they managed to maintain this dominance over a mixed system of supplementary health insurance? It was during the 1980s that the investor-owned insurers began to enter the market, and the mutuals benefitted from being there first. The impact of competition was lessened because they specialised in collective contracts to closed groups that were stable and that preferred to maintain the solidarity principles for which the societies were valued. The IOBs posed more of a direct challenge in the market for individual insurance, as they discriminated in favour of lower risk consumers and so could afford to charge lower prices. As a result, many mutuals began adopting similar practices, for instance varying non-group prices according to subscriber age and offering more choice of products. However, they were careful not to go too far; these adaptations enabled them to maintain their position in the market, without infringing their values of solidarity.

The three categories of insurers differ in their organisational objectives and in the way that they are regulated. The mutuals have always had a distinct set of values, emphasising mutual aid and solidarity, and this means they make very limited use of risk-rating or risk selection strategies. This gives them the right to exemption from a 7% premium tax on insurance contracts. Despite a threat from the European Union to impose more uniform regulations for the industry, the tax advantage has remained. Mutuals are financed almost entirely by payments and fees paid by subscribers, and complementary health insurance is their main line of business, representing 95% of outlays in 2000 (Buechmuller and Couffinhall 2004). In contrast, the investor-owned insurers see health cover as just one of many insurance products representing less than 5% of total revenue.

What affect have the mutuals had on the wider system of health care? They have been rather passive. The lists of reimbursable items have always been managed by the state, sometimes with advice from the health insurance funds and health professionals. They have tended to tie the level of benefits closely to that of the public system, and have not extended this to cover treatments that are not covered by social security. Yet they have held firm to the principle of solidarity, and prevented 'adverse selection' by investor-owned firms from becoming the norm.

How good is the quality of health care that results from this system? The World Health Organisation rated it number one in the world in 2001. In a survey conducted in 1996, 15% of French people were dissatisfied with their health care system compared to 41% in Britain (Green and Irvine, 2001). The causes of such high satisfaction are various, including the high level of total expenditure on health, and the system of direct payments from patient to doctor, and the wide amount of choice that goes with it. However, like most health care systems it is under pressure from increasing demand and costs. The government is considering increasing the scope of benefits provided by voluntary health insurers. It is interesting that the commercial insurance industry supports the idea of shifting the responsibility, but the *mutuelles* are less supportive of reducing the role of the public system; being motivated less by profit they can see the need for solidarity.

4. Residual funding by the state

In the USA, one might have expected fraternal societies to come to dominate the market in sickness benefits and health insurance. They had a head start over the investor-owned companies, and had inbuilt comparative advantages. Because they were small in size and culturally homogeneous, they were able largely to overcome the problems of asymmetric information, which is that the insured knows more than the insurer about his or her condition. Because the reputation of members mattered to each other, they could avoid moral hazard, which is the tendency of the insured person to exaggerate his or her need (Siddeley, 1992). Yet the movement reached its peak in 1925 with 120,000 lodges and then fell back. By 1986 only 52,000 lodges remained. Why did they decline? One historian blames actuarial problems originating in faulty assessments made between 1870 and 1910. The equal premium system came under strain with an ageing membership, higher fees had to be levied, and so younger people dropped out. There was a painful transition to premiums based on risk and many smaller societies were forced out of business. Then, legal impediments from medical societies closed off the growing health insurance market. The growth of the government's social welfare role weakened it; statutory workers' compensation made the societies withdraw gradually from providing industrial accident insurance (Beito, 1990).

Group insurance funded by employers became the main way in which workers and their families were insured against sickness and health care costs. Because deductions were made from payrolls, and the involvement of employers meant problems of adverse selection and moral hazard were not important, commercial insurers were able to offer low cost group contracts. In France the mutuals grew as the dominant supplementary insurance providers within a statutory health insurance system. Yet in the USA, where the health system was almost completely market-dominated, the mutuals were not able to make much impact. There are a few co-operative health providers, but we will be introducing them in the next chapter, when looking at consumer co-operatives in health care.

The current situation of friendly societies

In Britain, after losing their role in social insurance in 1948, friendly societies struggled to find a new role. They found it in provision of a variety of supplementary insurance and savings products. There are currently 57 societies and mutual insurance companies in membership of their national association, Association of Financial Mutuals, who between them have 12 million members, and assets under management of £80 billion. In the USA, the National Fraternal Congress (NFCA) has 67 member-societies and 31 state fraternal congresses in membership, with 9.3 million 'fraternalists' in 37,000 local chapters, making it one of America's largest member-volunteer networks. Combined, the NFCA's member-societies maintain more than $353 billions of life insurance-in-force and, in 2008 alone, contributed almost $424 million to charitable and fraternal programs, and volunteered nearly 94 million hours for community-service projects (National Fraternal Congress, 2010). In Canada a Canadian Fraternal Association claims 17 member-societies, with 400,000 members. In Australia the national federation (Friendly Societies of Australia) has 32 societies in membership, whose main products are funeral bonds, insurance-based savings, and insurance for aged care. So it seems that in all of these countries the friendly societies have lost their dominant role but have managed to survive and, to some extent, reinvent themselves.

Type 2: Mutual insurance companies

There are a variety of needs for insurance that can be met through MOBs. For consumers, insurance comes in two major forms; 'non-life' which covers all sorts of risks to property and person, and life insurance, which is a payment to a beneficiary on someone's death.

The founding period

Non-life insurance began with the need to spread the risks from fire. Its origin can be traced precisely to the Great Fire of London in 1666 that destroyed more than 13,000 homes. There are two ways to mitigate loss by fire; one is to put the fire out and the other to restore the monetary loss. The first began in 1696; a society with the improbably long title of 'Contributors for Insuring Houses, Chambers or Rooms from Loss by Fire by Amicable Contributionship' (commonly known as the Hand-in-Hand because of its distinctive fire mark) provided fire engines and crews to put out fires in houses owned by its members (Mutual Assurance, 2010). The idea spread to America, where Benjamin Franklin helped set up a volunteer fire fighting association in Philadelphia called the Union Fire Company that provided a model for many others. However, Franklin realised that insurance was also needed, and in 1752 he set up a society called The Philadelphia Contributionship. Because, in America, volunteer fire fighters were doing the job of putting out the fires, the society could concentrate on insurance against loss. A second company was formed in Philadelphia and a third in New York (though this converted to an IOB in 1809, which must be the earliest example of demutualisation we can find). The Baltimore Equitable Society was formed in 1794, and it remains the second oldest mutual fire insurance company still in business in America.

The first life insurance mutual was probably Equitable Life, founded in London in 1762. It was made possible by advances in the scientific understanding of risk undertaken by Charles Dodson, who calculated premiums using mortality tables and probability studies. This meant that the policyholder's premium could be fixed throughout the term of the policy and the amount paid on death was guaranteed. As early as 1777 the Society was able to reduce all premiums by 10%. Another reduction in premiums followed and a regular system of bonuses was subsequently developed. This combination of fair dealing and regular bonuses attracted new business and by 1799 there were 5,000 policies in force for sums totalling around £4 million. By 1810, membership had approached 10,000, and notable policyholders included such esteemed characters as Samuel Taylor Coleridge, William Wilberforce and Sir Walter Scott (Equitable Life, 2010).

However, it was in America that the mutual life insurance sector became fully developed. Commercial life insurance began in the USA during the colonial period, but companies rarely survived for long and sold few policies (Murphy, 2010). Suddenly in the 1840s it took off, for two reasons. First, there were legislative changes that allowed women to insure their husbands' lives and to benefit from the payout. Second, mutual life companies began to emerge that redistributed annual profits to policyholders rather than stockholders. They did not really need to raise large amounts of capital from a separate group of stockholders; if they grew quickly their size would soon ensure that they could meet claims out of their own reserves. Also, their mutual status reassured potential customers of their trustworthiness at a time when there was little state regulation. The Mutual Life Insurance Company of New York issued its first policy in 1843, the New England Mutual Life in 1844, and at least 15 more mutuals were chartered by 1849. They grew quickly through aggressive advertising and were popular with policyholders because of the annual dividends they paid not on capital but in reduced premium payments. However, investor-owned life insurers fought back, lobbying for legislation in New York State for a law to limit the operation of mutuals. As a result, mutuals were forced to find an initial deposit of $100,000 in order to start business, and this caused real damage. As one historian says, it 'dampened the movement towards mutualisation until the 1890s' (Murphy, 2010: 4).

A period of growth and consolidation

From the early part of the 19th century, the idea of mutual insurance spread throughout America, moving west with the population and becoming the normal way in which fire insurance was organised. Fire insurance then became bundled up with other risks and sold as home insurance. Auto insurance began that covered both damage to the vehicle and legal liabilities arising out of accidents. A variety of insured risks to the person began to be insured, such as accident and disability cover, designed to mitigate loss of earnings. A major innovation begun by the Equitable Life Assurance Society was the deferred dividend policy, whereby people could insure their life and share dividends from an investment fund when they retired. By the end of the 19th century the life insurance business had become dominated by the mutual companies and the fraternal societies. Between 1885 and 1905 the mutuals began doing business internationally; the Equitable provided insurance in almost 100 countries, the New York Life in almost 50 and the Mutual in about 20 (Murphy, 2010).

In 1905 an investigation was made into the mutuals, which found that like some of the collecting societies in Britain there were abuses

such as excessive management costs, high expenses and political lobbying, and proxy voting was being used to frustrate control by policyholders. Legislation was passed to combat this, and another surge in the
growth of mutuals began; while there had been 106 companies in 1904,
by 1914 another 288 had been founded, and they continued to dominate
the market until the demutualisation trend began in the 1980s.

Type 3: Insurers set up as secondary co-operatives

There is yet another important mutual insurance sector; member-owned
insurance societies set up by consumer co-operatives and similar organisations in order to meet their own needs as businesses as well as the
needs of their members. These are often called 'secondary co-ops', and
they can take any one of three forms: co-operatives, mutuals or stock
companies owned by co-operatives. In 1997, for instance, 51% were
co-ops, 28% mutuals and 21% stock companies (Kennedy, 1999). There
is not much information about the sector, but it is represented internationally by an International Co-operative and Mutual Insurance Federation (ICMIF) whose membership list more or less defines the sector.
The criteria for joining the Federation are that members have to conform to co-operative principles; they have to pay a dividend on business
done by members with the co-operative, offer open and voluntary membership and provide only limited interest on capital (Kennedy, 1999).

The founding period

The earliest example of this type is the Co-operative Insurance Society,
founded in Britain 1867 by the consumer co-operative movement to
meet the needs of its societies for fire and property insurance, and then
by extension to meet their members' need for personal insurance. The
second was Les Artisans Coopvie, founded in Quebec in 1876 to provide life insurance, and the third was La Prevoyance Sociale, founded in
Belgium in 1907 by the Belgian Workers Party as a reaction against poorly
managed private insurers, providing both life and fire insurance.

Thereafter, the history of the sector is really the history of individual
secondary co-ops founded by a variety of sponsors: consumer co-operatives,
farmer co-operatives, trade unions, churches and so on. Not many were
founded by individuals, as it is difficult for individuals needing insurance
to overcome the collective action problem. Also, while a mutual insurance provider does not need large amounts of capital to get going, it
does need to grow quickly if it is to gain the protection of numbers that
makes its commitments less risky. This is best done through an existing

organisation that can provide it with a guaranteed market and invest enough capital to get it over the initial period of growth when it is not able to meet all its commitments. Also, in some countries there are laws against primary co-operative insurers and so only secondary agencies have been able to do it.

A period of growth

There has been a steady growth in the numbers and size of member-organisations of the ICMIF. In 1922, when the Federation was founded it had just 21 member co-ops. By 1969 it had 57 societies from 25 countries insuring over 60 million people, and by 1999 it had over 100 members from 60 countries with nearly 9% of the world's market for insurance. At that time, the diverse origins of member-organisations were investigated; 15% had a base in agricultural co-operatives, 29% in trade unions and professional groups, 19% in multi-purpose co-operatives from developing countries, 19% in credit unions and 18% in other categories (Kennedy, 1999: 227). By 2009 this number has risen to 216 members with approximately one-third of the membership in Europe, a further third in the Americas and the remainder representing Asia and Oceania, Africa and the Middle East. The members in turn represent over 400 insurance organisations with assets approaching $1 trillion; spread across more than 70 countries, these organisations employ over 300,000 people. A further 1700 mutual insurers are indirect members of ICMIF through their national mutual trade associations (ICMIF, 2010).

In virtually every developed country one or two co-operative insurers will be among the top ten. The Nationwide Mutual Insurance Company started as an auto insurer for Ohio farmers, and is now one of the largest insurance and financial companies in the world, ranked 108 in the Fortune 500 listing. It has almost $15.5 billion in statutory assets, and has more than 16 million policies. The Debeka Group provides life and health insurance mainly for civil servants; it is the top private health insurer and the fourth largest direct insurance company in Germany. Unipol was founded by one of Italy's co-operative federations, Legacoop to meet its members' needs for insurance. It is now the fourth largest insurer with a market share of over 10%. The Co-operators in Canada is the largest Canadian multi-product insurer. It was started in 1945 by Saskatchewan Wheat Pool, owned by co-operatives and credit unions, and it provides a mixture of individual and farm insurance. Ethias is the second largest in Belgium, Folksam is dominant in Sweden, Mobillar dominant in Switzerland, while Glensiddige Forsikring is the second largest non-life insurer in Norway. MACIF is largest automobile insurer in France with a 14% market share, Cattolical Assicurazioni is the fifth largest in Italy in non-life and life insurance, La Mondiale in France is an international leader in pension and estate planning insurance, and so on. In Asia there are several large co-operative insurers; Zenkyoren set up to meet the needs of Japanese farmers, Zenrosai the needs of trade unions and consumer co-ops, while NTUC Income, set up by the trade union congress in Singapore, is now one of the most successful in the region. CUNA Mutual is a massive, international insurer owned by credit unions, for whom it markets a range of products.

However, the problem in researching this particular type of member-owned business is that it is a shifting category. Insurers that began servicing one distinct group of members have diversified. Most are now both producer and consumer oriented. Also, there is more and more integration between the insurance and banking sectors; soon it may be impossible to identify them as a separate sector. For instance, OP Bank group is the largest financial services group in Finland, with over 30% of domestic loans and deposits and 25% of the domestic non-life insurance market. It may be possible to shift to a broader definition, in which member-ownership can still be clearly distinguished in their governance structures. However, some of the largest, notably Nationwide in the USA, have set up IOBs from which to do their business and so member-ownership is hidden behind the IOB in a holding company.

Demutualisation of life insurance mutuals

The boundaries between different types of ownership can never be taken for granted. In the insurance industry there have been periods of mutualisation and demutualisation. For instance, the UK-based insurer, Standard Life, was founded in 1825 as an IOB, in 1925 it converted to a mutual and in 2006 it converted back again to an IOB. There has also been one period in which mutuals were nationalised and became POBs! It seems that insurance business has been fought over by competing ownership types, each of which is thought to have built-in advantages over the others.

The first move was towards mutuality. Early on in the evolution of insurance, several investor-owned companies in the USA and the UK such as Standard Life and Equitable Life decided to switch to mutual status, because it gave them advantages in the market; at that time, with little or no government regulation, customers did not trust the IOB model. Then, with better regulation by governments some traffic began to flow the other way: by the end of the 1970s in the USA 100 life companies and about the same number of non-life companies had demutualised (Franklin and Lee, 1988), and the 135 that were left had a market share of 43% (down from 69% in 1954 – Hansmann, 1985). The process was slowed by laws passed in the 1920s in New York State and several other states because of insiders benefitting from wind-fall profits, and it only got going in the 1980s when deregulation' of the industry took place. In other countries demutualisation was not an issue and there was some movement in the other direction; in the 1960s several IOBs in the UK converted to mutual form in order to 'escape from the attentions of the corporate raiders of the time' (Franklin and Lee, 1988: 89). In another twist to the tale, in the 1970s several insurance companies in France and Germany, and auto insurers in several states in Canada, were nationalised. In the UK the consumer co-operative owned CIS had to fight hard against nationalisation of the whole industry.

The recent trend has all been in the direction of the IOB, both in the USA and in the UK and other countries such as South Africa and Australia and even Japan. In the USA, an important moment was the demutualisation of Union Mutual in 1986. From then onwards some of the largest mutuals such as Prudential, MetLife, John Hancock and Sun Life converted. The boards of others such as Northwestern, New York Life and Penn Mutual decided to stay mutual, but in the USA now fewer than 80 remain. The process did not begin in the UK until the 1990s, but then within 10 years 12 large mutuals had converted, two by flotation and 10 being bought by a bank or insurance company. By 2004, the mutuals had only 16% of the market, and then in 2006 the largest of the remaining societies, Standard Life, demutualised. It had suffered a reduced capital base when the stock markets fell between 2001 and 2003, and its board decided it could no longer provide the kinds of benefits with-profits policyholders expected from a mutual. It also needed to seek additional capital to meet its commitments, and so in 2006 it converted back to investor-ownership (Standard Life, 2010). Now the mutual share in the UK is only 4.5% (ICMIF, 2009). It consists of one large mutual insurance company, Royal London, a few insurers owned by other types of MOB such as CIS and the NFU Mutual, and a large number of friendly societies some of which are very small.

What were the reasons for demutualisation? It is important to know, because if these are compelling we can expect demutualisation to continue, but if they are weak or specific to certain times and places then the future is more hopeful. An early analysis of the subject concluded that 'The motivation will vary from country to country, depending on the particular economic and institutional background' (Franklin and

Lee, 1988: 89). However, the main reason for demutualisation seems to be to gain access to the capital that new investors bring in. It might be thought that a business that recycles money to and from its customers cannot be in need of extra capital; one of the main advantages of a financial mutual (including the banks we will be exploring in Chapter 7) is that it merely invests money on behalf of its customers. Why then does it need capital from outside? Sometimes a mutual has to demutualise and seek new capital because it has got things wrong. For instance, the UK's largest mutual, Standard Life suffered a reduced capital base when the stock markets fell between 2001 and 2003, and its board decided it could no longer provide the kinds of benefits with-profits policyholders expected from a mutual. It also needed to seek additional capital to meet its commitments, and so in 2006 it converted back to investor-ownership (Standard Life, 2010).

However, in most cases the main reason for demutualisation is so mutual can enter new markets that are riskier than the ones they are in. The obvious counter argument is that they do not need to do this; they exist to serve a particular type of need not to grow just for the sake of it. However, managers are often motivated by a desire to emulate IOB competitors, and to grow the business so they themselves can profit through higher salaries and bonuses. If the mutual is not governed well on the members' behalf, this motivation can divert the business from its ethic of service to one of 'mimetic isomorphism'; managers just want to be like everyone else. More concretely, managers cannot benefit in a mutual from share-based incentive plans. It is no accident that the wave of demutualisations has coincided with a wave of stock option plans for managers of their IOB equivalents.

We now know the consequences of unrestrained growth in financial services companies that put short-term profit through share values before long-term stability. The spectacular failures of Enron and Worldcom, the current banking crisis that we will be reviewing in Chapter 7, point to the need for a reappraisal of the benefits of mutuality; the constraints they impose on their managers are now seen as a comparative advantage rather than a disadvantage, and the benefits of mutuality are beginning to be seen as outweighing those of conversion. This brings us to another supposed advantage of IOBs over MOBs; they are found by some economists to be more efficient. Demutualisation is a kind of natural experiment, and we can measure the relative efficiency of the two types before and after conversion. The results are clear; mutuals are shown to return more of the value to their members, to have lower average costs and, because they do not pay out dividends to shareholders retain more of the surplus to support growth. As Armitage and Kirk put it, 'the evidence... suggests that mutual status in the life industry is associated with greater competitiveness and efficiency, not less' (1994: 256). Why then do mutuals convert? It is tempting to revert to the simplest explanation that it is in the interests of managers but not of members.

Demutualisation points up the issue of policyholder rights, discussions over which indirectly show the inherent advantages of mutuals. Court judgements concerning demutualisations in the USA and South Africa in the 1970s and 1980s established that only the with-profits policyholders should benefit, as they were found to be entitled to all the stock. Courts insisted that after demutualisation member should be protected by receiving benefits and dividends that are at least as good as they would have received without demutualisation. It is possible to go further and argue that they need compensating for loss of their membership rights to control the business (Franklin and Lee, 1988). This raises the question of who owns a mutual. There are two theories about this. The 'entity theory' asserts that it is not owned by current members but exists for the benefit of current and future members, using reserves built up by previous members who did not take all the profits they could have taken but left some to accrue for the benefit of future generations. The 'revolving fund theory' asserts that the mutual *is* owned by current members because the business operates on a cost-price basis, returning surpluses to members regularly so as to adjust the price down to what it costs to provide the service (Franklin and Lee, 1988). The resulting discussion is rather theological, but it points to the difficulty in reassigning ownership rights from a form of organisation that is based on service to one based on profit. What is certain is that it seems unfair for managers and new owners to benefit from a windfall that they have not earned or taken any risks to obtain.

The strongest argument in favour of conversion is based on a theoretical understanding of the relationship between governance and management. If managers can be more effectively controlled in an IOB (or to put it another way, can be incentivised to align their interests with those of the owners), and if the costs of control are lower, then we can predict that IOBs will be more efficient. Mutuals are deemed to be less efficient because they cannot offer stock options to managers, they do not have share prices to signal how they are performing, and they do not have to face competition between rival groups of managers for control. Corporate governance is a problem in MOBs, particularly when they contain large numbers of members who have heterogeneous interests and who face high costs in trying to influence decision-making. Because their interest is so widely dispersed, there is no equivalent of the large institutional shareholder in an ILO that can oversee the company. A recent review of the governance of life insurance mutuals in the UK confirms that in some mutuals this is a serious problem (Myners, 2004).

The review came about because of the governance failures implicit in the demise of one of the largest mutuals, Equitable Life. In 2000 Equitable lost a court case which meant it had to honour an agreement to service high interest-bearing life insurance policies entered into many years previously when interest rates were much higher. In the subsequent financial crisis it had to sell off parts of the business and cease to write new policies. An Inquiry into the collapse by Lord Penrose found that there had been 'ineffective scrutiny and challenge of the executive of the Society', the board had insufficient skills, was totally dependent on actuarial advice, and 'was never fully advised of the financial implications of the decisions that were said to be open to them'. Crucially, the board itself was 'not subject to effective external scrutiny or discipline'. Yet under the articles 'policyholders were effectively powerless, and the Board was a self-perpetuating oligarchy amenable to policyholder pressure only at its discretion' (Penrose, quoted in Myners, 2004: 113). To make matters worse, not all customers were members, but only those who had with-profits policies.

Rather than tackling the underlying problem of the lack of member participation, Penrose recommended that the Financial Services Authority appoint an expert to a board who would report back to the FSA. The Myners Review commissioned research that found that members value their membership and had a very positive view of mutuality. They had high levels of trust and believed mutuals could deliver superior performance. The majority were not interested in taking part in governance, but there was a substantial cohort who were interested in becoming engaged, suggesting that 'while engaging members may be difficult, it is certainly not impossible' (Myners, 2004: 102). The Review went further than Penrose, recommending that mutuals find ways of connecting with their members and calling for their trade associations to provide best practice guidance in member relations. It set out detailed principles for fair and accessible voting procedures, and called for mutuals to be obliged to notify members of major transactions and to have to seek their permission for very major changes. Many of their recommendations have been implemented, and the situation is now much improved.

The current situation of insurance mutuals

Surprisingly, demutualisation has not dented the sector as much as we might have expected. In 2007, the global market share of mutual and co-operative insurers (all the types we have been discussing so far) was still 22.6% (ICMIF, 2009). Its share of the US market was 28.7%, of Japan 41.6%, of France 38.2%, of Germany 43.5%, of the Netherlands 25.8%, of Canada 16.1%, of Italy 13.6%, and so on. Another way to look at the same figures is to list the top ten countries where the mutual market share is largest. At number 1 is Finland with a 71% market share, followed by Germany with 43.5%. Then follow Denmark, Japan, France, Norway, Austria, Iceland, Tunisia and the USA. This shows how dominant the sector still is in most countries in Europe and in Japan. If we look at the figures by region we find that North America, Europe and Asia/Oceania have similar shares of the mutual market (28%, 21% and 21% respectively), with Latin America taking 6% and Africa just over 1%. If we split life and non-life insurance we find that the global market share is 20% in life and 26.5% in non-life business. Is the mutual share growing or contracting? Between 2006 and 2007 it fell from 23.6% to 22.6%, not because of demutualisation but because of a reduced share of the fast growing life insurance market. It seems, then, that from a global perspective the sector is now quite stable.

Future prospects

We began the chapter by tracing the origins and development of three distinct streams of member-owned insurance: friendly societies, mutual insurers and insurance companies owned by other types of MOB. Early in their history, friendly societies provided a strong mixture of health and sickness insurance and conviviality, but they came up against the medical establishment and then had to learn to survive in an uncomfortable place somewhere between the market and the welfare state, their status determined more by public policy than by any comparative advantages they may have had. Mutual insurers grew by selling the mutual proposition of a less risky product beneficial to customers as members, but their commitment was never backed up by the sense of being part of a social movement. Their managers often saw their chance to switch between member- and investor-ownership as it suited them, and because of governance failures they and a self-selected group of directors became the de facto owners. Co-operative and mutual insurers grew steadily from a secure base in consumer- or producer-ownership, their governance being held indirectly by members of another organisation, and so in a curious way their status has been protected and they have been allowed to serve their members more single-mindedly without the threat of demutualisation.

No three streams have all flowed into one river of mutual insurance, and it is becoming harder to distinguish between them. In some countries they share the same trade association and they all work in the same markets. Increasingly there is a confluence of insurance with banking, so that the category of mutual insurance is increasingly being relabelled as 'mutual financial services'. Soon the stories told in this chapter may become, in a more negative sense, history. In this sector, globalisation is not really an issue, or rather it is one that has been around for a long time. Some of the big American mutuals have operated across national boundaries, and the credit unions' CUNA Mutual has been a truly global company. It is not difficult for life insurers to offer membership to policy-holders wherever they live but this will exacerbate their inherent prob-lems of governance. However, if they take seriously the recommendations of the Myners Review and similar pressure points in other countries, they should be able to work out a viable membership strategy. While this will never turn mutual insurance into the mass movement that the friendly societies once achieved, it should involve enough active members to ensure good governance. We will return to this subject of membership strategy in the last chapter.

Insurance can seem a dull subject, but in an uncertain world we cannot do without it. Life insurance and pensions in particular hold the key to the welfare of whole generations of citizens, and in countries that do not pay for health care directly out of taxation health insurance will remain a contentious issue. We can expect that public policies will continue to be made that impinge directly on the sector. For instance, in the USA, there is at the time of writing (2010) a serious attempt to reform the health care system to make it accessible to the 30 million Americans who it is said do not have any insurance cover at all. Barack Obama proposed publicly-funded health care, but a counter proposal is for a health insurance co-operative. Their advocates say this would expand coverage to 94% of all eligible Americans. Co-ops could cover 12 million people, but they need a critical mass of over 500,000 to become strong enough to enter the market in order to affect the price of health care. They would be able to combat market monopolies, and would be consumer owned and so would keep down costs and keep up quality. Group Health Co-operative, which we will be discussing in Chapter 6, is the inspiration, and we await the outcome of this debate to see whether co-operative health insurance is really on the agenda.

5
Consumer-ownership of Housing

One of the most important needs is for shelter, and here housing co-ops have filled an important niche, though rarely achieving a dominant position in a housing market. Before we even begin to consider this type of MOB, we have to make a crucial distinction between *building co-ops* and *permanent housing co-ops*. Building co-ops are set up to enable people mutually to build housing; they are the counterpart to the terminating building society that used to provide finance for the same purpose, and when the housing is finished the society ceases to exist. They are often conflated with permanent housing co-ops. For instance, they are common in Ireland, and this leads to a claim that 4% of housing in Ireland is co-operative when in fact there is only a very small permanent housing co-operative sector (CCMH, 2009). They have been a major tool for urban development in Turkey, Pakistan and India, using land given by government to create whole neighbourhoods for owner-occupation. Building co-ops have provided 1.4 million dwellings – 25% of the housing stock – in Turkey, but they have nearly all dissolved on completion. In India there are said to be 92,000 housing co-ops, but these include terminating and permanent societies, as well as building societies for mortgage lending (ICA Housing, 2010).

Permanent co-operative housing tends to develop among low- to middle-income people as an alternative to owning or renting. It has two basic advantages over other forms of tenure. First, compared to other commodities housing is what the economists call 'sticky': it requires a large investment, is immovable, lasts for a long time, and so on. The costs of acquiring a home are high but the costs of leaving it are even higher, particularly for people on low incomes who do not have much choice in the market. Housing supply often does not keep up with demand, and just getting a home can be an achievement. Hirschmann's distinction between exit and voice is relevant here; the more restricted one's choice the more important is voice, and in this respect the principle of one person one vote is an advantage that is built into co-operative housing but not into any other type of tenure. Second, unlike other commodities, the value of a home is related intimately to the quality value of its setting in an apartment block or neighbourhood. Housing may be of good quality in itself but if the environment is unsafe it loses its use value to the dweller. Housing co-ops offer a unique form of collective control over the environment that neither owner-occupation nor renting can match. These advantages explain why, in the face of fierce competition from bigger tenure forms, we find small co-operative housing sectors in most developed countries.

There is another advantage that relates particularly to apartment blocks. When people live in multi-dwelling blocks, it is in the nature of the building that they share ownership of the land and responsibility for maintaining common parts such as the roof, drainage systems, stairways and gardens. Different countries have very different legal systems to deal with this issue. In England the land and common parts are owned by a freeholder who leases the dwelling to a leaseholder, but this solution has proved unpopular and has been avoided elsewhere. In Scotland a system of 'feuhold' applies with responsibility shared between the residents but it has no mechanisms for resolving conflicts other than through the courts. Co-operative housing provides such a mechanism, with a mix of individual rights and collective duties that maximise the use value of the home (Birchall, 1988). In this it has a serious competitor – the condominium. The differences between the two forms are not large. In a condominium, an apartment is bought at market value and the buyer also gets joint ownership in a company that owns the land and common parts. There is usually a monthly fee for management and maintenance. In a co-operative, the right to occupy the apartment is granted after the prospective member buys a share in the co-operative. The advantage of a 'condo' is its simplicity, which sometimes makes it easier to obtain a mortgage loan. The advantages of a co-op are that it enables dwellers to gain a cheaper collective mortgage, to raise money collectively for repairs and refurbishment, and – subject to equal opportunities laws – to choose who to allow into the scheme.

However, there is one disadvantage to the co-operative form. Because housing is such an expensive and fixed commodity and paying for it demands a steady income stream, it is not as resilient as other types of MOB during a recession. During the 1930s some housing co-ops in New York went out of business because their members could not afford to pay the rent. In the postwar period there has been a sustained growth in housing co-ops in several countries in Europe and North America, but in order to make it accessible to people on low incomes it has been subsidised by governments with low-cost land, low-interest mortgages and sometimes rent subsidies to individual members. This explains why there are not many genuine housing co-ops in developing countries, because they are simply too expensive to promote when compared with informal self-building.

Housing co-ops fall into three types depending on the extent to which the value locked in the housing is owned individually or in common. In a full equity co-op, people buy a share that is equal to the value of the apartment they are to live in, which entitles them to membership in the co-operative and a 'right to occupy' their individual home. When they leave, they can sell their share at market value. In a non-equity co-op, people pay a nominal amount for a membership share, are allocated a home on the basis of need and then 'rent' from the co-op; when they leave they only get their nominal share back. In between are limited equity co-ops that attempt a compromise between affordability and increase in market value; when they leave, members receive a payment based on a formula that revalues the original share, taking into account inflation and the amount the member has paid off the collective mortgage. Roughly speaking, full equity co-ops correspond to owner-occupation while non-equity co-ops correspond to renting, which is why they are sometimes referred to as 'ownership co-ops' and 'rental co-ops'. Limited equity co-ops are somewhere in between. However, the significance of a co-operative depends on the nature of the housing market it is in, and this varies greatly between countries. In a housing market dominated by individual owner-occupation, non-equity co-ops are seen as social housing that people only gain access to if they cannot house themselves in the 'normal' way. In a housing market dominated by renting, it is seen as one option among others within the normal market. Thus, co-ops in Britain and Switzerland may look the same but be understood quite differently. The meaning also varies depending on the size of the sector relative to other sectors, and its density in a particular city or region. Co-operative housing is a minor tenure in the USA, but in New York it is a major player in the housing market for apartment blocks and is seen as 'normal' to the extent that celebrities such as John Lennon have often chosen to live in one.

Some false starts in Britain

The first attempt to set up a housing co-operative was made by some of the Rochdale Pioneers. In 1861 they set up a Rochdale Co-operative

Land and Building Company (Birchall, 1995b). Though it was registered as an ordinary joint stock company, it was expected that the tenants as well as outside shareholders would invest in it, so that it would be the 'joint property of the occupiers and others taking out shares' (Cole, 1944: 92). Only 25 homes were built, and the company soon got into financial difficulty because members were so poor they could not afford the rents. In 1868 the board of the main Pioneer society were asking for payments on a £2000 loan, and by 1869 all references to the Company had ceased (though the descendants of one of the Pioneers were still collecting rents on some of the houses in the 1980s and so it must have converted to private renting). The difficulties the Land and Building Company got into contrasted with the growing problem in consumer co-ops of what to do with the surplus capital invested with them, and the logical solution was for the Rochdale Pioneers society itself to begin building. It was the first of several consumer co-operatives to branch out into building housing estates to rent for its members. Members of the society who were also tenants could, of course, exercise some rights at general meetings, but it was an indirect form of control at best.

The next attempt was made in 1887 by a co-operative activist Owen Greening, and the London manager of the Co-operative Wholesale Society Benjamin Jones, who founded Tenant Co-operators Ltd. The main problem was still how to provide good quality housing for low-income people, given the inevitably high initial financial commitment. A state loan (from the Public Works Loan Board) was by now available to Industrial and Provident Societies, but this would not cover more than two-thirds of the cost. The Society was financed by a small group of wealthy people such as Vansittart Neale who, as well as being pillars of the consumer co-operative movement were also highly influential liberal politicians and businessmen, who could raise the necessary capital from among their friends. This proved to be a fatal weakness. Despite buying up or building a total of 210 dwellings, it never became a tenant-led organisation but remained more like a philanthropic housing association.

Yet the scheme was commercially sound, and it provided the basis for a successful wave of tenant co-partnerships which began in 1901 at Ealing in West London. A rule-change was crucial; the tenant share-holding was increased to £50, payable in instalments, which guaranteed commitment but limited the schemes to better-off skilled workers and clerks. At least 14 societies were formed between 1901 and 1912, building 6595 dwellings for a population of 30–35,000 people (and this author's research has found up to another 40 that were built outside the aegis of the national federation – Birchall, 1995b). It was linked to an influential social movement led by Ebenezer Howard for the development of garden cities and suburbs, with Raymond Unwin as its architect. Garden suburbs were built at Ealing and Hampstead that set a very high standard in estate design, and the model was also used at Letchworth Garden City. However, it had two fatal flaws. In areas where property values increased dramatically during the 1920s there was a growing temptation to privatise the estates. In Hampstead and Ealing Garden Suburbs, large capital gains were offered to shareholders and property speculators gained control. Also, the requirement for a large shareholding excluded low-income people, and so when the central government wanted to find a way of subsidising housing for the working classes after the First World War, it rejected co-partnership and turned to the public landlord model of local authority 'council housing'. There is no better illustration of the idea of the 'critical moment' in history that changes everything.

Co-operative housing in Western Europe

During the late 19th century housing co-ops were founded in Germany, Austria, and Switzerland. Their growth was checked in all but Switzerland by fascist governments, but in the postwar period the idea of co-operative housing was still on the agenda and was seen as a normal way of housing people. In all three countries co-operatives take their place as part of a larger 'limited dividend' sector. The Federal German Housing and Real Estate Organization (GdW) includes in its membership 2000 housing co-operatives, 723 municipal housing organisations and 160 private housing companies. GdW and its 14 regional federations provide a powerful interest group to look after the interests of co-operatives, and provide legal, financial and technical advice and auditing to the primary societies, for whom membership is mandatory. The Austrian Federation of Limited-Profit Housing Associations (GBV) also unites co-operative and limited-profit companies under one single organisation, with 101 housing co-ops and 92 companies. Again, membership is mandatory. The *Schweizerischer Verband für Wohnungswesen* (SVW/ASH) is the national Swiss co-operative housing federation whose membership includes housing co-operatives, non-profit building contractors and foundations. It has around 1000 members, of whom 900 are co-ops.

In each country, co-ops were given a small but assured role in policies to ease the postwar housing shortages, with low interest loans and tax advantages. With the gradual easing of housing shortages, this state support has tailed off. In Germany, the decline in state involvement began in 1986 and in 1990 the non-profit law was abolished. In Austria, co-operatives can still gain public financing for specific projects, provided they target their housing at low-income people and allow local authorities to make referrals. In Switzerland there has been a gradual decrease in new schemes since the 1970s. However, in all three countries the result has been that co-operatives are a stable if minor form of tenure. Now their share of the housing stock is 8% in Germany, 6% in Austria, and 5% in Switzerland. In Germany, there are 2,000 housing co-operatives with three million members, in Austria 101 co-operatives with 412,000 members, and in Switzerland 1500 co-ops with 160,000 members (ICA Housing, 2010). In Germany and Switzerland, all are regarded as 'rental' or non-equity co-ops, while in Austria there is a mix of two thirds rental (non-equity) and a third owner-occupied (full equity).

Italy provides a slightly different story. Here, development also began in the late 19th century and the numbers of housing co-operatives grew rapidly. However, the fascist government took them all over and denied them any autonomy. During the postwar period, instead of being part of a larger limited-profit housing sector, they have been fully integrated from the start into the wider co-operative sector. There are four national federations, each one of which is a specialist part of a larger apex federation representing all types of co-operative: consumer, worker, savings and credit and so on. They have concentrated until recently on developing the full equity or 'owner-occupied' type and so have drawn on the resources of the wider movement rather than relying on government. Recently, with a shift of policy from national to regional government and a growing housing shortage, they have begun to develop non-equity co-ops for low-income people. One source estimates that there are 6100 co-ops with 575,000 members, and with the full equity type outnumbering the rental co-ops by five to one (CECODHAS, 2008). However, another source also estimates 11,000 co-ops; the splitting of the movement into four separate federations makes a full estimate difficult (ICA Housing, 2010).

Co-operative housing in Scandinavia

Norway and Sweden have an even bigger concentration of co-operatives with their own distinctive character. In 1923, HSB (Tenants' Savings Bank and Housing Association) was founded in Sweden as a combined savings bank and housing co-operative developer; it acted as a 'mother' to 'daughter' societies, setting them up and then, through regional associations, offering them management services. Prospective 'tenant-owners' had to save with the savings bank before becoming eligible for a co-op apartment, and so the whole system of building, managing, and financing a co-operative was contained in the one organisation. In 1940 the other big Swedish co-operative development agency, Riksbyggen, was founded by building trade unions, initially to provide work for their members but then to act in the same way as HSB, offering membership to 'daughter' co-ops and managing the queue for housing through savings. They were helped by a law of 1930 that prevented other forms of owner-occupation in apartment blocks, so that co-operatives became the only way people could gain access to housing other than through renting. Though the purchase of a membership share was significant, the co-ops took a limited equity form; the price of entry was controlled by the societies so as to ensure affordability.

In 1929 a similar organisation, OBOS, was set up in Norway by trade unions, modelled on HSB and producing limited equity housing. However, it quickly got involved in the social renting sector. In contrast to Britain, in 1935 the Oslo city council gave OBOS the task of providing all future municipal housing and in 1947 went further and began transferring its estates to tenant co-operatives. The co-operative housing sector in Sweden grew steadily during the second half of the 20th century. By 1971 it had provided 25% of all postwar housing development and now has 18% of the total stock – 750,000 apartments. HSB and Ryksbiggen have 75% of co-operatives in membership, with the other 25% being independent. HSB has 540,000 members, of whom 360,000 are tenant-owners (the rest are waiting for a home), and it has 3845 co-ops in membership of the 33 HSB regional societies. Riksbyggen has 170,000 tenant-members, 1700 co-ops and 35 delegate bodies. A similar period of growth in Norway led, by the late 1980s, to the sector having 19% of the total housing stock, with a concentration of 45% of the stock in Oslo (Birchall, 1988). Now OBOS has 226,000 members. In Oslo it still has 25% of the stock in 350 primary co-operatives and in total it manages 128,000 homes for 950 co-operatives (OBOS, 2010).

In both countries, eventually the limited equity form began to be questioned. In 1969, after a lot of pressure from members, HSB allowed transfers at market rates; from then on, a member would simply be able to sell their 'right to occupy' at whatever the purchaser was willing to pay. Riksbyggen made the same decision around the same time. The lifting of price controls was done in the context of a market in which supply had overtaken demand, and so it only became a contentious issue when prices began to rise. From the mid-1980s, banks began to accept a tenant-ownership certificate as collateral for long-term loans, and this contributed to the soaring price of co-operative flats. Low-income households were priced out, especially in central Stockholm and other big cities. HSB and Riksbyggen began to develop more specialised housing for the elderly, young households, and so on, but were not able to reinstate price control. Some commentators think it is now a commodified tenure, similar to owner-occupation (Lundquist et al, 1990), but others see it more as just a tendency away from the 'social' aims of the past (Svensson, 1995). The high price of co-operative housing has recently led to a new interest in non-equity or rental co-ops, and new ones have been established on the basis of trial legislation. But political support for them has been patchy, and they remain marginal in the housing market.

In Norway, a similar process of gradual commodification of co-ops has occurred. In the early postwar period, there were strict controls on the exchange of second hand co-op dwellings, with deposits for new entrants set at an initial price plus some allowance for inflation. During the 1970s, a widening gulf between owner-occupiers and co-op members led to a black market in sales of co-op dwellings. Some independent co-ops dissolved in order that their members could sell on the open market. In 1981, following the election of a Conservative Government, price ceilings were adjusted upwards substantially and then entirely abolished everywhere except in Oslo and 11 other areas of high housing demand (Birchall, 2009). If a bill that is currently under consideration is passed by Parliament, people will be able to own new apartments as owner-occupiers. If the right to convert existing co-ops to owner-occupation were also granted the sector could shrink dramatically, but there is an agreement among political parties that owner-occupation can only apply to new buildings.

Just at the time when the Scandinavian co-operatives were converting into full equity form, co-operative promoters in Britain began to use the Scandinavian model to argue for a new form of limited equity co-operative, the co-ownership society. There were two advantages to the idea. As a group, co-owners could be seen as owner-occupiers and so were eligible for tax relief on their joint mortgage, and if they built up an equity stake over time this would help them to gain access to owner-occupation. Between 1961 and 1977, 1222 co-ownership societies were formed, producing over 40,000 dwellings. They were aided by a new development agency, the Housing Corporation, established in 1964 with £100 million of Treasury funding and a pledge of £200 million from building societies. However, the idea was constrained from the start by the 'top-down' way in which the schemes were developed. A new society would be registered by founder members who were usually the committee members and staff of a local housing association. They had the scheme designed and built, selected the first co-owners, and then tied them to a management agreement with the association for anything up to seven years. They were supposed to ensure that, six months after letting the scheme, resident members would be elected and take over, but sometimes the agents failed to get round to doing this. The co-operative nature of the schemes was played down, only being mentioned where it had to be in the model loan agreement and rules (Birchall, 1988). In 1979, when the Conservative government brought in a right to buy for council tenants, co-ownership society members persuaded the Prime Minister to grant them a right to sell, whereby societies could be broken up and individual dwellings sold to their members. Most of the sector then disappeared into owner-occupation.

Co-operative housing in North America

Despite the significant achievements in Scandinavia, probably the densest concentration of housing co-operatives in the world is in New York. Here there are around 600,000 co-op homes, and co-operatives have become the main form of apartment ownership. It is still preferred to the other main form of apartment-owning, a condominium, because it gives exist-ing residents much more control over their estate (in particular control over who can become a resident). The idea has also spread to other cities; altogether there are over 1.5 million co-operative housing units, with large numbers also in Washington DC, Chicago, Miami, Minneapolis, Detroit, Atlanta and San Francisco. In the form of 'seniors co-ops' it has also begun to spread to rural areas.

The first housing co-operative was the Finnish Home Building Associ-ation, founded in 1918 in the South Bronx, but it was after 1926 when New York State passed a Limited Dividends Housing Companies Act that the movement really got started. The legislation had the goal of promot-ing the construction of more affordable housing developments, and it gave municipalities the right to condemn land for large-scale construc-tion, and to provide companies with a 20-year exemption from muni-cipal real estate taxes in return for rent regulation and limitation by a newly created Housing Board (Co-op Village, 2010). It provided incen-tives for private capital to construct affordable housing, yet prospective landlords were put off by the rent regulation. Trade union leaders saw the opportunity, and in 1927 the Amalgamated Clothing Workers Union set up the first limited dividend company, the Amalgamated Housing Cor-poration, appointing Abraham Kazan, the president of the ACW's credit union, as its president. Their first project was Amalgamated Houses in the

Bronx, and then in 1930 they completed Amalgamated Dwellings on the Lower East Side. During the 1930s there was steady growth, though some of the new co-ops were unable to survive the depression.

After the Second World War, there was a period of acute housing shortage and in 1949 the Federal Government passed a National Housing Act that enabled New York City to clear slums and release land for new subsidised housing. In 1951 the United Housing Foundation (UHF) was set up to do the development, and it built 13 new housing co-ops. Then in 1955 a new affordable housing act was passed by the State of New York. Called the Mitchell-Lama Housing Programme, it provided low interest mortgages and tax abatements for development of affordable housing, both rental and co-operative. A total of 269 developments with over 105,000 apartments were built under the programme. They included several huge schemes that were influenced by Le Corbusier's concept of the 'city in the park', with giant high-rise buildings and their own schools, shopping malls, generating stations and even police forces. The largest is Co-op City, with 15,372 units in 35 high-rise buildings; it is the largest single residential development in the USA. The second largest is Rochdale Village (named after the Rochdale Pioneers) with 5860 apartments in 20 high-rise blocks in the South Jamaica district of Queens.

Like many other mass housing schemes around the world that were developed in the postwar period, these co-operatives were designed and built without any input from the future residents. In Co-op City, in 1975 mismanagement, shoddy construction and corruption led to a default on the co-op's loan from the State. Abraham Kazan's board resigned and the state took control. Co-operators were faced with a 25% increase in their monthly maintenance fees and so they went on a rent strike. They held out for 13 months before a compromise was agreed; they had to remit $20 millions in back pay, but got to take over management of the complex and set their own fees. From 2000 onwards they oversaw a $240 million renovation, and by 2008 the arrears were paid off (Co-op City, 2010). The sorry history of the co-operative shows that member-ownership is not on its own a guarantee of housing quality. Yet it also shows that, because of their co-operative governance structure, it was possible for residents to take control and put right some of the mistakes.

Like the Scandinavian co-operatives, the New York co-ops have been subjected to pressure to convert to full equity and allow members to buy and sell the right to occupy their apartments at market value. Schemes that were funded under the Mitchell-Lama programme were released from any obligation to keep to limited equity rules once their mortgage was paid, and between 1990 and 2005 the programme lost 34% of its stock. In housing co-ops, members can decide to demutualise, permitting them to sell their apartments. This means they lose tax abatement, but flip taxes on resales can mitigate these and members can gain a potentially large capital receipt on leaving the co-op. For instance, in Co-op Village, the vote to abandon limited equity led to a price increase of up to five times a member's equity stake. However, some co-ops have refused to convert. At Penn South a large majority voted for a 25-year phase-in of real estate taxes, which allowed the co-op to keep carrying charges well below market rates and preserve the limited-equity character of the co-operative for the future generation. However, the increase in asset values causes problems for limited equity co-ops, since it allows the City to increase property taxes sharply. At Penn South this was solved by an agreement to apply the Mitchell-Lama tax rule, which isolates the development from rising neighborhood values and instead ties taxes to the co-op's income (Penn South, 2010). Not surprisingly, given its problems with debt, Co-op City is also still limited equity, and it is able to charge comparatively low prices for an apartment and to keep a minimum and maximum income requirement.

During the 1980s, there was a trend for privately-rented buildings built during the period between the 1920s and 1950s to convert into co-ops: in fact, most of the housing co-ops in New York are conversions. In the heavily controlled environment of major cities it is difficult to make renting pay. Instead, landlords convert to 'co-op', and tenants are given an option to buy into the co-op, while rent controlled tenants who do not want to buy are protected. During the 1990s and 2000s similar conversions were made in Chicago, Washington DC and Miami, illustrating that the full equity co-op model is more than holding its own against other competing forms of tenure.

A more dramatic kind of conversion from private renting began in New York during the 1970s when new co-ops began to be formed by tenants to take over blocks abandoned by private landlords. Though they were open to people on very low incomes and so might have been expected to take a non-equity form, they were limited equity; relying on voluntary labour to renovate the blocks, they rewarded members with a modest increase in their equity stake when they left. The opportunity was created when, during the 1960s, the City of New York began foreclosing on thousands of landlord-owned properties for non-payment of taxes. The landlords responded by abandoning their tenement blocks or setting fire to them to get the insurance; by the end of the decade an average of 38,000 units a year were being abandoned. Squatters moved into empty buildings, and tenants fought back by forming campaigning organisations and clubbing together to renovate their homes. The City Council responded positively, selling the tenements for a dollar to tenant co-operatives and giving them low-interest loans for renovation. Tenants used their own 'sweat-equity', learning building skills and renovating their tenements themselves, and in the process increased their employability in the local job market. Later projects built on this with an on-the-job training component funded by an employment training act programme.

In 1975 the City of New York had a major financial crisis, and most of the funding programmes collapsed. However, the institutions for co-operative development had by then been developed; neighbourhood housing developers had formed their own federation, and a co-operative development agency, the Urban Homestead Assistance Board (UHAB), had been founded. There were delays in funding that sapped people's morale, friction with contractors, and internal disagreements about the amount of sweat-equity individuals were putting in. But the movement was unstoppable, and the City began a community management programme whereby tenants could manage their blocks and prepare more carefully for tenant-ownership. The tenant groups, led mainly by women, went on to challenge new threats to their homes from hospitals wishing to expand into surrounding areas, and from landlords wanting to evict them so as to get round rent restrictions and rent to higher-income tenants. The result is that now more than 27,000 families live in low-income co-operatives (Birchall, 2003).

Conversions have been going on for 25 years. UHAB works with more than 1,300 buildings, offering technical assistance, management training classes and emergency support programmes. It has recently secured funding from a federal 'connecting communities' grant to provide wiring, computers, and computer training for tenants, most of whom earn less than US\$15,000 a year. This develops employment skills, self-confidence and civic activism. Co-operative leaders have formed neighbourhood networks which are active in crime prevention, cleaning up parks, creating fuel co-operatives to deliver cheaper fuel to their members, and so on. A citywide coalition of co-operative leaders is active in the political arena. A recent study has found that resident participation reduces operating costs compared to other forms of rental housing. There are intangible benefits too, such as the empowerment of low-income people, increasing civic participation, the development of social capital, increased job opportunities, and the chance to accumulate some wealth. One tangible benefit seems to be increased incomes. The average income in a city-owned building is US$9,709. After joining the Tenant Interim Lease Scheme, the average rises to US$11,948. When this develops into a tenant co-operative, the average rises again to US$14,782. It is not that the original tenants are displaced by higher-income tenants; co-operatives have the longest length of residency. Upward economic mobility is the only explanation (Birchall, 2003).

This form of co-operative is spreading to other parts of the United States; there is one already in New Jersey, and the co-operative development specialists at UHAB have been advising Russian housing specialists. This form has the potential to solve the huge problems of disrepair and poor management in apartment blocks left behind by the demise of the Soviet Union. It is being tried in South Africa, where a mutual housing agency, COPE, began in 1997 to transform itself from being a donor-funded NGO into a member-based housing association, establishing housing co-operatives that are similar in structure to those in New York. The circumstances are similar, too; in Johannesburg there are thousands of people living in apartment blocks abandoned by their owners.

In Canada, co-operative housing began in Toronto in the 1930s along the same lines as the New York co-ops, and it also began to suffer from competition when condominiums were allowed in 1973. Then a new movement began that was quite different, being based strictly on the non-equity model, and designed to provide an alternative to renting rather than owner-occupation. It was promoted strongly by other types of co-operative in agriculture, retailing and insurance. By 1968 a Co-operative Housing Foundation had been set up that then became a federation, with 23 regional federations in membership. They formed a powerful lobby that resulted in legislation providing startup funding and mortgage financing from the federal and provincial governments through the Canada Mortgage and Housing Corporation, and the encouragement of resource groups to do the promotion and development of primary co-ops. Loan assistance was granted on condition the co-ops provided 15–20% of their homes for people on low incomes, and funding was provided to the co-operative to bring the revenue from each dwelling up to the full rate. This allowed the co-operatives to be mixed-income communities. However, the government stopped its funding in 1992, and the provinces followed in 1995; there was political pressure from private landlords who resented the competition, and also criticism from supporters of other forms of social renting who claimed the co-operatives were not housing those in most need (Quarter, 1992).

Since then, the sector has almost come to a standstill; in 1999 there were 2133 housing co-ops, with nearly 90,000 units (Goldblatt, 2000), but ten years on there are 2200 co-ops with 92,000 units. During the last decade, a debate has begun about how to meet a growing housing shortage among people on low incomes, but because co-ops are committed to the mixed-income concept they cannot take advantage of the new opportunities. It seems they are being squeezed between two other tenure forms – private renting and social renting – whose advocates also have political resources. However, no other form has yet been able to achieve that elusive goal of the mixed-income community.

A small non-equity sector struggles to emerge in Britain

In Britain, despite all the efforts at developing the form, only 0.6% of the housing stock is co-operative. We have noted already how attempts to promote co-partnership and then co-ownership failed because the forms chosen proved unstable, deforming under market pressures into more conventional tenures. The latest attempt to develop co-operatives focused on the non-equity type, relying on government sponsorship and placing them among a much larger social housing sector. In England this consisted of public sector 'council housing' and a housing association sector dominated by large, charitable associations and more commercial limited dividend associations dating back to the Victorian era. In this climate it was not easy for tenant-controlled organisations to make headway. In Scotland, co-operatives began as conversions from public sector housing, and then took their place among a much larger community-based housing association sector that made it hard for them to maintain a distinct identity.

In England, during the late 1960s and early 1970s three types of need were identified to which co-ops might provide solutions: those of inner city residents whose homes were threatened by clearance programmes, of squatters living illegally in empty property, and of tenants living on badly run council estates. Three new types of co-operative were developed in response: non-equity, short-life and tenant management. From the early 1970s, around 260 non-equity co-ops were formed in England, of which half were in London, with concentrations in other cities such as Liverpool. They were sponsored through the Housing Corporation, receiving Housing Association Grant in the same way as other, more traditional housing associations. They tended to be quite small (averaging 40–50 households), having been developed at a time when there was a consensus that 'small is beautiful' (Birchall, 1995). Tenant self-management developed as a response to failures in housing management by local authorities, and at their peak there were around 70 in England and 30 in Scotland; they managed estates as agents for the landlords. There was a concentration in London and Glasgow, and they tended to be larger than ownership co-ops on estates of up to 1000 homes. A less strenuous form of co-operation was then developed in the form of estate management board which specialised in the management of difficult to let estates of up to 1500 homes. Here, tenants shared responsibility for management with housing managers and local councillors, though always being a majority on the board. Short-life co-ops managed housing for a short time, usually from public sector landlords who intended to refurbish or demolish it but had left it empty for the moment. At their peak there were about 200 of them, mostly quite small, and nearly all based in London (Birchall, 1988).

During the 1980s pressure built up for local authorities to transfer their huge housing stocks to housing associations, and as part of this movement a few new housing co-operatives have resulted. However, the dominance of housing professionals in the process has meant that the preferred model has been a housing association with some tenant representation, and those co-operatives that have been produced under a 'community gateway' scheme have had to compromise on their governance, with tenants often being in the minority. Tenant self-management has also diffused into a wider set of options, and the numbers of tenant management co-ops has been in decline. Some of the non-equity co-ops have been closed down as they cannot meet the stringent monitoring standards imposed by regulators, but most survive. In Scotland, however, there are only 15 left, occupying a small niche in the community housing association sector. The difference between these two forms is small; the governance structure of the associations is wider with local people allowed to be members as well as tenants, while in co-operative only tenants can be members though others can be co-opted on to the board. There has been unintentional discrimination against co-ops that has seen many of them convert to conventional housing associations. In 2002 a law was repealed that allowed associations to claim a grant reimbursing them for the tax liability on their surpluses. Associations then began to apply for charitable status that exempted them from tax. Co-operatives were not eligible for charitable status because they were set up to benefit their members rather than the wider public and so most of the co-ops converted to association status (Birchall, 2009). Recently a Commission for Co-operative and Mutual Housing has recommended numerous ways in which co-operative housing can be supported, but it is hard going (2009).

Future prospects for co-operative housing

Explanations for the success or failure of co-operative housing as a form of tenure are not hard to find. First, expansion has taken place whenever there has been a shortage of housing that has gained the attention of both reforming organisations and governments. It has taken a co-operative form when the reformers have been convinced that this form is best; trade unions in particular have been influential, but also other types of co-operative that were inheritors of the 'Rochdale tradition'. Even more than other types of MOB, housing co-ops have needed government support through legislation to establish the tenure form, and because of the high initial cost of housing have needed some form of subsidy, through cheap loans, loan guarantees or tax breaks. This has meant that more than any other type they have depended on a sympathetic political environment, and when the environment changes their growth is stalled. Their growth is also affected by the relative attractiveness of other tenures. Where the alternative is private renting people value the control that co-operation brings for tenants who are their own landlord. Where the alternative is owner-occupation, in multi-occupied blocks full equity co-ops can outperform other forms of tenure. Where the alternative is a more authoritarian form of social-rented housing, they consistently outperform their rivals, though dependence on state patronage and the support of housing professionals can make them vulnerable (CCMH, 2009). They always do better when the wider environment supports other types of MOB, because this gives them institutional sources for the political support they need.

Given its mixed history, on a pessimistic view it is tempting to see co-operative housing as an unstable form that tends to deform into one of the majority tenures; equity co-ops into individual owner-occupation, non-equity co-ops into a wider social-rented sector. Yet this is an over-generalisation; in Scandinavia and parts of the USA and continental Europe it has held its own, and sometimes other tenures have converted to co-operative ownership. It depends on the support they get in the wider cultural and political environment.

6
Consumer-ownership in Public Services and Utilities

In this chapter we will be describing and analysing sectors in which consumer-ownership is sometimes found, but in which the public interest is often dominant and there is a strong political interest in the way the service is funded and produced: health care, education, utilities and leisure. In some countries this leads to the public sector not only funding the provision but also providing it through local government or public corporations. They are sectors in which producer groups also have an interest and are sometimes reluctant to let consumers wholly own and control the organisation that delivers the service. Producers may prefer to own it themselves, or to take part in multi-stakeholder governance through a hybrid form that also includes consumers and employees. If the governance is likely to be contentious, the stakeholder groups may prefer to leave governance to a set of trustees in a non-profit, or to a public body that is governed by elected members.

Governments have an interest because there is a vital need to be met, because it has made a service compulsory for all citizens, or because the sector is a natural monopoly and politicians do not want consumers to be exploited. The idea of membership may be challenged by public bodies that want ownership to be vested in citizens in general, want control to be exercised by elected representatives and want the benefits to be shared out according to criteria of need or fairness. We can expect competition between different types of owner. Sometimes there will be competition between consumer-owned and producer-owned businesses, sometimes between member-owned businesses and the public sector, sometimes in a managed market between MOBs, IOBs and NPBs. This is why, in the sectors we are analysing here, member-owned businesses are rarely dominant, often in a minority, and overshadowed by other types. In some countries they cannot get started at all because the state will not allow them to exist.

106

Type 1: Health care

It is not easy for patients to take the opportunity to provide health care for themselves. The collective-action problem in getting started is acute. The costs borne by the founders are much higher than in other types of MOB. Consumers can set up their own store, farmers can jointly supply themselves with seeds or fertiliser, much more easily than patients can organise their own health care. It is not surprising that most examples of member-owned health provision are outgrowths from other types. For instance, we have noted in Chapter 4 how friendly societies that began by offering insurance that met the costs of medical care soon found themselves organising medical centres, pharmacies and even, in some countries, hospital care. We also described how mutual insurers in France have carried on this tradition by running a wide range of medical facilities. There are economic incentives for doing this; by bringing provision of care into ownership, health insurers can better control costs and ensure quality. We have also noted in Chapter 3 how retail consumer co-ops in Europe have extended their range to include pharmacies, and will see in Chapter 8 how farmer co-ops in Japan provide a comprehensive health care system in rural areas. However, the activities of other MOBs are not always so benign. Sometimes medical doctors set up their own MOB to provide services to consumers, and they occupy the exact same space in the market that a consumer co-operative might want to occupy. We will also be looking at this option in Chapter 8.

The first condition for development of a health co-operative must be unmet needs. The need for health care is one of the most basic, and it is not surprising that one of the earliest recognisably modern forms of mutual aid – the friendly society – grew up in order to insure members against the costs of its purchase. Why should consumers organise to provide their own health care rather than leaving it to the medical profession to produce it? There are two reasons. One is that coverage may be poor or non-existent because doctors cannot be persuaded to provide it. People living in remote rural areas face particular problems in this respect, but sometimes urban dwellers are also excluded because of lack of purchasing power. The second reason is that consumers may resent the power of the medical profession and want to gain more control over the terms under which health care is provided.

Where consumers decide to provide their own health care we can expect them to begin with a simple act such as a group hiring their own doctor, but it is a big leap from there to running their own health centre or hospital. We can also expect them to need help from existing

MOBs such as farmer co-ops or consumer co-ops that are prepared to bear some of the promotional costs. They will also need a sympathetic attitude from at least some members of the medical profession, but we have noted how the development of friendly societies in Britain, the USA and Australia, was seriously held back by resistance from medical associations that resented consumer control. The initiative may not even get started. Then, if it is successful governments may want to provide public funding. This comes at a cost, because the funder may insist on the MOB offering coverage to non-members, which in the long run will undermine the incentive for being a member. Eventually, the co-operative may provide a comprehensive service to a whole community and become, in practice, an NPB or a POB. It is hard to deny care to non-members who are in need, particularly in rural areas where the co-operative may be the only provider. It is hard to deny other stakeholders a share in governance when much of the funding is from the public purse.

Founding period

The first recorded health co-operative was founded in Serbia in 1920 in a rural area served by a small town called Pozega. The promoters included a federation of co-operatives and a local doctor (Dr Kojik), and they got help from the Serbian Child Welfare Association of America (UN, 1997). Pozega became a model for a substantial health co-operative movement; by 1938 there were 134 societies with their own national federation. There was a total membership of 65,600 households representing 390,000 people, and they employed 95 doctors, operated 25 health centres and a mobile dental clinic. They were financed by member contributions supplemented by an insurance fund, and although contributions were voluntary they could be made compulsory by decision of a general meeting (the problem of how to cover a whole population with a system relying on voluntary membership was already making itself felt). From 1927 onwards government began to provide technical and financial support, and in 1930 legislation provided permanent financial assistance and made them partners in a public health service.

The co-operatives employed doctors and nurses at fixed prices according to rates agreed by the national federation, supplemented by a variable salary decided on by the local co-operative. At first, each one set up a clinic, a dispensary and rooms for nursing seriously ill patients, but conditions improved; the first fully equipped health centre was set up in 1928. The cost of services was estimated at a third of private for-profit provision. However, they went much further than just providing curative health services. They undertook vaccination programmes and operated day nurseries and preventive programmes for children. Sanitary conditions were improved and health education was provided, youth and women's sections were encouraged, and area-based representatives were appointed to give preventive health advice, encourage improved hygiene and promote healthy living (UN, 1997: 58–59).

It was the model for a similar movement in Poland that began in 1936 with 500 members from seven villages employing a doctor and a dentist. By the outbreak of the War there were 12 co-operatives. Amazingly, the idea also spread to India. A superintendent of a village welfare department in Bengal made a study visit to Serbia in 1930, and began to establish similar co-operatives in a district North West of Calcutta; by 1938 there were 12 such co-operatives with their own federation. Again the emphasis was on preventive health care, with priority given to care of mothers and children.

In the USA rural health co-ops began in the late 1920s. They began under similar circumstances: rural areas poorly served by medical services; a local population used to working co-operatively in agricultural co-ops; resources provided by existing co-ops for starting up; and a federal government keen to find ways of improving services to rural areas. It is not surprising that they 'reinvented the same wheel'. The first health co-operative began in 1929 in Oklahoma, with over 2000 families contributing share capital of $50 each to build and equip a community hospital. They paid an annual membership fee of $25, which gave free care from salaried doctors. Again it was the initiative of a doctor, Michael Shadid, who saw it as a middle way between public and commercial medicine. In the Great Plains states, the populist tradition and already existing agricultural co-ops meant a favourable environment for the idea. Shadid argued that it would also be good for doctors as it provided financial security and opportunities for professional development, but it was opposed by the American Medical Association, and from 1939 onwards state medical associations succeeded in getting legislation in 26 states barring consumer-controlled health plans. Shadid managed to get a health co-op going in Elk City, Oklahoma with help from the Oklahoma Farmers Union, and in spite of the opposition during the 1930s many others were established, mostly in Oklahoma and Texas. By 1950 there were 101, more than half of which were in Texas where state legislation actually promoted them. Along with farmer and electricity co-ops, they received government support under the New Deal rural health programme. Similarly, in rural Canada health co-ops were set up by grain marketing co-ops, consumer co-ops and credit unions, and by 1945 there were 271 of these with over 14,000 members (UN, 1997).

It was not long before the idea began to be applied to urban areas. In Japan, in 1931 the well-known co-operative promoter, Dr Kagawa, set up a Tokyo Medical Co-operative Society, and by 1940 there were 89 hospitals and 137 clinics all for low-income people (Birchall, 1997). This then formed the basis for a revived urban health co-operative movement after the War. In the USA the first urban health co-operative was set up in 1947 (Group Health Co-operative). It was the initiative of farmer co-operatives, trade unions, and members of consumer and student co-ops in Seattle, Washington state. The immediate catalyst was the prospect of going back to a totally private system of medical care after having experienced a system of prepaid care during the War. Some doctors wanted a prepaid system as well, but the local medical society opposed the idea, preferring the traditional 'fee for service' model. In 1947 the co-operative bought a small hospital funded by member share capital and limited interest bonds, and it employed the doctors who worked there on contract. However, the medical society remained opposed and prevented the co-operative from using specialists, and it was only after the co-op won a legal battle against 'conspiracy in restraint of trade' that it was able to grow.

A period of decline in some areas, growth in others

There was a tendency almost everywhere for rural health co-operatives to evolve into, or be taken over by, the public sector. In Serbia and Poland, after World War Two the new communist regimes set up a public health service in rural areas and the co-operatives were absorbed into it. In the USA, growing affluence and a reduction in federal support led to both consumers and doctors becoming less interested in participating in the rural co-ops, and by 1949 only 54 remained. After the introduction of Medicare and Medicaid in 1965, federal and state governments promoted community-based rural health centres that had a wider constituency of community representatives and that did not require patients to be members. By 1995 there were still 37 health co-ops but they were hard to distinguish as a separate type because they had become part of a wider, government sponsored community health service (UN, 1997). Similarly, in Canada user-owned health co-operatives were set up to meet gaps in provision in rural areas, but as they could not restrict access to non-members it was a challenge to make membership meaningful (Girard, 2000). There are still a few primary health care co-ops in Quebec, but their governance structure shades into that of community-based POBs.

However, the urban co-operatives have fared better, being part of a competitive market in which patients have the chance to choose between providers; Group Health Co-operative in the USA and the urban health co-operatives in Japan have experienced continued growth up to the present day. In 1951 Group Health Co-operative won its case and relations with the medical profession began to be normalised. There were still considerable tensions between consumer and producer interests in governance, but by 1955 these had been largely overcome through a joint committee responsible for resolving differences, and medical staff got the autonomy they needed by becoming self-managing on a joint contract with the Board. The co-operative grew fast; by 1984 membership had grown to 332,000 and it had expanded to adjacent regions in Washington state, and then to Idaho through an affiliate, Group Health Northwest. It took its place in the American health care system as a consumer-owned health maintenance organisation (HMO), employing its own staff augmented with a primary care network of selected community physicians. During the 1980s competition grew from non-co-operative HMOs, and yet its innovative management kept it ahead. In 1990 it set up Group Health Options to offer health insurance to local employers. By 1994 it had 510,000 members and enrolees, 86% of whom were covered by group health insurance contracts with their employer. The co-operative covered nearly 10% of the population of Washington. In 1997, doctors became completely self-employed, contracting with the co-operative through their own Group Health Permanente medical group rather than as salaried staff.

Now the co-operative has 628,000 members, with a revenue in 2009 of $2.8 billion. It has over 9000 staff working in one hospital, 26 primary care medical centres, six specialty care units, seven behavioural health clinics, 14 eye care clinics, seven audiology clinics and eight speech, language and learning services clinics (Group Health, 2010). It even has its own research institute and a charitable foundation. The governance structure is complex and provides plenty of opportunities for members to get involved; they have a board of trustees, three regional councils, 23 local advisory councils, and special interest groups. It is ranked seventh largest non-profit HMO and 18th largest of all HMOs in the USA, and it regularly wins awards for member satisfaction. It is affiliated to another HMO, Kaiser Permanente, sharing marketing and best practice and providing full member reciprocity. Kaiser is a non-profit but is not a co-operative, and the relationship begs an interesting question about how distinctive is Group Health's governance structure when compared to that of others. There is only one other fully consumer-owned and controlled co-operative in the USA; Health Partners in the Minnesota-Wisconsin region which is of roughly equal size with 630,000 members and 9600 staff working in 50 locations. The Group Health system has proved successful, then, but has not yet succeeded in out-competing other types of HMO.

In Japan, a law of 1948 allowed for health co-operatives, but it is interesting to note that it prohibited non-members from using them except in the case of emergency services; there was going to be no deformation into community-ownership here. From the start, the health co-ops were seen as part of a wider consumer co-operative movement, and their association was set up as a specialist section of the Japanese Consumer Co-operatives Union. In 1961 comprehensive health insurance came in, with most of the costs of health care paid by the state but, as in France, with some topping up of payments by consumers. At the time it was thought that the health co-ops would lose their reason to exist, but the public health system allowed for a variety of providers all designated as non-profits under the law, and so co-operatives were able to find a niche as one set of providers among others. They found a market niche by emphasising preventive health and then long term care for the elderly, and unlike other providers they had a strong commitment to consumer voice. From 1969 onwards they started a policy of encouraging small 'han' groups of members that met to provide health education and preventive care (Hino, 1996).

Co-ops grew both in membership and turnover during the 1970s and 1980s. The funding system was experiencing increasing strain, and the patients' top up payments reached 30% of total costs. In response, patients were becoming more assertive; in 1991 the co-operatives introduced a charter of patients' rights, putting them in the forefront of demands for more consumer voice and a more equal relationship with the medical profession. Now there are 116 health co-ops with a membership of 2.6 million, the average age of whom is over 60. Share capital has increased as co-ops have made calls on members to finance new developments; it now stands at Y67 billion (25,700 yen per member). The turnover of the sector is an impressive Y280 billion, but it amounts to a modest 0.8% of total Japanese health care expenditure. They have 81 hospitals, 351 clinics, and 222 visiting nurse stations. They run 18 health facilities for the elderly, 20 group homes for dementia, 16 service houses for the elderly, 185 home-help stations and 315 day-care centres. Some co-ops have set up social-welfare corporations to run nursing homes for the elderly, while others operate fitness centres and preschools for children (Kurimoto, 2010). 300,000 of the members (11.5%) belong to

27,000 Han groups, which undertake activities such as self-health monitoring and health education.

Future prospects

What are the prospects for consumer-owned health co-operatives? We can expect that in countries like Canada isolated rural communities may continue to find this type useful as a vehicle for achieving health services where there are no services at all. However, we can also expect it to continue to convert into a more inclusive POB type over time. In the USA the Group Health model may be set for dramatic expansion if it is chosen by government to lead the current health reforms, delivering health care to the 30 million people who are currently without any coverage. In Japan we can expect the consumer-owned health co-ops to continue to be a small but stable part of the health sector, with a distinctive role in advocating health consumers' rights. What should be the respective roles of medical staff and patient-members in a consumer-led health care organisation? The USA and Japan provide two models; the former has a separate producer co-operative contracting with the consumer co-operative, while the latter invites producers to become members and participate in one integrated governance structure. In this model, the producers are vastly outnumbered but there is a tradition that each board is chaired by a medical doctor.

Type 2: Education

If governments demand that all children be educated to a certain standard and agree to pay for the service to be provided, it would seem there is no room for a member-based organisation to deliver it. There are two pragmatic reasons why MOBs have been involved. One is in providing education and training to their members so as to make them capable of taking part in governance; co-operatives subscribe to a set of 'Rochdale principles' that include education and often allocate a set percentage of surpluses for that purpose. For similar reasons, credit unions in developing countries often link development of new unions to adult literacy and numeracy programmes, and they work very well. The other reason is that, where governments lack the resources or the will to provide basic education for children, MOBs sometimes step in. As with health care, in rural areas where governments have failed to provide the service it is quite common for MOBs such as agricultural co-ops and credit unions to fill the gap. In Tanzania, for instance, coffee marketing co-ops used to run primary schools and provide scholarships to send children to secondary schools. However, they did this because the public sector was not doing it, not because there was a clear comparative advantage to be provided by being an MOB. As in health care, there is a tendency for governments to take over as soon as they are able.

Under certain conditions MOBs can provide a clear advantage in offering membership-based education. Again these are similar to health care. Government must have the will to let go of providing the service directly and create a managed market with a range of different types of provider. It must provide enough funding so as to ensure fairness and equality of access for all. There has to be a real choice between providers so that MOBs can offer membership; if they have a monopoly then parents (like patients) have to become members and so it ceases to be voluntary. This means urban rather than rural areas, where there is sufficient population to support more than one provider. If these conditions are fulfilled, then member-owned education can begin.

There is, in fact, only one country where these conditions have been fulfilled and a consumer-owned provider has emerged – Sweden. Here, child care co-ops began in the early 1980s, and were given a boost by the decision of local governments to switch from being a monopoly provider to giving parents vouchers so they could choose between independent providers. By 1995, helped by a network of co-operative development agencies, around 1300 parent-owned child care co-operatives had been set up (with another 129 had been set up by the other vital stakeholder group, employees – Stryjan and Wijkstrom, 1996). The child care co-ops have continued to be popular, and have proved superior to municipal, non-profit and for-profit providers on a range of indicators. In particular, they encourage participation by parents to a much larger extent than the other types.

Co-operative schools came about in a similar way, when in 1992 the Swedish Government gave a general right for all parents with children in the compulsory age-range (7–16) and upper secondary age range (16–18) to choose their child's school. At the same time, the funding for each pupil was decoupled from the local authority budget and given to parents as a voucher, which meant they could choose to send their child to an independent school. A general right was also given for anyone to open an independent school, which meant parents were able to start their own schools. There are limits to what they can do: new schools have to be approved by central government, they cannot ask for top-up fees, and selection on the grounds of academic merit is not allowed. The sector has grown from 90 'seven to sixteen' schools and 57 'upper' schools in 1992, to 585 and 266 respectively in 2005. They make up 12% of the 7–16 schools and 33% of the upper schools. During the same period, under competition from the independents the number of municipal schools decreased by 252. In 2007 there were 600 applications to open new independent schools, and so the trend is towards greater diversity and independence (Cowen, 2008). The new schools can be run as for-profit companies, non-profits or co-ops, though nobody (neither the government department nor the schools federation) seems to know how many of them genuine, parent-owned co-ops. Will this trend towards co-operative provision continue? According to a leading academic writer, Sweden has 'now reached a historic juncture where a greater role for citizen participation and the third sector provision of welfare services is fully possible' (Pestoff, 2009). The challenges of an ageing population, austerity in public finances and a growing democratic deficit, have all contributed to the change of mood. Co-operatives are no longer seen as a 'private' alternative but as a way in which service-users can gain membership and some control over the services they receive.

In Britain, the national consumer co-operative *Co-operative Group* and the *Co-operative College* are involved in turning existing state schools into 'co-operative schools'; ten have been designated so far, and there are around 100 keenly interested in the idea. Unlike the Swedish schools, they are multi-stakeholder co-ops in which parents, pupils, staff and the wider community can become members. Also, they will be less independent because they are to remain part of the local authority sector, though they will have more control over the curriculum and discipline policy (Dept for Children, Schools and Families, 2009). There are other ways of looking at co-operation in education. As well as co-operative schools there are school co-operatives, student-owned co-ops that provide services within the school or otherwise encourage them to set up a business. These are common in developing countries such as Sri Lanka. The UK Co-operative College has set up 300 Young Co-operatives encouraging young people to form co-operatives to sell fair trade products, and this scheme is to be extended into schools. The College is also working with schools to develop curriculum materials that enable students to understand better the co-operative business option. However, all of this falls far short of the pure, parent-owned school that is possible in Sweden. As in other services dominated by a public sector ethos, it is hard for the idea of membership to get a grip, and multi-stakeholding seems to be the price paid by consumers to the vested interests of producers (in this case the teaching profession) and politicians.

Type 3: Utilities

There is some ambiguity in what we mean by a 'utility'. If something has utility it means it is useful to people. It nearly always comes with the prefix 'public', but this can mean either that it is provided by a public body or that it is used by the public, which are two different things. It also refers to the supply of goods that rely on a fixed distribution system such as pipes, lines or cables, and so the business sectors that are referred to as utilities are water supply, electricity, gas, telecommunications and some forms of transport. There are natural monopolies involved, because the costs of installing the system that carries the utility are usually large, and once it is built there are high barriers to entry. Also, because the commodity is often vital for human life and consumers cannot do without it, they cannot avoid purchasing it even at a high price. It is vital that the organisation that owns the distribution system is accountable to the public; otherwise it will charge monopoly prices and enrich its owners unfairly, and may stop short of providing the service to people in rural areas or on low incomes if this is not profitable. It is no wonder that governments get involved either to regulate the industry on behalf of its citizens or simply to deliver the service itself. It is also often in the interests of the industry to have efficient regulation, because in the early days in which the distribution system is laid down lack of co-ordination can be damaging; in England during the rush to build railways in the 19th century the lack of regulation resulted in eight different gauges of railway track (Birchall, 2002). Also, independent producers of water, electricity, or gas have to find a way to sell their products, and arrangements can be made with the owner of the distribution system to carry these. Yet again the problem of monopoly arises as the producers are in the same disadvantageous position as the end-users. It is not surprising that in many instances publicly corporations simply own the lot. Where private companies are allowed to be the owners, there is likely to be demand from the public and from other business interests for heavy and persistent regulation by governments.

There are obvious theoretical advantages in member-owned businesses running utilities. If consumers are supplying themselves it does not matter that there is a monopoly. If they make a profit they can redistribute it in lower prices, operating an automatic cost-price mechanism that, like other consumer co-ops, excludes the 'middleman'. There may be disadvantages if they cannot raise capital as easily or as cheaply as their competitors. Where they have succeeded in becoming established they usually receive low interest loans or other favourable treatment from government, but this is also true of other providers (NRECA, 2010). What opportunities have there been for member-owned businesses to compete in these sectors? First, there are situations where there is no distribution system at all, a local economy is only just reaching the stage where it is needed and governments choose to offer the monopoly to a member-owned business; this happened in the 1880s in Finland in water and telecoms, and in the 1930s in the USA in electricity supply. Second, there are opportunities to deliver energy to a distribution system that allows competing suppliers; consumer-owned businesses now supply wind-generated electricity in Denmark, and solar and hydro powered electricity in Switzerland. Third, there are situations in which either POBs or IOBs have failed and consumers have turned to their own solutions; this has happened in water supply in Bolivia.

Water co-operatives

Probably the earliest consumer-owned utility is the water co-operatives that supply rural areas in Finland. Here, local government took responsibility for providing water and sewage facilities to urban areas, but because the rural areas had sparse populations and there was a long tradition of self-help, towards the end of the 19th century consumer co-ops became the preferred option. Now, as well as 400 municipal utilities, there are 902 co-operatives. Some are quite large, serving more than 10,000 people, and they supply rural areas and small towns. They began with drinking water but many have expanded to sewerage and waste water treatment. Not many countries have followed Finland's lead, but water co-operatives are important in Argentina, Chile, Colombia and Bolivia. Here, the provision of water has been surrounded by controversy over what sort of ownership structure works best. During the 1990s, the World Bank supported privatisation to large transnational water companies, but the UN came out against such privatisation because private companies had found ways of excluding poor people. The UN Development Report for 2003 said that service provision was best provided by local communities and firms, and that it was the government's role to build their capacity (UNESCO, 2003). In Santa Cruz, Bolivia, a consumer co-operative known as Saguapac has been providing the city's water since 1979. Visiting consultants from USAID had advocated a co-operative model, and citizens were receptive to the idea; they had their own tradition of small-scale co-operative banking, and had co-operatives already in the telecoms and electricity sectors. All of these factors provided a favourable environment for the water co-operative. Saguapac is a true consumer co-operative, and all 96,000 domestic customers are automatically members. It has been copied elsewhere in Bolivia and has proved to be efficient and effective (Birchall, 2003).

How does it compare with other forms of water delivery? A study undertaken by Birmingham University economists has found that it is one of the best-run water companies in Latin America, with a low level of water leakage, a high level of staff productivity and universal metering. It has a low average tariff and high collection efficiency. It is also efficient in its use of foreign loan finance for investment, outperforming two private companies (Nickson, 2000). Its co-operative structure is the main reason for its good performance; the co-operative shields managers from the kind of political interference that weakens municipal water companies, it allows for continuity in administration, and the electoral system works against corruption.

Electricity co-ops

During the 1930s, electricity co-ops began to be developed in rural USA. As in Finland, by the 1930s the idea of co-operation had become deeply rooted in rural areas through agricultural and credit co-operatives. President Roosevelt's New Deal programme brought these into partnership with the government in a drive to develop the rural economy. Power companies were uninterested in supplying electricity to farmers; they were uncertain about the demand and wary of committing the huge amount of capital investment needed to create a transmission system. In 1935 the government created the Rural Electrification Administration which offered low-interest loans to electricity co-ops and in 1937 began to establish four public power companies to generate electricity from federal dams and offer it at low prices to the co-operatives. By 1953, more than 90% of US farms had electricity. Now there are 864 distribution co-ops and 66 generation and transmission co-ops in the system, providing power to 12% of the population (42 million people) in 47 states. They have 42% of the distribution lines, deliver 10% and generate nearly 5% of the power used in the USA each year (NRECA, 2010). Their 10% of power delivered compares with public bodies that deliver 16% and private companies 74%; they are the third in importance but are predominant in rural areas and their share of the market seems assured.

The American model of rural electricity co-ops has been exported via the international arm of the National Rural Electricity Co-operative Association (NRECA), with funding from USAID and the Department of Agriculture. In the Philippines, acting on advice from NRECA International, the government established a National Electrification Administration to work towards universal electrification, primarily through the establishment of new rural co-operatives. Over the past four decades 119 co-ops have been established, providing electricity to over 80% of the rural population. As in the USA in the 1930s, this has improved rural living conditions and resulted in sustained economic development, especially in value-added agriculture (NRECA, 2010). Since 1962, NRECA International has developed dozens of rural electrification projects throughout Bolivia. The electrical counterpart to the water co-op in Santa Cruz, *Cooperativa de Eléctrificacion Rural,* has over 300,000 consumer members and is now one of the largest rural electric co-operatives in the world. NRECA has been working in Costa Rica since 1963, and now there are four electric co-operatives representing approximately 15% of the total electric distribution market in the country and roughly 40% of the rural-area service.

Undoubtedly the success story for NRECA is Bangladesh. Here a national rural electrification programme began in 1977, and within 25 years over 70 rural electric co-operatives have been created, with four million metered connections serving 25 million people in rural areas. Such an infrastructure does not come cheap – an investment of $1 billion has been necessary, funded by 13 donor agencies. The system is still expanding, with 1000 new connections daily. System losses are less than 15% and collection rates over 97%; a growing number of co-operatives are reaching the point where they are financially self-sustaining. A sample survey of 3700 households has provided these findings: there has been a 16% increase in the income of rural electrified households; infant mortality in these households is 35% less than the national rural average; new employment opportunities have resulted in people migrating to the electrified village; crop yields under powered irrigation are 24% higher than those using diesel. A variety of new industries have been started, leading to expansion of rural markets. At the household level, rural electricity has contributed to: fuel savings; reduced fertility rates and infant mortality; improved hygiene and awareness of public health issues; increased literacy; women's spatial mobility; income; awareness of gender issues; women's empowerment; school enrolment; and immunisation coverage (Birchall, 2004).

How does the co-operative model compare with alternatives? In the Philippines, the co-operatives achieve 95% revenue collection, and their overall performance compares well with neighbouring private utilities. In contrast, public companies do not have a good track record; there are technical failures, losses of power due to deteriorating networks, poor management, inability to make consumers pay their bills, and sometimes corruption (in India, for example, utility losses and subsidies amount to an estimated $3 billion a year). Private for-profit companies have experience the same disincentives that prevented them from electrifying rural USA in the 1930s; a mix of funds is needed, including commercial loans, government grants and consumer contributions, and the co-operative model tends to deliver a result that is affordable. NRECA says 'our experience has demonstrated that a focus on serving the consumer results in the most efficiently run systems'. Co-operatives have the advantage of being consumer-driven, putting the key stakeholder in the centre of the business, being able to access capital but keeping bills affordable, and using the new energy to help people find new ways of making a living. It is no exaggeration to say that electricity releases the creative energy of the people who use it (NRECA International, 2010).

Electricity co-ops are also important in Brazil, Chile and Argentina. In Denmark, they have been leading the way in development of wind farms. Here, like in the USA, in rural areas the networks are owned by the consumers. Despite liberalisation of the market in 2002, suppliers continue to have a monopoly; a large part of the price of electricity consists of energy taxes, and so suppliers cannot really compete on price and have to compete at the margins on service quality. It helps, therefore, that the co-operative model guarantees accountability to consumers, has price transparency and a non-distribution rule that means profits are returned to consumers in lower prices. Despite privatisation, co-operatives remain a popular option. Denmark has invested heavily in energy technology over the last 25 years and has pioneered energy taxation, designed to reduce CO_2 emissions and support renewable forms of energy. The result is that renewables now supply 20% of the country's electricity. The grid has hundreds of small-scale distributed generators, using wind power and a range of fuels such as wood, straw, biogas and bio-oil. Denmark leads the world in wind power, and co-operatives have played a surprisingly large part in its development. The idea is not new; even in the 1930s there were 30,000 windmills, some of which were producing electricity and so when modern turbines began to appear they were not seen as controversial. Local communities became involved on the principle that they should own their own power source, and then when schemes became larger and moved offshore ownership was opened up to the whole population. Between 1978 and 1994 co-ops had over 50% market share, but this has now fallen to around 23% as landowners and larger investors have entered the market. By 2004, no new wind farms were being planned because of a cut in subsidies, but the sector had become established:

150,000 families are members of wind-energy co-operatives, owning over 3000 turbines (Birchall, 2009).

Denmark is also a world leader in district heating networks which now account for over 50% of space heating, and allow cheaper, low grade fuels to be used. The decision was made 30 years ago to invest in district heating rather than individual connections to natural gas networks. From 1986 onwards, the emphasis was put on combined heat and power plants which were more efficient and allowed for fuel flexibility; natural gas, biogas, woodchip, straw, bio-oil and even solar thermal can be used, and excess heat from power stations can be circulated to city heating grids. In order for the new system to work, local authorities were given the power to force consumers to connect to the system, and this was counter-balanced by a commitment to the consumer control and price transparency that co-operatives provided. Of the 430 district heating companies in 2001, 85% were co-operatives, though they only account for 37% of the heat sales because the larger ones are owned by local authorities. They are, however, recognised as being more efficient and responsive to consumers than the local authority district heating systems (Birchall, 2009).

Switzerland provides a twist to the same tale; here there are around 50 solar energy co-ops that provide an opportunity for consumers to invest. Some are also developing small hydro-power schemes. However, a comparison with Scotland shows why some countries may lag behind in these new developments; as a new market develops and matures later entrants find it harder to gain access. In Scotland, a support organisation, Energy4All, has developed several co-operatives on an asset-ownership model pioneered by the Baywind Co-operative in Cumbria. It has four wind co-ops in development in Scotland, and aims to create a national co-operative 'Caledonia' that will become a national Scottish renewable energy co-operative. This makes sense, as many people in urban areas want to invest in renewables and as wind farms are being developed off-shore. Yet, compared with Denmark where the whole system has been co-operative, Scotland has had to make do with co-ops that are merely one investor among others, relying on private companies to do the development.

Telecoms co-ops

In Finland, the development of telephone networks began at the same time as the water co-ops. The Telecoms company, Elisa Oyj was founded in 1882 and it soon became dominant in the rural market (though it was demutualised in 2000). Another 27 local telephone associations banded together in the Finnet Group, which has a mobile phone network called

DNA Finland, and a market share of 18% of the fixed telephone lines (Birchall, 2009). Again, to find the next example we have to make a leap of the imagination from Finland to Latin America, where Argentina has 130 telecoms co-ops.

A new area of development is broadband for rural areas. Using wireless technology or fibre optic cables, around 40 broadband co-ops are in development in Britain. They are backed by government, and by the national federation Co-operatives UK. One interesting variant that is likely to become much more common is the linkup between housing co-ops and broadband. In Scotland, new homes are being built for the West Whitlawburn Housing Co-operative that will have fibre optic cables installed giving next generation broadband access. A communications co-operative Whitcomm is being set up that will provide TV, phone and internet services at reduced costs compared to major providers. In the context of a low-income community, 60% of whom are reliant on housing benefit to help pay their rents to the co-operative, this is a major step towards 'digital inclusion'. It is expected that this model will spread to other socially and digitally excluded communities. Similar examples are being developed in housing co-operatives in New York.

Transport

There is not much evidence of consumer-ownership of transport systems such as roads and railways. The collective action costs of start-ups have been too high, it is difficult to exclude non-members, and also consumers do not form a coherent interest group. It is possible to envisage a quasi-membership organisation that owns a rail network, but it would have to be multi-stakeholder-based and non-profit (Birchall, 2002). However, there is one area where consumer-ownership has begun to thrive. Car sharing co-operatives began in Switzerland and Germany during the 1980s as a way of enabling people to cut down on their car use and make better use of resources. One example is Mobility, a Swiss car sharing co-operative that provides over 2200 vehicles at 1000 stations throughout Switzerland. It has 80,000 customers, including more than 2100 businesses. Members of the co-operative can book online and use various types of credit and ID cards to gain access to the vehicle without having to use keys. The idea has spread throughout Europe, and there are several such co-operatives in Canada and Australia (Birchall, 2009).

Type 4: Leisure services

In provision of leisure services, co-operatives shade into the related category of associations. Basically, an association that provides services to its members through trading is a co-operative. An association that provides services to a broader 'community' and for whom membership is not a requirement is a non-profit business (NPB). One that has a membership but does not trade, such as a village hall association, remains simply a voluntary association. Our comparator countries all have a large, thriving associational sector based on the idea of membership, but they are not seen as MOBs. In the UK there is a long tradition of working men's clubs that developed in parallel with other movements in the 19th century, such as the consumer co-operatives. These provide a social venue for their members and, though they also have broader aims they trade in a serious way in alcoholic drinks and entertainment; until recently they had their own brewery. They are non-profit distributing, but it could be argued that this conforms to co-operative principles; like other consumer co-ops they provide their product as near as possible to cost price, and like water utility co-ops they return the surplus not in dividend on purchases but in lower prices. The Club and Institute Union (CIU) estimates there are around 2500 of these in the UK. The sector has been in decline since the 1970s, when there were more than 4000, and the remaining 2500 clubs have seen membership halved in the last 20 years. Some clubs have managed to shed their old-fashioned 'cloth cap' image, but most are struggling.

Where there is decline there is also renewal. In the early 20th century, the same era that working men's clubs became established, most football clubs in Britain were industrial and provident societies, owned by their supporters, but the commercialisation of sport has meant most are now IOBs owned by the mega-rich. A new type of mutual has arisen called a supporters' trust. The idea is for fans to buy shares in their club, and then pool the voting rights that come with these to the trust which will then be able to represent them. If supporters buy enough shares they can, in this way, eventually take over the club and even own it outright. The model for such buyouts is Spanish football clubs such as Barcelona that are, by law, wholly owned by their supporters, and German clubs that are 51% owned. The trust movement has grown rapidly over the last few years. They are working in over 160 clubs in the UK, with 120,000 members. Sixty clubs now have supporter-directors, and 15 clubs have become completely member-owned (Supporters Direct, 2010). Its success has led the European football governing body, UEFA, to sponsor research to determine how to apply the supporters' trust model into other countries. There is no reason why the idea should not be exported to other countries. Also, the trusts, along with the wind farm co-operatives in Britain, show that there is another category of member organisation we might call an investment co-operative; its purpose is to enable consumers to invest in another organisation. This idea may catch on in other areas where consumers feel excluded from ownership and control of an IOB.

Future prospects for consumer-ownership in public services

In public utilities, consumer-owned businesses first became established in a few countries where they were granted a monopoly by governments; they did the job that the public sector or a heavily regulated IOB sector did elsewhere. In the same way, they are finding opportunities as 'first mover' into the market in developing countries. Where the market has opened up to competing suppliers, they can sometimes enter as a minor player through exploiting new opportunities such as renewable energy or broadband networks. In health care and education, opportunities are equally dependent on government policies and the MOB option only proves stable in markets where competing suppliers are tolerated. There may be an opportunity opening up in health care reform in the USA for a whole sector to be based on the rather impressive achievements of two existing health care co-operatives. Opportunities in education are opening up in England for co-operative schools, based on the popular Swedish independent school model.

However, MOBs in services that have a public character face fierce competition from other types of ownership and control. Their competitors are not just IOBs and POBs but the non-profit or voluntary sector that traditionally in many countries has had a major role in provision. In Britain, a new hybrid form has been created called a public benefit company (PBC). It is a non-profit that has a multi-stakeholder membership representing consumers, employees and the wider community, and it has some of the qualities of an MOB. Examples include foundation hospitals, leisure trusts and water and rail utilities. On closer inspection we find that the idea of membership in PBCs is not always what it seems. It varies from proxy representation of consumers by people who are appointed by the board of the PBC, through indirect representation by people appointed by other membership organisations, to direct representation of members by members (Birchall, 2002). The least mutual are Network Rail and Welsh Water, which have a bizarre way of recruiting members to a membership council; the board of directors appoints the members, who then oversee the board. Then there are leisure trusts with a multi-stakeholder board that includes worker representatives as well as local authority councillors and other community interests, sometimes but not always including consumers.

Then there are the foundation hospital trusts that have a two-tier board structure, with a board of governors (often called a member council) and a management board. People join directly as patient, employee or community members, and then they elect the board of governors which has some powers over the management board. It is a mixed system of accountability but it seems to be working well, with a great deal of member-interest; so far over a million people have become members and elections have been strongly contested (Ham and Hunt, 2008). It seems that there is a taste for a hybrid form of member/public organisation, provided it has a genuinely democratic governance structure.

In Italy, similar organisations that deliver social care services and employment services to vulnerable and dependent people are called social co-operatives. There are around 7000 of them, and they fall into two types: those that provide social services and have workers, beneficiaries and volunteers in membership, and those that integrate vulnerable people into paid work and have different types of worker in membership. In both types, the interests of the public and of funding agencies are also represented. If we accept that multi-stakeholding is as valid as single stakeholding, and that dependence on public funding is inevitable in some sectors, and if we accept that such restrictions as a lock on the assets and non-profit distribution do not compromise the idea of member-owners, then these can also be considered MOBs. The idea is catching on in other countries, and it is certainly a way of democratising previously hierarchical governance structures in public service delivery organisations. Like the British public benefit company it attempts to balance the interests of service-users, employees and the wider public, and while it extends the idea of membership it also has the potential to dilute it.

7
Consumer/Producer-owned Banks

Before the industrial revolution and the development of a modern, market-based society there were really only two types of bank; the private bank for the rich and the mutual aid society for the poor. Neither was what we would recognise as a formal organisation. The first was a set of private arrangements between investors, merchants and manufacturers. The second was a club that provided mutual savings and credit on the simplest of terms. Like the friendly societies it consisted of a group of people who regularly put money into a box and, depending on whether they wanted to provide loans or regular savings, took turns to borrow from it or shared it out at the end of the year. One of the reasons why co-operative banking has done so well in so many countries is that it builds on this almost universal tradition of box clubs, slates, tontines, sou sou, syndicats, kootu, and so on (MacPherson, 1999). The informal system is still important in developing countries where formal banking does not meet the needs of the majority, but in the developed world it has been overtaken by member-owned banks that offer the same kind of services, drawing on the same impulse to mutual aid, but in forms appropriate to a modern society.

We have noted in Chapter 3 how the system developed for consumer co-operation by the Rochdale Pioneers became universal; there was really only one story to tell. However, like the mutual insurance sector we described in Chapter 4, the co-operative banking sector has more than one origin. At first sight it looks as if there are several types, because different traditions have evolved that use alternative names for the same type of business; savings and loans instead of building societies, credit unions or savings-and-credit co-ops instead of co-operative banks. There are really only two main types: building societies/savings and loans and co-operative banks/credit unions.

Like some insurance mutuals, co-operative banks are owned by two classes of member – producers and consumers – who are sometimes different people, sometimes the same people expressing both business and personal needs. The building societies began in the 18th century providing mainly for consumption (of housing) by members, but when they became permanent in the mid-19th century they also began to lend to developers and landlords whose business was to provide housing for rent. The co-operative banks started in the mid-19th century as a way of providing capital for production, and then during the consumer revolution of the early 20th century became providers of capital for consumption. Does all this make the distinction between producer and consumer invalid? Not really, because keeping the distinction highlights an important question (familiar to researchers into micro-credit in developing countries) – what is credit for? It may be lent for productive purposes to enable people to escape from poverty, yet money borrowed for a business often leaks into personal consumption. Does this matter? The general feeling among promoters of microcredit is that anything that stops people from having to go to moneylenders is good, and one of the ways in which people get into debt is when they have expenses towards a wedding, or funeral, or a period of sickness, or a child starting school. In the developed world, borrowing for consumption is normal but the same issue of usury arises; here, the usurers are not just money lenders but commercial banks that charge high interest rates on credit cards and in their own way can also force poor people deeper into poverty.

Type 1: Building societies/savings and loans

There is a distinct category of savings and credit society that attracts many small lenders in order to finance house purchase. Known as building societies in Britain, and Savings and Loans in the USA, this is another MOB type that, from humble beginnings in the 18th century, has spread around the world.

Founding period

Like the friendly societies, building societies emerged in Britain as a simple way of meeting people's needs, in this case for housing finance; the first was probably started in 1775 at the Golden Cross Inn in Birmingham, and they became strong in areas such as Birmingham, Leeds and South Wales. They were 'terminating societies' whose members deposited their 'club money' in a box in a public house until there was enough to start building. Then houses were allocated by ballot or by auction as they become available, and loans were sometimes taken to speed up the process. By 1825 there were well over 250 of these societies, terminating eventually when all members were housed. However, they had a more limited appeal than the friendly societies because the rates of subscription were too high for poorer working men. Like other mutuals, at first they had no legal status and so no redress against fraud. The 1832 Reform Act extended the parliamentary vote to smaller property owners, and this greatly increased their business, because working class people could gain the vote provided they qualified as property owners. Freehold land societies began with the express purpose of dividing up land to offer as freeholds, and a number of them registered as building societies. The 1836 Building Societies Act regularised them, and made them exempt from stamp duty on shares, a vital concession if they were able to prosper. From then onwards there was tremendous growth. The statistics are disputed: by 1869 there were, according to one source about 2000 societies with 800,000 members and according to another 1500 societies with 300,000 members (Gosden, 1973), but as a sector this form of mutual had become well established.

In the USA, they were called 'building and loans', later 'savings and loans' (S&Ls for short), but most people referred to them as 'thrifts'. We will refer to them as S&Ls. Like the British building societies, which they copied, they began as terminating then developed into permanent societies. The first one was the Oxford Provident Building Society in Frankfort Pennsylvania, founded in 1831. There was slow progress until the 1870s, when urban growth related to the second industrial revolution led to their numbers increasing rapidly (Mason, 2010). By 1890 they had spread to all the states; Philadelphia, Chicago and New York had over 300 each. They were small and local and granted governance rights based on the amount of capital held on deposit. In contrast, National Building and Loans were formed that were nationally based and with local branches. These were investor-owned 'for-profits', that paid very high interest on savings and charged higher rates on loans, but the 1893 depression resulted in a decline and by the end of the century nearly all of these had gone out of business! A national association emerged, and legislation began to protect the real S&Ls from deforming; by 1914 there were 6600 of them.

Period of growth

The growth of the building societies in Britain was helped by the invention of the permanent building society'; the first of these, the Metropolitan Equitable, began in 1845. We can understand how this happened.

First, when they terminated some societies ended up with a surplus which they would lend to other societies. Second, new terminating societies would be formed to replace the old, so as to accommodate new members. In 1847 the idea was set out in detail by a reformer, Arthur Scratchley; they should separate the borrower from the investor and run the society like a bank with depositors and mortgage loan holders. This meant the length of term of the loan could be increased, and as long as the income from borrowers covered the interest to saving members (plus management expenses) they were sound. Generally, both savers and borrowers could become members; it was realised that if borrowers were excluded the societies would become more like investment clubs for the wealthy. In effect, they became savings banks, accepting money on deposit and paying depositors at lower rates than shareholders. In this they were very secure. There is an old joke in building society circles that sums up the simplicity of the form:

You borrow at one percent, lend at two percent and you are on the golf course by three

Of course it was not so easy. The movement was in need of its own legislation, which it got in 1874. Crucially, the right of societies to borrow was limited to two-thirds of the amounts secured on mortgages, but poor regulation and the depression that began in 1875 caused difficulties. These were compounded by the invention in the 1860s of a new form, the Starr-Bowkett society. These societies, named after their inventors, proved popular; there were more than 1000 of them by 1892. They invited people to invest small sums and then enter a lottery, the winner of which got an interest-free loan for housing. However, this was more like gambling, and the high salaries of the officers and their rules that prevented office-holders from being dismissed made them notorious. In 1892 two societies collapsed through fraud and in 1894 a new Act was passed that made the lottery illegal in newly formed societies and toughened the law against dishonesty. Powers of inspection were given to the Chief Registrar, societies were required to make an annual return, and members were given the power to dissolve a society. By then, much good had been done; it was estimated that between 1836 and 1896 at least 250,000 people had become home owners because of the societies. By 1910 there were 1723 societies with 626,000 members, and assets of over £76 million (BSA, 2010).

In the USA, by 1930 there were nearly 12,000 S&Ls, with 22% of all mortgages and 10% of the population in membership. During the Great

Depression they tended to survive better than banks; for instance, in 1931 20% of banks went out of business, while only 2% of S&Ls failed. Their numbers did fall during the 1930s to just over 9000 in 1937, but this was mainly through mergers. In 1932 their trade association worked with Congress to create a Federal Home Loan Bank to make loans to S&Ls facing fund shortages. A source of liquidity and low cost financing, it was organised through 12 regional banks that were federally sponsored but owned by the S&Ls through stock holdings. Also, a Federal Savings and Loans Insurance Corporation was founded to insure against risks, and this was put under the authority of the Bank; by 1934 federal chartering of S&Ls and an insurance scheme were in place, and a close association began between the S&Ls and their regulators.

Their competitors were insurance companies that lent on short term and required a large payment at the end, or lent on an interest only basis; they could not match the products the S&Ls were able to offer. Banks also offered only short-term deposits with penalties for early withdrawals. The S&Ls offered longer-term savings to members, who earned compound interest as profits were distributed to share balances, and they had a distinct social movement approach to their work, an attitude of 'social uplift' that gave them a moral edge. In the postwar period there was a baby boom, a surge in suburban home construction, and strong expansion; in 1945 they had had 7% of consumer savings and 23% of home loans, but by 1965 they had increased their share of the market to 26% of consumer savings and 46% of home loans. They increased in size rather than in numbers of societies, which remained stable at just over 6000.

A period of crisis in the 1980s

The idea spread to many other countries, notably Australia, New Zealand, Ireland, and Jamaica. It also caught on in continental Europe, with societies in Germany, Austria and Finland. By the 1970s, the building society/savings and loans model was well developed and a significant player in savings and mortgage loan markets in many countries. It was a dull but worthy sector, whose main task was to attract savings and recycle them into home loans. It did this rather well; its management costs were modest and its transactions relatively low risk, so it required only a light and routinised form of regulation. All of this changed – in the late 1970s in the USA, and from the late 1980s in other countries – so that, for reasons we will explore, the sector is now much smaller and most of its assets have been transferred, either through conversion or takeover, to the investor-owned business model.

Problems began in the late 1970s in the USA, when the world oil crises led to rapid inflation, and governments began to try to combat this with ever higher interest rates. In the British model, mortgages were set at a percentage above the Bank of England base rate, which meant that though there was increasing pain for mortgage-holders (and gain for savers) the societies remained sound. In America the S&Ls lent on fixed interest rates, which meant that when the return to savers overtook the return from loans the societies quickly ran into trouble. In response, Congress passed two laws to deregulate the industry, allowing a wider array of savings products and expanded lending authority, with more lenient accounting rules. At this time, only 80% of the S&Ls were member-owned; the rest were investor-owned 'stock associations' that had very restrictive rules to make sure they were owned by large numbers of local people, no one of whom could gain a controlling interest. They had to have 400 stockholders, each with no more than 10% of the stock, no controlling group could own more than 25%, and 75% of owners had to reside or do business in the market area. For these stock associations, the rules were swept aside and it became possible for anyone to buy their own S&L. The results were dramatic. In 45 years only 143 S&Ls had failed, but in the early 1980s 118 societies failed, with many more merging in order to survive (FDIC, 1999).

Why did so many fail? First, they were specialised financial institutions, lending long and borrowing fairly long. To meet the competition they had to be deregulated to offer higher interest rates, but because they lacked the authority to make variable rate mortgages they were unable to generate higher incomes. Second, there was a decline in regulatory oversight and so unscrupulous managers were able to avoid scrutiny and use the S&Ls for their own gain, and insider mismanagement and fraud resulted. Managers pursued a 'go for broke' lending strategy, making high risk loans as a way to recover, knowing that if the loans were defaulted on Federal insurance would cover the losses. Also, many managers lacked the experience to calculate risks in deregulated areas; bad loans were made from well-intentioned decisions. Third, regulation of the sector was faulty. The regulator, Federal Home Loans Bank Board was small and used to overseeing a public service industry with low risk; it was not designed to function in the new environment of the 1980s. Also, the sector was regulated by one body and insured by another, which meant that poor inspection reports were not followed up. Fourth, the stock associations became targets for speculators, and new owners came in who just wanted to make money; they were prepared to make high risk loans and pay high interest on deposits.

A drop in interest rates in 1982 helped the sector to return to solvency. Between 1982 and 1985 there was very rapid growth, with 492 new S&Ls being founded and the sector's total assets increasing by 56%. Yet conversion from MOB to IOB status meant there was an opportunity for new people to gain control and milk a society for high salaries and dividends. Healthy S&Ls became contaminated by having to keep up with the rest, illustrating the old saying that 'bad money drives out good'. In 1989 the federal government finally created a programme to resolve the crisis by *reregulating* the sector through a new Office of Thrift Supervision. A report from the Federal Deposit Insurance Corporation estimates that during the 1980s 747 S&Ls had failed at cost of $160 billion, of which $132 billion were paid by federal tax payers. Coupled with the larger failure of 1530 commercial banks taking with them more than $230 billion in assets, it had been the most expensive financial collapse in American history (FDIC, 1999).

Demutualisation and discovery of the advantages of mutuality

The conversion of member-owned S&Ls to investor-owned status was a major part of the disaster. At the start of the crisis, only 20% were IOBs (controlling 27% of the industry assets) while the rest were MOBs; at the end most of the mutuals had been converted. Commentators say both deregulation and the change in type of ownership were to blame. However, we should not overestimate the extent of involvement of members in the governance of the MOBs. They tended to be controlled by 'a self-perpetuating management group', with no incentive to members to participate, particularly since their deposits were covered by federal insurance. However, with demutualisation managers were free to become owners and maximise their own interests, which usually meant pursuing higher risk strategies. A similar process has been blamed as one of the causes of the boom and bust real estate cycle in New England during the mid to late 1980s that led to the failure of mutual savings banks (FDIC, 1999).

The legislation of 1989 prevented the crisis from occurring again, but by end of the century the S&Ls' share of the residential mortgage market had halved from 40% (in 1980) to less than 20%. Yet remarkably they continue to thrive; in 2000 there were 1103 S&Ls, with $863 billion in assets. They have remained the second largest sector in consumer savings, though they are now virtually indistinguishable from the banks. With hindsight we can see that the original problem was not deregulation but over-regulation; in the 1970s this prevented them from adapting to market conditions. Deposit insurance made things worse by ensuring that investors' money flowed to the riskiest firms that gave the highest returns. It was a mishandled industry-restructuring problem that, if it had been handled better, would not have led to demutualisation. In Britain, demutualisation occurred in a completely different context. Building societies were basically sound, but had been chafing at the restrictions put on them by the regulator (the Building Societies Commission) and wanted powers to compete with the commercial banks. The 1986 Act gave them these wider powers to engage in personal banking, but it also gave them the option to convert to IOBs providing 75% of their members voted in favour. In 1989 Abbey National resolved to convert. Then in 1995 Cheltenham and Gloucester converted and was taken over by Lloyds Bank Group. An Act of 1997 then provided the societies with the more flexible operating regime they had been looking for, though in return they had to take measures to increase accountability of boards to members. This satisfied some society boards, who began to take steps to resist calls for demutualisation, but ten of the biggest societies converted, taking with them around 70% of the sector's assets. Among the biggest, only the Nationwide resisted the siren call.

The official reason for conversion was to seek a more liberalised trading regime and to be able to raise more capital. However, from 1997 onwards the building societies felt they had a liberal enough regime, and did not need to raise capital on the stock markets. After all, their main business proposition had always been that they recycled small savings into mortgages for house purchase. The real reasons for demutualisation were greed on the part of management (who benefitted through enhanced salaries and bonuses and stock options) and on the part of members (who benefitted from windfall profits on conversion of their member shares to stock). The whole process was made notorious by a process of 'carpetbagging' whereby people would open new accounts in building societies in the hope of getting a windfall profit on conversion. By the late 1990s most of the remaining societies had modified their rules to make this more difficult; anyone joining a society would have to sign away any profit from demutualisation to a charity. With the chance of a quick profit removed, the wave of demutualisations came to an end.

The demutualisation trend is uneven. It seems to have occurred in the Anglophone countries but not in continental Europe. In Australia, a similar deregulation of the finance industry in the 1980s led to a spate of demutualisations, with at least 18 building societies converting (Delisted, 2010). The smaller societies were taken over while some of the largest became banks. In New Zealand, the finance company crash of 2006–2008 and the flow on from the credit crisis have led to merger and demutualisation.

One side-effect of demutualisations has been a clearer realisation of the comparative advantages of mutuals. In the UK, studies have found that demutualised societies' rates on deposits and mortgages are more favourable to shareholders than to customers, with the remaining mutual building societies offering consistently better rates (Heffernan, 2003). Societies began to turn to their advantage the fact that they had no investors to cream off the profits. Then in 2008 the collapse of two former building societies, Northern Rock and Bradford and Bingley, underlined the benefits of having a less risky mutual sector. Now there is a reduced sector of 52 societies but they are self-confident and much clearer about the benefits of mutuality.

UK Building societies have seen their assets grow from £171 billion in 2001 to £335 billion in 2010. Mutuality has become an attractive business model and customers are switching from the demutualised banks. A recent House of Commons report has found that any windfall the members may get on conversion soon disappears in lower returns and higher costs. Customers typically lose their windfalls to higher charges and less competitive rates within four years of demutualisation. Mutuals are winning awards and regularly outperforming their competitors in business league tables, occupying over half of the top 25 positions in the sector. They are also more committed to keeping open local branches; since 1995 the banks have reduced their network by 27%, the mutuals by just 5% (All-Party Parliamentary Group, 2006). The former societies are now banks and are driven by profits and shareholder returns. Building societies are owned by their members and are governed by their own Act of Parliament. This restricts their exposure to the wholesale money markets where many of the difficulties for the banks arose. Northern Rock borrowed much of its money from other businesses – which means when the credit crunch hit, it struggled. Building societies have avoided the problem because most of the money they lend comes from their own savers. In the first half of 2008, nearly £6.3 billion of customer money flowed into building society savings accounts. This compares with just £3.8 billion for the same period in 2007 – before the collapse and government bailout of Northern Rock.

The Achilles heel of the building society movement had, for a long time, been its poor record of member relations. When the demutualisations were being promoted, many members were not aware that they were in fact members, and saw the prospect of a windfall payout as a win-win situation with no negative effects. The realisation that mutuals can outperform their rivals, and that they are safer and more risk-averse, has been coupled with a modest reconnection between the remaining societies and their members. Using a variety of methods including member panels, roadshows and interactive websites, they have increased member interest and participation, and in so doing have increased the quality of governance. They have improved their arrangements for voting and annual meetings, making it easier for members to take part, though so far few member-nominated directors have emerged. The importance of membership is signalled by the way in which member relations strategies are being pursued, often led directly by the chief executive (Building Societies Association, 2010). There is a new confidence. In 2005 Britannia Building Society bought the savings and branch business of Bristol and West in what might be the first of a series of remutualisations; the UK government is considering remutualising Northern Rock.

Type 2: Co-operative banks/credit unions

In bad times of famine or economic depression informal lending and borrowing fails, because people run out of money and have to borrow from moneylenders. Because they have no collateral the interest rate charged is amazingly high, and because they have only their productive capacity (their labour, their children's labour, tools, livestock, next year's crop) to set against the loan, they can fall deeper into debt. This is one of the main reasons why, once they have become poor, people tend to remain poor. The promoters of co-operative banking began from the need to stamp out the 'curse of usury' by what they called 'loan banking'. On the other side of the same coin, they wanted to encourage people on low to middle incomes to be thrifty, to help themselves through 'savings banking'. Taken together, credit and savings would then be put to good use in raising productive capacity so that local economies could grow and everyone would be better off (see Wolff, 1907 introduction).

Founding period

It was in Germany that a viable model for co-operative banking was first invented. Why Germany? Here, a market society developed before large-scale industrialisation, and small business people, artisans and farmers needed access to capital if they were to survive. They needed to take advantage of new markets yet the commercial banks, set up to service richer customers, were unwilling to provide for their needs. Philanthropic banks set up by the rich to lend to working people were unpopular because they seemed more like charity than self-help. As Henry Wolff put it, capital was not equal to the demands made on it. People remained poor through lack of capital, and lacked capital because they were poor

(Wolff, 1893: 20). There was a need to find a way to give credit to those who had no security to offer in exchange. The great Italian promoter, Luigi Luzzatti, talked of the need to find a moral guarantee, a means for the 'capitalisation of honesty' (Wolff, 1893: 23). Another, Leon Say, summed up the task as 'the democratisation of credit'. There was an urgent need to find a way of releasing all the productive power that lay latent in the working people for want of capital. For this to happen reformers had to find a way, as Luzzatti put it, of 'aspiring to descend'.

There was plenty of social capital around; urban dwellers had a strong sense of identity derived from the continuing bonds of the guild system that was only just beginning to break down. In rural areas, villages were still small and had a real communal life (MacPherson, 1999). There was a pervasive religious culture in which religion provided cohesion and, crucially, leadership through the local priest or pastor (Wolff, 1893) Thanks to two reformers, Schulze-Delitzsch and Raiffeisen, there were also two viable business models, one for the town and one for the country.

The idea of co-operative banking was first explored in a series of pamphlets by Victor Aime Huber (a doctor who preferred co-operation to medicine), who travelled extensively around Europe and became an enthusiast for the co-operative philosophers Robert Owen and Saint Simon, and an advocate for the British consumer and French worker co-op models. Hermann Schulze was the mayor of Delitzsch and, after the 1848 revolution, a politician – a member of the Prussian National Assembly (Fay, 1938). He was influenced by the British friendly societies which gave him the idea of thrift, and more directly by Huber who gave him the idea of co-operative banking. First he set up a friendly society providing sickness benefits, then a supply association for joint purchase of raw material for shoemakers, and then in 1850 a credit association. This was a philanthropic venture with capital supplied by rich founder members, but it was co-operative in its insistence that borrowers also become members.

At the same time a colleague, Dr Bernhardi, set up a bank at Eilenburg that was more genuinely co-operative, so in 1852 Schulze modified his own bank to become self-supporting with the members contributing share capital. He was a great organiser and propagandist, and he travelled round the country expounding his system. In 1856 he published a book, and in 1859 organised the first congress of banks which resulted in for-mation of a national federation. In 1867 he secured the first co-operative law in Prussia, and then four years later a wider German law, and went on to create a superstructure of regional and national banks to service the local banks. He did not have an easy time of it; Wolff comments that, being a liberal, he was harassed by the government and deliberately excluded by Bismarck in drafting the law on co-operation. However, he single-mindedly stuck to his programme and by the time of his death in 1883 he had organised 1900 societies with 466,000 members (MacPherson, 1999). Because many banks did not join his union, Wolff gives a higher estimate of 4000 associations organised on his rules, with 1.2 million members (1893).

Friedrich Raiffeisen was burgomaster of the villages of Weyerbusch and Flammersfeld, and then became mayor of Heddesdorf. It was a terrible famine of 1846–7 that was the catalyst for action. He began by distributing bread and potatoes to the poor, established a co-operative bakery that halved the price of bread, and set up a cattle purchase association. He then began to tackle what he saw as the underlying problem of usury. In 1849, with £300 raised from rich supporters, he set up his first loan bank at Flammersfeld. Then in 1854 he formed a second bank at Heddesdorf but it was only by 1862 that in his third society at Anhausen the borrowing farmers were themselves the members (Fay, 1938). Like Schulze he wrote a book expounding his system, and in 1877 set up a national federation of rural co-operative societies. When he died in 1888 he had set up 423 local banks.

Who was the first in the field? Most historians give Raiffeisen the credit, but since both promoters relied on rich founder members and took time to develop a self-help model, it is probably Schulze who was first; 1852 compared with 1862 for Raiffeisen. Table 7.1 summarises the similarities and differences in their systems.

In Schulze's system, every member took up one share that was set at a high level but payable by instalments, which committed a member to a long course of saving (Wolff said the share could be between £10 and £30, and Fay said at least £6). It is no wonder his banks appealed to small tradesmen, clerks, and artisans but tended to exclude the poor. Raiffeisen had no joining fee or share capital, so the poor could afford to join and he avoided the risk of a bank being run for the benefit of a few non-borrowing shareholders. In a law of 1889, the German Chancellor Bismarck overruled him and insisted shares be issued, so from then on Raiffeisen's banks asked for a nominal share. Schulze saw the need to allow dividend on share capital, though he wanted it to reduce over time as he was well aware that big dividends could divert the association from its proper purpose (as Wolff tersely commented, they should be fighting usury not practicing it). He was right to be concerned; some of his banks pursued high dividends and then demutualised into joint stock companies so the shareholders could profit even more. Raiffeisen's rules made

Table 7.1   Differences between the Schulze-Delitzsch and Raiffeisen systems

	Schulze-Delitsch system	*Raiffeisen system*
Entry conditions	Membership share, set at high level, paid in instalments	No member share, or if forced by law, a nominal one
Dividend on share capital	Yes, sometimes high %	No, all surpluses go to reserve
Voting rights and governance structure	One vote per member, with management committee and supervisory committee	The same
Remuneration to committee members/ managers?	Yes, and also commissions to managers for business gained	No, except for cashier
Type of lending	Short, three months as norm (to meet needs of traders, artisans). High interest rates	Long, up to ten years (to meet needs of farmers). Interest rates as low as possible
Attitude to growth of association	Based on one town but with large catchment area. Otherwise unlimited growth	Parish, minimum 400 population. Limited growth
Type of guarantee	Commercial – mortgages, bills, guarantors etc	Reputation, unlimited liability
Type of liability	Unlimited at first, later limited	Unlimited, later limited in Hungary

all the surpluses go to the bank's reserve; this was the backbone of the whole system, meeting any losses and making lending cheaper, though surpluses could also be passed on to members in higher interest rates on deposits and lower interest on loans. In order to make sure there was no incentive to demutualise, Raiffeisen's rules prevented the share out of reserves to members even if a society were dissolved; all the assets would have to go to a good cause.

Both systems had one person one vote and a two-tier system of management and supervisory boards. However, Schulze decided the directors should be paid salaries and commissions. His critics thought this would give an incentive to unsound lending (a concern echoed in recent arguments over whether bankers should receive high bonuses) and would prove costly. They had a point; in 1885 the salaries and commissions in the town banks averaged 12% of turnover (Wolff, 1893). Raiffeisen called for unpaid volunteers and in his societies only the cashier was paid. The type of lending was also very different; Schulze's banks gave short-term loans of three months, which meant they were good for urban businesses but useless for small farmers, while in Raiffeisen's banks long lending for up to ten years was the rule. Schulze's banks were based on a whole town and so could grow bigger whereas Raiffeisen's, being strictly confined to one parish, could not. This affected their attitude to risk; the urban banks asked no questions as to the purpose of the loan and they took any kind of security in pledges, land mortgages, collateral or good reputation (Fay, 1938). Critics said this effectively ruled out the poor who only had their reputation to offer. In the rural banks there was a sense of community and of common obligation which meant mutual knowledge was their only form of credit.

Both systems began with unlimited liability among the members, and gradually move to limited liability as their central banks and large reserves began to make lending less risky. It was a German tradition not to limit liability, and unlimited liability had two clear advantages: it made sure that new members were carefully vetted before being admitted, and ensured a high level of member participation. A law of 1889 allowed limited liability but there was no rush to convert; by 1905 only 284 of the rural 913 banks had made the change (Fay, 1938). In contrast, in other countries co-operative banks could not get going at all unless liability was limited; promoters in Italy and Hungary limited it right from the start.

Which system was better? Some people thought Raiffeisen, because although it raised much less money it had a firmer moral base and was much less risky. It was a purer form of co-operation in banking and, above all, it reached down to the poor. Yet as Fay pointed out, the controversy was unnecessary, because 'neither realised that their differences of method were due to, and justified by, differences of environment' (1938: 20). Each was right in his own way.

A first period of growth in Europe

In Germany the urban co-operative banks grew steadily until by 1892 there were 1044 of them in Schulze's Union plus a large number organised along same lines not belonging to the Union, making a total of around 4500 with 1.5 million members. However, this type was not entirely stable. Conversion to investor-owned banks was frequent; for instance, in Saxony in 1889 there were 115 credit associations, but two years later 12 of them had converted (Wolff, 1893: 55). Between 1875 and 1886 36 associations went bankrupt, and 174 more went into liquidation.

In 1892, one authority estimated that there had been 184 failures out of 1910 banks, an attrition rate of nearly 10%. Wolff said the cause was greed and carelessness; they had taken doubtful bills and lent freely to outsiders (until a law of 1889 compelled them to stop), and had lent carelessly on mortgages. He blamed the way in which Schulze's system had put temptation in their way by setting a premium on risky management (1893: 62). Experience had exposed the defects of the system, yet Schulze's followers continued to adhere to it, keeping the rules stationary when they should have been improved. The banks failed to provide enough security and the temptation of high dividends, salaries and commissions were one-sided benefits that in the long run undermined them. The Schulze-Delitzsch associations declined while their rivals grew.

Still, by 1905 the economist CR Fay could report that there were 1020 banks with 585,000 members and they were established in nearly every town of any importance. We know a few details about the members of the banks. Around 60% of them took credit, while the rest just used the bank for savings. A wide range of trades were represented but the percentage of hand workers was declining – the banks were becoming more middle class. However, Fay maintained that this was because they had succeeded in making their members better off rather than because they discriminated against working class people (Fay, 1907).

The Raiffeisen banks made a slow start, with growth only beginning in the 1880s. Perhaps they reflected Raiffeisen's own character in the unassuming and modest way they proclaimed their advantages. By 1893 there were over 1000 of them (but again that number could be doubled with societies that were not in the Raiffeisen Union). Then the movement really took off: by 1905 there were over 13,000 rural banks with nearly a million members, a staggering increase of nearly 800%. Despite there being many more banks than in the urban movement, they were small, only giving one-sixth of the credit, with a total membership twice as large than that of the town banks but with membership of each bank being on average seven times smaller. Nearly 50% of farmers were members of the rural banks, while 10% (chiefly the larger farmers) were in the urban banks.

Both movements were good at developing regional and national unions, central banks and commercial subsidiaries. The Raiffeisen movement set up a central bank and a trading firm supplying machinery, feed, manures, seeds, and coals to farmer-members. Supply associations were also set up in each district, but they were kept independent of the local banks so their business would not become mixed up. A co-operative insurance department was set up to insure cattle, and marketing co-ops followed in dairying, hops and wine. Credit from the banks meant that these could develop the now familiar system whereby farmers were paid in two stages for their produce, one payment on delivery of the produce and another when it had been marketed. The banks proved more stable than their urban cousins. Wolff was able to report in 1893 that in 43 years there had only been ten cases of fraud, in every case with losses made up out of reserves or sureties, and there had been no temptation to convert to IOB status.

From Germany the idea spread to Austria, Italy, Switzerland, Belgium and France. Germans living in Central Europe took it to Poland, while in the South East Serbs and Bulgarians created strong movements (MacPherson, 1999). There was great progress in Russia among the serfs, and the idea was also tried out in Egypt, Japan, China and the USA. By the 1890s Austria had nearly 1500 credit associations, Hungary 576, and Switzerland 900. In Italy, the outstanding leadership of Luigi Luzzatti (who was later to become Prime Minister) led to the establishment of 900 urban banks with a third of the banking market. Luzzatti was not afraid to adapt the form to Italian conditions, making the societies more democratic (with a large supervisory board and a specialised risks committee), limiting liability, giving preference to smaller loans, creating links with friendly societies and providing loans to worker co-ops. In parallel with Luzzatti another promoter, Dr Wollemborg, founded rural banks along Raiffeisen lines; by 1906 there were 1461 of them, mostly associated with the Catholic church. In Ireland the rural bank found a ready audience, despite as Fay put it 'the intense hopelessness of a nation distracted by political and religious quarrels' (1938: 74). As in most countries, it arose on the back of agricultural co-operation (a story we will continue in Chapter 8). By 1905 there were 200 banks, the majority in the poor West. Because of the dire poverty of their members they were not able to develop as savings banks but lent money on from government and from private banks.

Despite this rapid growth throughout Europe, there were natural limits to this type of MOB. In France and Belgium the movement got off to a slow start because of competition from savings banks that the government was subsidising with high interest rates, and because the first 'credit mutuels' were swept away in the war of 1870. By 1906 there were only 17 in France and 18 in Belgium (Fay, 1907). In Britain the industrial revolution was more complete, and because of the conversion of most working people to a wage-earning class there was much less need for credit. Private banking reached lower, meeting the needs of farmers and urban business people, while working class people could deposit their savings in consumer co-operative share accounts, savings banks and building societies. In Denmark farmers were mainly livestock growers, so had no need for credit to tide them over to the next harvest. Using the two-stage payment system, they got a constant stream of working capital from their marketing co-ops.

A second period of growth in North America

There is a particularly acute collective action problem in relation to co-operative banks. They are costly to set up, requiring much dedicated time and effort, the learning of new skills, and the building up of trust among large numbers of people. It also helps to have rich supporters who can invest the start-up capital. As in Europe, so in America, it took specialist promotion by individuals who were strongly motivated and well connected, such as Alphonse Desjardins in French-speaking Canada and Edward Filene in the USA. Desjardins was working as a translator in the Canadian House of Commons in 1887 when he observed a debate over usury that impressed him with the extent of the problem (MacPherson, 1999). He read Wolff and Luzzatti, and in 1900 opened the first caisse populaire in his home town of Levis, based on a combination of the ideas of Raiffeissen and Luzzatti. In the first seven years the caisse made 2900 loans without a single loss, forcing three moneylenders to give up business. The idea spread slowly through parishes throughout Quebec and other French speaking provinces, and by the time of his death in 1920, he had organised 175 caisses. The Great Depression of the 1930s forced the caisses populaires to become disciplined, with an integrated structure of four regional unions and a provincial federation and a rigorous auditing system. By 1940 there were 562 caisses with $25 million in assets. The pattern was set for a distinctive movement that enabled caisses to remain small and parish based, while benefitting from strong centrals and specialised subsidiaries providing other products such as life insurance.

In the USA, the movement began with Quebecois immigrants who had moved to New England. In 1908 a Catholic priest, Monsignor Hevey, invited Desjardins to Manchester New Hampshire to explain the system and a society was set up. The New Hampshire legislature then passed a law to provide statutory authority for it. Banking was a major issue at the time, with a widespread sense that the commercial banking system was not meeting the needs of working people and small businesses, and with the Federal government searching for ways to provide credit to farmers. Filene was a member of a merchant family with a large department store in Boston. He travelled round Europe looking at co-operative banks, read Wolff's books and visited Desjardins. Together with Pierre Jay, the state commissioner for banks, in 1909 he achieved a Massachusetts Credit Union Act (using the term credit union so as not to confuse it with the mutual building and loans societies that at the time were referred to as co-operative banks). The rules were mainly from Raiffeisen but with distribution of surpluses allowed as long as 20% went to a reserve fund.

For the next ten years there was slow progress but in 1920 Filene and Roy Bergengren set up a Credit Union National Extension Bureau that Bergengren then managed and Filene spent much of his personal fortune to finance. During the 1920s, with the growth of mass production, rising wages and improved transportation people began to become consumers, buying new items such as cars, refrigerators and radios. Retailers set up instalment plans but they charged high interest rates, and employees saw the benefits of being in a credit union. Expansion had to await enabling legislation; in 1921 there were only four state laws, but by 1934 there were 32, and a federal law of 1932 provided universal coverage. The movement continued to grow during the Great Depression and hardly lost any money; a Princeton University study found in 1937 that banks had lost 34.5% of their deposits, buildings and loans societies had lost 32%, but the credit unions had only lost 6.7% of their investments (MacPherson, 1999: 22).

Employment based credit unions became the norm, with their low administrative costs, easy deductions from salaries and low-risk loans. The idea was widely promoted by professional groups such as teachers, enlightened employers, trade unions, the Roman Catholic church, ethnic groups (who were aware of the European legacy), and the established consumer and agricultural co-operative movements. Using these networks, the resources provided by Filene, and strong state leagues, by the mid-1930s they had created over 3000 credit unions. In 1934 the extension bureau became the Credit Union National Association, and it formed two important subsidiaries: CUNA Mutual providing insurance, and CUNA Supply providing joint purchasing. By 1941 there were nearly 11,000 credit unions, and in a postwar explosion of consumer demand the sector grew even more: by 1954 there were 15,000 with more than seven million members.

In English-speaking Canada it was 1930 before Bergengren got round to organising the first credit union (at Welland, Ontario among a group of employees). What really got the movement going here was a combination of adult education and local economic development. The Extension Department of the St Francis Xavier University in Antigonish, Nova Scotia developed a method for study clubs under the direction of two priests, Jimmy Tompkins and Moses Coady. The method was simple; an organiser from the Extension Department would come to a community and set up a meeting. Local people would look at their needs and consider the possibilities and then, in study clubs that met weekly for a year or more, would establish a co-operative (MacPherson, 1999). The movement that grew out of this was different from the American in being community-based and linked to other types of co-operative. During the 1940s there was remarkable expansion; in 1941 there were nearly 1500 credit unions, and by 1954 there were 3800 with 1.5 million members. The movement expanded in the West, where it was taken up by farmers in the prairie region of Saskatchewan and Alberta. It reached Ontario and British Columbia, but here it was largely urban and employee-based. Why did it grow so fast? One underlying reason was that there were not much competition; there were no other community based banks, the larger banks did not meet people's needs, and unlike in the USA there were no savings and loans societies (which meant credit unions could offer mortgage loans).

In the late 1940s the idea reached Australia, where credit unions began to be formed along American lines, mainly as 'closed bond' employee unions; by 1962 there were 126 in New South Wales, and 36 in Victoria. In Ireland, there had been a false start when the promoter, AE Russell, had set up co-operative banks early in the 20th century, but in the turmoil of independence and the Irish civil war they had all collapsed. A new beginning was made in 1958 and by 1970 there were 366 unions with over 220,000 members.

A period of worldwide growth, and consolidation in North America and Europe

During the early 20th century colonial governments had begun to see the value in credit unions as a way of countering usury and enabling indigenous people to make the transition to a modern world of business and markets. Because the promotion of co-operatives had been paternalistic and their regulation excessive, the results were disappointing. Yet the idea had been planted and after independence in the 1950s and 1960s real credit union sectors began to emerge. While nationalist governments became very heavy handed in dealing with agricultural and consumer co-ops, they tended to leave the credit unions alone because they were small and, in the politicians' view, not very significant. From 1941 onwards catholic priests began to promote them in Jamaica using the Antigonish method. The idea travelled all round the Caribbean until by 1962 there were 406 unions in the region, with 62,000 members.

Jamaican immigrants then introduced them into Britain which, despite the efforts of Henry Wolff, had previously been unreceptive to the idea. In 1955 another priest introduced them into Latin America via Peru; by 1970 the region had 3000 credit unions organised in 15 leagues, with nearly a million members (MacPherson, 1999). Catholic activists also began to promote them in several Asian countries during the 1950s, and they began to be promoted actively in Africa through aid programmes. They were organised mainly along traditional Raiffeisen lines: small, volunteer-led, and based on a specific community or place of employment. The problem soon became how to stabilise a huge movement that was growing very quickly and lacked stability. In 1969, the Credit Union National Association was renamed the World Council of Credit Unions. It took on this process of stabilisation through a programme of international lending and technical assistance, overseeing a worldwide expansion in the sector that is still continuing.

In contrast, during the 1960s growth in new credit unions was slowing in the USA and Canada and in some areas had stopped. Unions were starting to diversify and amalgamate for economies of scale, and a minority were expanding because they really wanted to grow. The larger ones became more professionalised and evolved into a more 'managerial' type, with salaried staff, a wider range of financial 'products', growing technological sophistication and a more indirect form of member governance. With greater use of advertising and the introduction of teller lines in their branches, they were beginning to look more like the commercial banks. During the 1970s, the American movement continued to grow until in 1978 it had nearly half the total number of credit unions worldwide, but 72% of the total membership and 73% of the total assets (MacPherson, 1999: 106). In 1977 new legislation allowed them to give mortgages, then in the 1980s they experienced a heady mixture of deregulation, inflation, increased competition, and the introduction of electronic banking. Unlike the S&Ls they weathered the storm very well, resisting the temptation to demutualise and keeping their distinctive set of values while at the same time competing successfully with the IOB sector.

We left the history of co-operative banks in Europe at the period before the First World War when the Raiffeisen and Schulze systems were growing strongly throughout continental Europe. Unfortunately, their history in the 20th century still has to be written, but we know that they managed to survive a world war and takeover by fascist states that could not tolerate their independence. They then survived a second world war to see the restoration of savings and credit systems in the West and a long period of state control under communism in the East. Surprisingly, the

contours of the systems set up by Raiffeisen and Schulze are still dis-
cernible. In Germany, the two were merged in 1971 into one movement.
Now there are over a thousand local banks with two central banks. DZ
Bank has 1196 local banks in membership with 16.2 million customers,
of whom 54% are members (ECBA, 2008). It is the fifth largest bank in
Germany, with an 18.6% share of the market in deposits and a 16% share
in loans, and it provides 25% of all loans to small and medium-sized businesses (SMEs). WGZ is the central bank for 1400 local co-operative banks
that include three quarters of the Volksbanks and Raiffeisen banks in
Germany and Austria. In Austria and Italy, there are still two movements
corresponding to the Raiffeisen and Schulze traditions. In Austria, the
Raiffeisen banks are organised in a three tiered system of 541 local banks,
eight regional banks and one national. Together they have 3.6 million
clients and 1.65 million members. Their national bank, RZB is the third
largest bank in Austria, with a 38% market share of loans to SMEs, a 28.6%
share of deposits and 24.6% share of credits. There is also an Austrian Co-
operative Union that explicitly claims the legacy of Schulze; it has an 8%
market share of deposits and a 7.5% share of credits. In Italy, Federcasse is
the central bank for 432 local casse rurali with 940,000 members. It has a
market share of 8.9% of deposits, 7.2% of loans. There is also the National
Federation of the Banche Popolari which has 97 banks with 25% market
share of loans to SMEs, a 25% share of deposits and a 23% share of loans.

In Switzerland, Raiffeisen Switzerland has 350 local banks in membership with 1.65 million members and three million customers. It is third
in the Swiss banking market in terms of assets, with 21% of deposits, and
15% of mortgage market. In France, the largest bank, Credit Agricole was
founded in the 19th century by the government to meet the needs of
farmers, but in 1988 it was converted to a mutual, and then recently at
the national level it was converted again into an IOB. It is owned mainly
by over 2500 local banks federated in 39 regional banks with 6.2 million
members, and so the system remains at base a mutual one. It has 35% of
the SME loans market, 24% of deposits and 22% of credits. France still has
a Schulze-inspired group in the 20 regional Banques Populaires, and yet
another member-owned sector in the 17 mutual savings banks that form
the Caisses d'Epargne (these were converted to MOB status in 1999). In
2009, these two groups merged into a new group called BPCE; this is now
France's second-largest banking group with 22% of deposits and 23% of
real estate loans. The Raiffeisen legacy is represented by Credit Mutuel,
which has grown to become the third largest bank with 3300 caisses federated into 18 regional federations; its market share of deposits is 12%,
and of loans is 16.9%. In Luxembourg there is just one Banque Raiffeisen

with a 10% market share. Contrast the Netherlands, where Rabobank is among the top 25 financial institutions worldwide. It was formed in 1972 from the merger of the Raiffeisen and Boerenbond bank groups, and now serves 147 banks with 1.7 million members. It has a market share of 39% of loans to SMEs, 43% of deposits and 30% of loans in the Netherlands, but also has a huge international presence in the food and agriculture industries.

The Raiffeisen system eventually reached Scandinavia. In 1915 a bank was founded in Denmark and now there is a small group of 20 Raiffeisen banks. During the 1920s it spread to Finland where the great reformer, Hannes Gebhard adopted it. There are now 228 local banks grouped in 16 regional federations, with 1.2 million members whose main task is to elect people to the supervisory board of the OP-Pohjola Group which is Finland's largest financial services group; it has over 30% of domestic loans and deposits and 25% of domestic non-life insurance. The idea also reached Spain and Portugal where there are small rural co-operative banking sectors. As Henry Wolff noted on his travels in the 1890s, Raiffeisen sectors were being set up in central and eastern Europe, but these later lost their independence under communist states. With the fall of communism some of these have been reconstituted and there are growing sectors in Poland, Romania and Hungary. However, co-operative banks set up in Bulgaria and Slovenia have recently been converted to IOBs, and so here the future of co-operative banking is uncertain.

The current situation of co-operative banks/credit unions

We are fortunate that the World Council of Credit Unions collects statistics worldwide on its membership. This gives all the significant indicators for regions and countries that follow the credit union model. If we supplement these with similar statistics of the members of the European Co-operative Banking Association, who are not part of WOCCU but represent the 'old' Raiffeisen and Volksbank legacy, we will be close to a picture of the world of co-operative banking.

Table 7.2 summarises statistics from WOCCU comparing the situation worldwide in the years 2000 and 2008. In those eight years there was a giant burst of activity. In 2000 there were over 36,000 unions in membership from 92 countries, with over 108 million members. By 2008 there were nearly 54,000 unions from 97 countries, and the membership had almost doubled to nearly 186 million (WOCCU, 2010). It could be that credit unions have just become better at collecting statistics during the last decade, but there is no disputing the real increase in both unions and members. In numbers of unions Asia leads, followed by Africa, Europe

Table 7.2   Credit union statistics, comparing the years 2000 and 2008

Year	Region	No. of countries & market penetration		No. of credit unions	No. of members
2000	World	92		36,512	108.2m
2008		97	7.7%	53,689	185.8m
2000	Africa	27		3267	2.1m
2008		22	8.8%	18,220	20.1m
2000	Asia	12		13,934	8.8m
2008		21	2.6%	21,076	35m
2000	Caribbean	16		304	1.2m
2008		16	23.4%	439	2.5m
2000	Europe	11		5899	5m
2008		12	3.7%	2569	8.7m
2000	Latin America	19		1055	3.1m
2008		17	4.7%	1994	12.1m
2000	North America	3		11,763	84.7m
2008		3	44.1%	9109	103.5m
2000	Oceania	4	17.8%	290	3.2m
2008		6		282	3.9m

Source: Edited from WOCCU, 2010

and Latin America. In membership, North America has more than half, followed by Asia, Africa and Latin America. The market penetration worldwide is 7.7% but in North America is a staggering 44.1%, and in the Caribbean it has reached 23.4%.

If we add in similar statistics for European co-operative banks that are not part of WOCCU, we find in 2008 there were 4461 local banks with nearly 52 million members, organised in 26 national federations or banks, having a market share of 21% of deposits and 19% of loans (ECBA, 2008). There is no doubt that co-operative banking, just like co-operative and mutual insurance, is a force to be reckoned with.

The impact of globalisation and problems of governance

Credit unions are evolving from a volunteer-led movement to one that is heavily dependent on professional managers, and there is a consequent loss of motivation and a change of culture that some see as dangerous for the future of the movement. As we have noted, in developed countries pressures to keep down costs have resulted in mergers and in unions becoming bigger and more remote from their members. Still, the old federal system of primary societies and regional and national 'centrals' survives, and unions tend to restrict themselves to doing business in their own areas and with the people they see as having a 'common bond'. With a carefully managed member relations strategy they can keep their members engaged.

In Europe, the co-operative banking sector has also managed to preserve the essential features of the old federal systems, whereby central banks provide services and supervision, and the local banks are active in managing contacts with members and the local community. In contrast with the mutual insurance and savings and loans sectors, there have not been any noticeable governance failures, and the presence of the local banks ensures some check on managerial ambitions. Yet there is a growing distance between the banks and their members (Rabobank, 2009). Decisions are increasingly being made at the centre. However, the evolution towards a more centralised structure is not complete, and is more pronounced in some countries than others; for instance the Dutch group is one of the most centralised, while the Italian is still the most decentralised in Europe. There are still choices to be made about the relative weight to give to governance between the local and central banks.

Like the mutual insurers, in response to the pressures of increased competition and globalisation the banks have been internationalising and creating complex new subsidiaries that make it hard for the members to understand what is going on. Rabobank estimates that about 25% of European co-operative banks' net revenues is derived from outside their home country (2009: 18). Banks have either acquired foreign banks or entered into strategic alliances. For instance, Raiffeisen International (a subsidiary of Raiffeisen Austria) has set up a large number of retail operations in central and eastern Europe, largely through acquisitions of formerly public banks. Credit Agricole and Credit Mutuel recently acquired banks in Italy, Greece, Poland and Germany. Rabobank has made strategic acquisitions and new business start-ups, and now has 603 offices spread over 46 foreign countries. In almost all cases they have not converted the foreign banks to a co-operative model, nor have they offered membership to customers.

The banks have to answer the question of whether their diversification into corporate and investment banking is justified, and whether they should be chasing business in other countries. When they do so they could agree to limit themselves to strategic alliances with other co-operative banks and credit unions. As well as governance issues, there may be good business reasons for restraint. Rabobank has had a difficult time with its overseas operations. In 1999 the Bank made a decision to cut back its investment banking and overseas business, and to phase out lending to 'non-core customers outside the Netherlands' (Rabobank, 2009: 38). If co-operative banks are not very good at investment and corporate banking and at expanding beyond their borders, then perhaps they should concentrate on their core business and, at the same time, make it easier for local members to monitor their banks and maintain a high quality of governance.

The impact of the recent banking crisis

In the recent banking crisis the investor-owned banks made huge losses and had to be bailed out by their governments. How did this affect the co-operative banking sector? It is the job of the central co-operative banks and credit unions to reinvest surplus cash from the local banks and unions, and in some cases they did so unwisely by buying investment products from other banks that lost much of their value. Sask-Central, one of the provincial Centrals in Canada, posted a loss of over $45 million as it had a 51% million writedown on investments in asset backed commercial paper (Birchall and Hammond Ketilson, 2009). Desjardins in Quebec also experienced significant losses. In the USA, the two corporate credit unions, US Central Credit Union and Federal Credit Union were seized by US regulators at the beginning of 2009; they were also involved in the kind of mortgage backed securities that got banks into trouble. The US Central Corporate Credit Union is to get $1 billion in government aid, but it is interesting to note that the losses are not due to a failure in corporate governance; at the time the investments were rated as low risk products. The US credit unions have a three tier system; there are 8400 primary societies, 27 corporates and the Centrals. The corporate credit unions invested $64 billion from their members in mortgage-backed securities, and as these have declined in value by $18 billion they are being forced to acknowledge the decline.

In Europe, a report from Rabobank says

While all the large co-operative banks have suffered substantial losses on risky investments, they do seem to have been hit relatively less hard by the direct effects of the crisis than private and investment banks (2009: 9).

For instance, in Germany, the co-operative central bank, DZ, announced a loss of Eur1 billion for 2008 as a consequence of high risk investments. Rabobank incurred losses and writedowns of around 6% of its total equity, thought it did not need any form of aid as it was strongly capitalised. The biggest loss may have been in Japan, where the Norinchukin Bank lost $8 billion on investments and securitized products, making it the biggest loser in Asia from the crisis. The bank had continued to buy toxic assets while other banks disclosed losses, because the assets were bought cheap, and its managers under-estimated the severity of the crisis. It is owned by 32 million farmers and fishers through their producer co-operatives, and they will have to find 1.9 trillion yen of financial support. While the bank is still able to guarantee a return on its members' assets, it was unable to pay a dividend in 2009, and this will put pressure on a not very profitable farming sector.

Despite these losses, credit unions and co-operative banks seem to be doing rather well. In Canada 516 credit unions and caisses populaires outside of Quebec saw a six-month increase in assets in the second quarter of 2008. Similar reports from the provincial credit union associations highlight the stability of the system. In Manitoba for example, the 48 credit unions saw assets, loans and deposits increase by 10% or more in 2008. For credit unions in Saskatchewan, net income and total assets in 2008 were the highest ever. It was also a record year for credit unions in British Columbia where 2008 earnings increased by 10% to reach an all-time high for the province. With an increase in member numbers, deposits and assets of these financial institutions is also on the rise. Credit Unions in Manitoba saw their deposits increase by 11.5% to $13.4 billion in 2008. The National Association in the US expects deposits in credit unions to increase by 10% in 2009 (Birchall and Hammond Ketilson, 2009).

While a credit freeze by the large banks has been one of the characteristics of the financial crisis, this has not been the case for the majority of financial co-operatives in the United States and Canada. In the USA, loans by credit unions increased from $539 billion in 2007 to $575 billion in 2008. By comparison, 8300 US banks saw loans outstanding decrease $31 billion to $7.876 trillion from $7.907 trillion in 2007. Here is another way of putting the same point: credit union loan volume increase 6.7% in 2008 while lending from banks dropped by 40%. Small businesses are a driving force in the economy and in employment creation, and in a recession it is crucially important that lending to this sector continues. In Canada, many credit unions have increased the number of loans to small businesses – in British Columbia by 10%. Credit unions in the United States have reported a substantial increase in the number of mortgages and car loans. Loan accessibility, competitive rates, and institutional stability have translated into an increase in membership. Taking the US as a whole, membership rose to almost 90 million in 2008, from 85 million in 2004. Market share is expanding: in the province of Manitoba it reached a record high of 40.7% in 2008.

In previous banking crises, such as the Asian crisis of the 1990s, there was a 'flight to quality' among savers. The growing membership of credit unions suggests that this is also occurring in the present crisis. Consumers are looking for safer and more ethical alternatives to the banks. Drops in stock prices have also driven investors to withdraw from the stock market and put their money into credit union savings accounts. As banks continue to suffer huge losses they have increased interest rates and lowered credit limits on consumer credit cards to make up some of these debts. Credit unions have no need to do this, and they are meeting the current demands of the market for good rates, low risk and personal service while banks are increasing fees to make up for losses.

The picture is similar in Europe. In 2008, Rabobank saw its share of loans increase to 42% of the market, and its local member banks recorded a sharp influx of savings of 20%. In the UK, the very low interest rate set by the Bank of England has discouraged savings, but the building societies' share of the retail savings market increased from 20.2% at the end of February 2008 to 21.4% at the end of February 2009. More deposits mean greater liquidity for credit unions and co-operative banks, and so more money is available for lending.

Future prospects

The future for co-operative banking seems to be assured. The banking crisis has shown that they have significant organisational comparative advantages which customers are beginning to appreciate. Because they are *member-owned* they tend to be more risk averse than other financial institutions. Because they are not driven by profits or shareholder interests they do not feel compelled to force people into inappropriate loans. They have a different kind of governance structure, in which local credit unions and co-operative banks scrutinise the decisions of the central institutions. In this way, they are more aware of the fact that the loan they offer to their members is another member's money. The direct link of savings and loans, which may not be as apparent in some banks, acts as a moral constraint. They are not reliant upon the capital markets for funding, but are funded through member deposits. They are strong in retail banking, which is characterised by stable returns and comparatively good access to savings and deposits. They are not able to go to the markets to obtain easy money from investors, and so they tend to retain their profits and take fewer risks. During the recent economic turmoil, member-owned banks have experienced an increase in almost every facet of their business including: increase in assets and deposits; increased volume of lending; increase in membership; a better rate of interest; and greater stability (measured by capital adequacy ratios, and loan default rates). They have had very few losses on investments and so far have not needed government help.

However, as the recession deepens and lengthens, the sector is likely to have to deal with increased loan delinquency, and eventually a falling off in deposits as members' incomes begin to decline. Also, perversely, co-operatives have to compete with bankrupt investor-owned banks that have been recapitalised by governments which are offering very high deposit rates and forcing others to follow; this is unfair competition. Eventually, governments that now have substantial ownership shares in the troubled banks may break them up and create new retail-focused banks. The expected 'return to retail banking' may provide more competition for the co-operative banks and credit unions (Rabobank, 2009). There has not been much pressure to demutualise, and the advantages of co-operative banking to customers are becoming more apparent. However, if times become better for banks in general the threat of demutualisation may re-emerge (Davis, 2007).

Perhaps the most important contribution co-operative banking will make in the future is in financial deepening in developing countries. Here, credit unions will continue to be crucial to their members' well-being, and if they become as good at all-round banking as they are at community economic development they will be able to raise many more people out of poverty.

8
Producer-owned and Employee-owned Businesses

In this chapter the focus changes and we look directly at the needs of people who are producing goods and services through MOBs, either as self-employed business people or as employees. There are two basic types. First, there are businesses owned by self-employed people who need to co-operate together to provide themselves with services that aid their own production process. Second, there are businesses owned by their employees that are designed so that the value added to the business from the production process is captured by the workforce. Call them, for convenience, producer-owned businesses (POBs) and employee-owned businesses (EOBs). Sometimes the difference between the two is a fine one, particularly in co-operatives that are set up by professional people such as architects, graphic designers or investment managers. Here, the decision to be employees or to be self-employed is not all that important; what is important is that the MOB helps people to be productive and to share the costs of production. Similarly, in developing countries handicraft co-operatives are common, and it is often unclear whether their workforce is employed or self-employed. The best test is whether the returns from their labour are based on the value added to an individually or a collectively produced product; a sculpture co-op is likely to be a POB, a pottery co-op an EOB.

The distinction is sometimes obscured by the way in which the term 'producer' is used. Traditionally, statistics have been gathered on 'producer co-ops' that include any ownership structure as long as the business is in some kind of production. The resulting confusion is exemplified by the title of the international organisation that represents them: the *International Organisation of Industrial, Artisanal and Service Producer Co-operatives*. Its members are 'representative organisations of producers' co-operatives from different sectors: construction, industrial production, general services, transport, intellectual skills, artisanal activities, health, social care, etc' (CICOPA, 2010). There is also a confusion over the term 'consumer', with some analysts distinguishing between individual consumers and businesses that collectively join together to procure inputs who are called 'business consumers'; it seems easier just to classify everything that businesses do collectively to provide both inputs and outputs as producer-owned businesses. Armed with these distinctions, we can keep the distinction between POBs and EOBs, and then identify which market sectors they are involved in. The resulting taxonomy distinguishes three basic types of POB. The first is the *primary producer-owned business*, created mainly by farmers, foresters and fishers, designed to help them to produce, process and market their products. The second is the *retailer-owned business*, designed to provide wholesaling and distribution so that small retailers can survive in a market increasingly dominated by retail chains. The third is a wide range of businesses that provide *shared services* for self-employed people and networks of small businesses. We can then reserve the final category for the *employee-owned* business, often known as a worker co-operative, which is designed to enable people who work for a business to own and control it and reap the benefits.

Type 1: Primary producer co-operatives

Primary producers in farming, forestry and fishing have a lot in common. They are all involved in creating value in an uncertain encounter between humans and the natural world that depends on climate and topography and that, because it is only partially under human agency, carries risks. They all need inputs to their production in the form of tools, seeds, feeds, fertilisers, nets, machinery and so on, and, because the transforming process takes time, they also need inputs of credit to provide cash flow. They also need insurance to lessen the risks, though some of the uncertainties they face are uninsurable. Then, when the product has been created, they need to have it collected, put it through some basic processing and then marketed. If they are very well organised, instead of marketing their products right away they can extend their control along the value chain, transforming the product further and so capturing more of the realisable value. Fishers are different in one respect; they simply hunt and catch the product in the wild, and so they face the added uncertainty that comes from dipping into a 'common pool resource' that can easily be over-used and degraded. Farmers and foresters have a lot in common; in Sweden and Finland they are not separate types of producer, but small farmers who also own and manage forests.

They share the same co-operative heritage, and the national-level businesses they have created have an overlapping membership and similar characteristics.

Founding period

Like other types of MOB, primary producer co-ops were invented to help people survive in a new industrial society in which money values began to predominate and subsistence production gave way to production for the market. From the mid-18th century in Britain – later in other countries – what was produced gradually became a commodity whose worth was only established when it was sold. The farming process became more intensive, more reliant on machinery and so on capital investment. It began to need regular inputs of fertilisers, seeds and livestock whose quality became more controlled (Smith, 1961). It relied on the development of railways to enable perishable products to be marketed in the vastly enlarged towns and cities, and on new industrialised processes to maximise its value: preserving the crops, processing them into standardised food products, and preparing them for export to other countries (Burnett, 1989).

The first activity to be organised was *food processing*; in Switzerland and France, cheese-making societies can be traced back to medieval times. In their modern form they were first set up in the USA, where by 1867 there were 400 co-operative cheese factories and creameries (Smith, 1961). As so often happened, the idea rapidly took root elsewhere; a Danish delegation visited in 1876 and in 1884 set up their first creamery at Hjedding. Technology was one factor; in 1878 the cream separator was invented and this meant the process could be industrialised. The threat of monopoly was also a factor; in Ireland, entrepreneurs saw the opportunity, paid the farmers high prices for milk inducing them to give up home production, and then reduced their prices (Horace Plunkett, quoted in Smith, 1961). Co-operative creameries then began to be developed all over Europe.

Marketing co-ops began in the USA. Here the distances to market were great, and the threat of exploitation by middlemen was obvious. Pig farmers began joint marketing as early as 1820, while sheep farmers began wool marketing in 1844. Then with the coming of the railroads marketing co-ops really took off; in Canada the Saskatchewan and Alberta wheat pools were founded to enable farmers to ship their grain to Britain. *Supply co-ops* ought to have been easy to set up; like consumer co-ops they involve joint purchase of a simple good that can be divided up. They began in 1865 in Switzerland for the supply of fertiliser (Birchall, 1997). However, their growth was inhibited by the way in which farmers relied on supply merchants for credit and could not easily break free. It took the development of the Raiffeisen banks to allow European farmers to supply themselves. First they purchased in bulk through their banks and then formed separate supply societies. It was a rival group to Raiffeisen, the Hesse Union that began this type; beginning in 1872, by 1886 they had formed a wholesale society, and by the end of the century were big enough to challenge cartels.

If the origins of farmer co-operation are scattered among several countries, it can be said to have reached its full potential in Denmark. Here, the economic conditions for co-operative development were very favourable. Land reform had created the second largest number of freehold farms in Europe (after Norway), and so there was a class of independent small farmers. However, they only had an average of 40 acres each, so needed to co-operate to counter the disadvantages of small scale (Fay, 1907). Towards the end of the 19th century they had developed a large export trade in butter and bacon, and had an incentive to capture as much as possible of the value chain for themselves. The social conditions were also favourable. The population was homogeneous, with a deep reservoir of social capital springing from common religious allegiances, an egalitarian political tradition, and compulsory education. In particular, the folk high school movement had prepared people for co-operative development (in the same way that the Antigonish movement was to do for Canadians a few decades later). By 1900 there were over 1000 co-operative dairies, processing around 80% of the milk produced, 27 meat co-ops producing 66% of the pork, and 800 supply societies in several federations importing and manufacturing animal feeds (Fay, 1907). Denmark had become what one writer called a 'farmers' co-operative commonwealth' (Manniche, 1969).

Farmers in other countries followed the Danish example, but did not reach the same level of market penetration. In France they were organised in syndicates, voluntary associations of farmers whose activities were much more diverse but eventually laid the foundations of a more focused co-operative sector. In Italy, by the end of the century there were 800 supply societies, 100 wine co-ops, 600 dairies and a national wholesale society. However, in Ireland and Britain growth was disappointing, though for different reasons. In Ireland the reformer Horace Plunkett was frustrated by the slow progress and blamed the lack of technical education, and religious differences that made it difficult for farmers to trust each other (West, 1986). In Britain, the different sizes of farms and the split between freehold and tenant landholdings meant farmers were not a cohesive class.

A period of growth and state support

In the late 1930s, CR Fay distinguished two streams in Europe, the first having developed from credit to agricultural co-operation, and the second the other way around. The Raiffeisen credit movement had given rise to supply and marketing co-ops throughout continental Europe, while the Danish movement based essentially on dairying had spread through Scandinavia, Finland, the Netherlands, Britain and Ireland (Fay, 1938). This is probably an over-generalisation but it simplifies a picture that can seem confusing if looked at in more detail. The first 'stream' based on co-operative credit was choked off by fascism in Germany, Austria and Italy, but the second continued to grow. The Danish system became highly integrated, with cattle, pigs and poultry making a virtuous circle of production; for instance, skimmed milk from the dairies was fed back to the pig industry. They were backed up by agricultural supply and a wide range of specialist societies. In other countries, farmer co-operation varied with the topography. In Norway there was more diversity, with fishing and forestry co-ops as well as dairying, but they had a small market share; in such a thinly populated country, farmers still sold their produce through local markets rather than for export. Fay says the north of Sweden was like Norway, the south like Denmark. The south of Sweden was also like England, because there large farmers could meet their needs individually rather than through collective action (Fay, 1938). In Iceland, a comprehensive co-operative sector developed to organise exports, while in Finland four-fifths of the dairying and most of the forestry was in co-operative hands.

While in Europe there was a long transition from a feudal system of land tenure to modern, market-led farming, in America there were no such constraints. A cash-cropping, export-led agriculture grew up early, helped by three important new inventions: the railway, the steamship and refrigeration. However, the long distances involved gave middlemen potentially great power. This is why co-operation began with marketing and then extended back into farm supply and forward into food processing. By the mid-1930s they had made serious inroads into the markets for dairy, grain, livestock, and fruit and vegetables, and large, state-wide marketing co-ops had grown up with distinctive brands such as Sunkist for oranges and Land O'Lakes for dairy products (Birchall, 1997).

The Danish system was based on single-purpose societies that were entirely without state support, and with no special co-operative laws. So confident were farmers in their own ability to run their co-operatives that, even with the heavy capital investments needed for food processing for export, they did not seek limited liability. As in the early Raiffeisen system, the risks attached to unlimited liability gave them a keen interest in good governance! However, in the world economic crisis of the 1930s, governments began to get much more involved, and in some countries such as Britain, Australia and New Zealand marketing co-ops were replaced by statutory marketing boards, while in others such as Finland and the USA the co-operatives were given state support (Birchall, 2009). Governments in Europe and North America passed laws privileging farmer co-ops, and in several countries (as diverse as France, Finland, USA, and Japan), governments set up banks to supply them with the credit they needed for modernisation. In most developed countries agricultural co-operatives came to dominate most produce markets. They did this with the help of secondary co-operatives in banking and insurance that they set up themselves or in partnership with governments.

A period of consolidation and further growth

During the postwar period, this combination of managed markets and state support continued, so that by the mid-1990s there were massive, consolidated farmer co-operative sectors. There were 58,000 societies in Europe, with nearly 14 million farmer members and a turnover of $265 billion (Cote and Luc, 1996). There were over 4000 societies in the USA with a membership of nearly four million and a turnover of $89 billion. In Canada, there were 830 societies with nearly 600,000 members and a turnover of more than $10 billion. During this period the idea spread to Latin America, becoming particularly important in export-led economies such as Brazil; here by 1995 there were nearly 1400 co-ops with a membership of nearly a million, and an output of more than $12 billion (a bit more than Canada and only slightly less than Denmark).

It also spread to Asia and Africa but with more mixed results. We will be looking at MOBs in developing countries in Chapter 9. Briefly, wherever governments decided to use farmer co-operatives as tools of development, reorganising them and imposing their own priorities, co-operatives failed. Yet it was not the involvement of governments that was the problem, but the way in which they tried to accelerate the growth of co-operatives artificially, and ignored the fundamental principles of farmer-ownership, control and benefit that gave meaning to the idea of membership. In Japan, Korea, and in some sectors in India (notably sugar and dairy), government involvement was extensive but somehow independent co-operative sectors did emerge. By the mid-1990s output in Japan rivalled that of the USA at nearly $90 billion, and that of Korea rivalled Canada with $11 billion, and in both countries virtually all farmers and fishers were in membership. Co-operatives also dominated the export-led farming industries in New Zealand and Australia (Birchall, 1997).

In the communist countries of the Soviet Union and its satellites, the term 'agricultural co-operatives' often meant collective farms rather than farmer-owned businesses. The collapse of the communist system meant land reforms, the reinstatement of family farms and, unsurprisingly, a growing need for farmers to associate for their mutual benefit. With the help of donors such as USAID, farmers in central and Eastern Europe set up marketing associations so they could market their crops for the wider European market. It is understandable that, given the dubious use of the word 'co-operative' in their recent past, they preferred to use the term 'farmer association', but the same needs led to the same solutions as were found by farmers in the rest of Europe.

It should be possible at this point to outline the current shape of the agricultural co-operative sector around the world. In 1996 this was achieved by two Canadian academics (Cote and Luc, 1996) but it is has not been done since, and we are left with incomplete and inconsistent statistics. However, a short description can be made of some countries where co-operatives are still dominant. In the USA, there are 2675 farmer-owned co-operatives with a net business volume of $110.5 billion. They are major employers in rural areas, employing 123,000 full time and 57,000 seasonal workers. Their membership has dropped from 3.4 million in 1997 to 2.6 million in 2006, but this reflects the decrease in the number of farms in that period rather than a loss of faith in co-operatives. Most co-operatives are still small and serve local areas, but large co-ops account for most of the business; 3% of them have a business volume of more than $200 million, but they account for 65% of sales (USDA, 2007). In Japan there is still an integrated agricultural co-operative sector that has nearly all farmers in membership. It does not need to calculate market share because this is also nearly all co-operative! It provides a comprehensive service to farmers and rural areas, with farm guidance, better living guidance for health and recreation, marketing, supply and a range of other services such as welfare services for older people. The national federation has its own bank and insurance federation. It has nearly 9.5 million members, equally divided between full farmer members and associate members who join for benefits such as mutual credit and insurance. It has 226,000 employees, and a turnover of more than 7.6 trillion yen (Kurimoto, 2010b).

In Denmark, co-operatives still account for a massive 10% of GDP. There has been so much consolidation that the numbers of co-operatives tell us nothing about the size of the sector. There were 1400 dairies in 1935 but only 12 remain, yet the market share of butter is 98%, of milk 96% and of cheese is 87%. There were 62 meat co-operatives in 1961 but now only two remain, yet the market share of pork production is 87% and of beef is 57% (Danish Agricultural Council, 2007). In Brazil, there are over 1600 co-operatives with nearly a million members and 139,000 employees. Their share of agricultural GPD is 40%, and of total GDP is 5.4% (Organisation of Brazilian Co-operatives, 2010). In Canada, there are 267 agricultural co-operatives with revenues of $13 billion. The demutualisation of grain and poultry co-ops has lowered market share, which ranges from 40% for dairy down to 8% for grains (Govt of Canada, 2010). Finally, in New Zealand there has been a similar consolidation to that experienced in Denmark; in 1935 there were over 400 co-ops, but now just three. The largest, Fonterra, processes 95% of all milk nation-wide, exports to 140 countries and generates 20% of New Zealand's export earnings (Nilsson and Ohlsson, 2007). In other countries the effects are not so dramatic, but agricultural co-operatives are still a major component of the economy. However, it is no longer entirely clear what we mean by an agricultural co-operative; the form is transmuting and, while farmer-ownership and control are still mostly intact, there has been a profound shift in the way it is expressed.

A period of radical restructuring

During the 1990s, the rather cosy relationship between governments and farmers began to break down, under a combination of deregulation, reducing subsidies, globalisation and competition from transnational agri-food corporations. In the USA, the traditional relationship between local and regional or national co-operatives began to come under strain, as locals began to seek alternatives to the traditional federated structures (Hogeland, 2002). Co-operatives needed to raise lots of capital and to raise it quickly. In order to do so they created innovative new types of business that blended various combinations of farmer-owned and investor-owned capital. Traditional co-operatives have the disadvantage that ownership rights are not transferable and do not appreciate with the value of the business so there is no incentive for members to put in more capital than is absolutely necessary. What they can do is to invest in joint ventures and strategic alliances with companies that do have capital. They can also insist that members provide capital in proportion to patronage (the business done with the co-operative), or go further and distribute dividends in proportion to shares as well as patronage. The furthest they can go while retaining full member-ownership is the new generation co-operative that insists members provide capital in proportion to delivery rights; the shares are then tradable among members. To gain access to outside capital, co-operatives can set up a separate business that investors can buy into, or they can offer them a different class of share in the co-operative itself, or they can convert to an IOB model and float the co-operative on the stock market (Cook and Chaddad, 2004). This last option looks like demutualisation, but if farmers maintain majority ownership it does not mean they lose control. They can also keep the co-operative as a holding company behind the IOB. It can be argued as long as these IOBs do not affect the fundamental principle of member benefit, we can still consider them to be member-owned (Nilsson, 2001). Here are some examples, using a typology developed by Chaddad and Cook (2004).

1. Proportional investment co-operative

Numerous well-known American co-operatives have made investment proportional, by designing a 'base capital plan' that aligns member capital with their patronage. Riceland, Land O'Lakes, Dairy Farmers of America are good examples.

2. Member-investor co-operative

Here, the co-operative distributes net earnings in proportion to member shareholdings rather than patronage. The best example is Fonterra, the giant New Zealand dairy co-operative that requires members to hold redeemable preference shares in proportion to the quantity of milk produced.

3. New generation co-operatives

Here, members contribute capital in proportion to the amount of product they intend to supply to a processing co-op. The resulting share confers a right to supply, and can be traded among farmers at market value. In return, they get a guarantee from the co-op to return all the value from processing back to the farmers, again in proportion to the amount they have supplied. This new form of co-op, of which there are around 200, is raising the incomes of farmers dramatically, and revitalising the local economies of North Dakota, Minnesota and neighbouring states (Merrett and Walzer, 2001). However, it is proving controversial. In most co-operatives members still have only one vote each, but some now link voting rights to shares and there is a tendency for those that want to grow rapidly to demutualise.

4. Co-operatives with capital-seeking entities

In this model, co-operatives avoid giving away ownership rights by setting up strategic alliances, trust companies or subsidiaries. Examples include Kerry Creameries and five other co-operatives in Ireland that set up investor-owned subsidiaries and transferred all their assets to them, receiving back majority equity ownership.

5. Investor-share co-operatives

In this model, the co-operative issues a separate class of equity share without voting rights. One of the largest co-ops in the USA, CHS, does this by offering preferred stock. CHS is a conglomerate in the grain marketing, petroleum refining, and food processing industries, that is ranked 166 in the Fortune 500 listing, and in 2008 it provided returns to its owners of $388 million in cash and preferred stock. In 1996, Saskatchewan Wheat Pool raised risk capital through converting member equity to non-voting common stock, allowed them to trade in house, and then issued the stock on the Toronto stock exchange. This has become a popular method of raising capital among Australian co-ops.

6. Investor-oriented firms

With all the experiments in new organisational structures and mixtures of member and non-member ownership, it is surprising that demutual-isation is not such a big issue in this sector. Perhaps all these other options have made it less attractive. In the USA there have only been a few; Chaddad and Cook list only seven since the 1980s (2004: 358). In Western Canada a number of well-known co-operatives have con-verted or been taken over by IOBs, including three wheat pools, a poultry processor and a dairy co-operative. Lack of access to capital, growing heterogeneity among members and growing individualism in the wider society have been cited as causes, but a good case has been made for management over-confidence coupled with lack of oversight by boards of directors (Fulton and Larson, 2009).

What makes co-operatives choose one of these options rather than another? An organisation's structure is linked to its strategy, and co-operatives tend to choose a strategy depending on the market conditions (Nilsson and Ohlsson, 2007). Traditional co-operatives are well adapted to providing farm inputs and marketing high volumes of product at low cost, but have problems when they want to go further along the value chain; as soon as they begin manufactur-ing farm inputs and processing outputs, they begin to need more capital and different kinds of expertise. Governance become more difficult as the incentives for farmers become less clear, and farmers themselves demand different kinds of service and reward from the co-operative. Yet in the current market, characterised by over-production and declining subsidies, fierce competition and lower margins, co-operatives may not have the option of keeping their traditional structure.

The effects of globalisation

The extent of globalisation in farmer co-operatives is truly astonishing. Here are some examples. Arla Foods is a dairy co-operative that was formed in 2000 in a merger between Sweden's Arla and Denmark's MD Foods. It is the largest dairy company in Europe, the eighth largest in the world, with well-known brands such as Lurpak and Anchor butter. It is owned by nearly 8000 Danish and Swedish farmers in roughly equal proportions, and they are represented through 50 districts and seven regional councils on a 140 member board of representatives. The United Kingdom is now its largest market, accounting for 27% of sales, which is a great achievement but it means Swedish and Danish farmers benefit from profits while British farmers do not. In Finland, The Valio Group is Finland's largest milk processor, a traditionally structured co-operative processing 82% of the raw milk taken in by Finnish dairies. It is owned by 22 dairy co-ops with nearly 11,000 farmers in membership. It has subsidiaries in several European countries, and its international business accounts for a third of its turnover. The forestry co-operative, Metsaliitto has grown massively since Finland joined the EU. Like the large farmer-owned agri-food businesses, it is active throughout Europe and markets its products worldwide. The Group is now the tenth largest producer of forest industry products in the world, and Europe's largest wood producer, and it is still owned by the forest owners, all 130,000 of them (Birchall, 2009). We can expect this trend towards international-isation to continue. It will make it more difficult for the idea of member-ship to remain meaningful, particularly if farmers in the home country have membership rights that are denied to others. However, Arla has recently decided to bring British and Finnish farmers gradually into owner-ship, pointing the way towards a transnational co-operative governance structure.

Fishing co-operatives

Finally, we need to add a short note on fishing co-operatives. These can be found in small numbers in most countries, but are strongest in South-East Asia. In Japan there are over 450,000 fishers in 2300 co-ops, federated at regional and national levels in the Zengyoren system. Because of declining fish stocks and the drift of young people to the cities, they are in some difficulty financially and a programme of mergers is under way. In Korea, co-ops have a market share of over 70%, but again there are difficulties with overfishing and a government programme is attempting to buy back boats and slim the industry down (Birchall, 2008). The problems of constantly dipping into a 'common pool resource' are plainly illustrated.

Type 2: Retailer-owned businesses

When independent retailers began to face serious competition from consumer co-ops and saw the massive advantages their rivals were gaining from vertical integration, they began to organise their own wholesale supply co-ops. Like the Rochdale co-ops, they began in a small way: Unified Grocers in the USA was founded in 1922 by 15 retailers who shared out a car load of soap. This parallel movement has built up a formidable set of retailer-owned businesses that are now trying to match the buying power of a newer rival, the multiple chains such as Tesco and Walmart.

Now, retailer suppliers are strong in Western Europe. Rewe, based in Germany, is a group of independent retailers and chain stores operating 7330 stores, and is the third largest player in the European food trade. Edeka is the fourth largest, with 4100 stores. In France, Leclerc has 17% of the market, Intermarche 11.3% and Systeme U 8.3% (Baron, 2007). Pharmacy chains are also very strong; Noweda Apothek is the top pharmacy wholesaler in Germany, with 6000 member pharmacies, and Cooperativa Farmaceutica Espanola is the largest in Spain. They are also strong in Scandinavia; Kesko is the largest trading company in Finland, with 30% of the market. It is the parent corporation of the K-Group comprising some 2400 independent retailer-shareholders who operate nearly 2700 stores specializing in groceries, leisure goods, and consumer durables. In the USA the Wakefern Food Corporation is the largest, with 43 members owning 200 Shoprite superstores, while Associated Wholesale Grocers, the second largest, serves 1900 stores in 21 states. In New Zealand, three co-operative buying groups called Foodstuffs form the second largest grocery distributor.

There are interesting national variations; in the USA separate groups supply hardware stores, whereas in Europe the groups supply, and also own directly, a wide range of types of business. There are also complications in the type of ownership. Some groups are wholly owned by the retailers, some wholly owned by the wholesalers, and some are mixed. Some have floated on the stock market and so have a mixed ownership structure, including independent store owners, large retail chains and wholesalers. They tend to operate through franchises, and their members have to accept the discipline of the group. This raises the question of who holds the power in a franchise; it could be argued that because the relationship is unequal it is better if franchisees collectively own the franchisor. The retailer-owned wholesaler model has distinct advantages, as it creates an interesting mix of individual ownership of stores and group discipline that is self-imposed and, over time, can evolve quite sophisticated ways of aligning member interests and avoiding opportunistic behaviour. The Leclerc chain, for instance, has rules that enable the co-operative to control when stores can be sold and to negotiate the price, while allowing individual owners to own their own stores, balancing short-term gain against long-term benefits (Baron, 2007).

There are occasional demutualisations; in Britain, Londis used to be retailer-owned but they sold out to a group of wholesalers. However, the mixed ownership structure makes the whole issue more complicated, and there is another interesting trend towards retailer-ownership and consumer co-operatives coming together for joint supply. The Spar Group is the world's biggest retail chain, and its ownership varies from one country to another. In Finland, the consumer co-operative S-Group is now the majority shareholder in Spar, which means it can supply independent retailers as well as consumer co-operative stores. In contrast, Spar Scotland is wholly-owned by a wholesaler, and retailers enter into a franchise agreement to gain access to the Spar brand. However, in 2006 the Co-operative Group and Spar entered into an alliance in which they agreed to pool their 'own label' volumes and jointly purchase from suppliers.

Here, as in farming, the member-owned type of business has demonstrated its effectiveness in shifting the balance decisively towards the small producer. Yet it is interesting to note that the retail buying groups are strongest in countries where there are few consumer co-ops: France, Germany, the USA. Faced with a strong consumer movement, Conad in Italy has become the country's second largest distributor but lags well behind Co-op Italia. Competition between different types of MOB can be just as serious as between MOBs and IOBs. Yet, as the S-Group in Finland and Cooperative Group in Scotland illustrate, the future may be with strategic alliances between consumer-owned and retailer-owned businesses against the challenge from the IOB sector.

Type 3: Shared service co-operatives

The idea that businesses should band together to supply themselves with whatever they need has obvious advantages. It helps self-employed and small business people to save on the costs of marketing, purchasing and shared services, doing away with the 'middleman' and enabling the members to retain the maximum surplus value from their work. It provides critical mass and economies of scale so that a product can be supplied in sufficient quantities and with continuity over time, both of which are important for anyone trying to sell to supermarkets. It shares risks and development costs so that new markets can be developed, and shares the cost of facilities such as retail outlets and workspaces. It allows the producers to keep control over standards and quality of work, and provides mutual support for lone traders. Often it enables businesses to develop an ethical approach, expressing and reinforcing distinctive values (Co-operatives UK, 2010).

The idea has been applied in many different ways. One of the earliest examples is mutual marine insurance, where ship-owners come together to insure each others' ships against the risk of loss. Like some of the early friendly societies and savings clubs, they began in the early 19th century based at several ports in Britain and Norway (Johnstad, 2000). At first they only insured the hull of the ship and so were known as 'hull societies'. However, when people started to emigrate in large numbers from Britain and Ireland, ship-owners began to be sued for damages and so from 1855 onwards protection and liability clubs began to be formed, insuring against loss of cargo, collision damage, liabilities to passengers and so on. It is easy to see how they came about and became so dominant in their market niche; they had a 'great stock of social capital' based on good social relations and high levels of mutual trust between ship-owners (Johnstad, 2000: 551). They had entrepreneurial skills and so could easily master the technicalities of mutual insurance. Economic explanations are also important. The business was characterised by asymmetric information concerning risk and a related moral hazard problem about verifying claims, that only those intimately involved with the business could solve. There was market failure, with limited competition among investor-owned insurers who consequently charged high prices. There was homogeneity in members' interests that made governance relatively straight forward (Johnstad, 2000). Now there are 13 clubs that are part of the International Group of P & I Clubs and, despite competition from investor-owned insurers such as Lloyds of London, they insure 90% of the world's shipping (Doe, 2010).

The more general history of this type began in Germany, where the founder of the urban co-operative banks, Schulze-Delitzsch, was also instrumental in setting up what we would call shared service co-ops to help sustain small enterprises to compete. One of his first initiatives was a co-operative that supplied materials to shoemakers. As a result, they are still a recognised category within the apex body, the German Co-operative and Raiffeisen Union, called 'small-scale industry commodity and service co-operatives'. There are over 1000 of them, providing economic support for their members who are described as 'traders, craftsmen and self-employed persons' in over 45 lines of business. Some of them are worker co-ops and some producer co-ops, and they have set up seven central co-operatives, two in the retail sector and five in trades and crafts (Sudradjat, 2010). This type of MOB is also beginning to be recognised in other countries. In the UK, they are called co-operative consortia, and they have become common in marketing of locally produced food and drink, arts and crafts, tourism, market trading, provision of out of hours medical coverage, home care services, specialist teaching services, and actors' agencies, as well as in the longer-established sectors of taxi driving and consultancy services (Co-operatives UK, 2010).

The biggest individual shared service co-operative may be the UNIMED system in Brazil. Here, 109,000 doctors have banded together in 375 medical co-operatives to provide a complete system of health care to 83% of the country. We have noted already how doctors do not like working for someone else, whether it be a friendly society or the government; with some honourable exceptions, they prefer to remain as independent practitioners. This is all very well, if there is a health care system to contract one's services to, but in Brazil the lack of basic infrastructure meant doctors were unable to find work, and so in 1967 they joined together in the city of Santos to found Unimed. In 1975 they founded a national federation, in 1983 they opened their first hospital and now they have 103 owned hospitals and 3244 accredited hospitals with which they have contracts. They also run their own ambulance and emergency services. They provide care to more than 16 million people who pay for the service through a user-owned health insurance co-operative called Usimed that has 34% of the national market in health plans. This Brazilian model has been followed in Chile, Colombia, Costa Rica, Paraguay and Argentina.

Other very large shared service co-ops can be found in media services. The National Cable Television Co-operative is owned by 1100 cable companies and supplies 12 million subscribers in the USA. Associated Press supplies news from 243 offices in 97 countries to its owners, who are 1500 daily newspapers. At the other end of the scale, in developing countries there are some interesting examples such as co-operatives of shoe-shiners and market stallholders, and the shared-ownership co-operative has been recognised as the only way of supporting workers in the informal economy (Birchall, 2004; Smith and Ross, 2006).

Type 4: Employee-owned businesses

Employee-owned businesses are usually referred to as worker co-ops, but there are good reasons why we should use the longer, if less inspiring, term. First, producer-owners such as farmers, transport operators and small businesses are also workers, but they are not employees. Second, like the farmers who increasingly have a stake in agri-food co-ops that have converted to investor-ownership, employees often have a stake in the business but are not outright owners. Arguably, the flexibility this brings to farmers in terms of ability to raise capital and move quickly into new areas of business is necessary in a rapidly globalising age. The important principle may not be ownership but control; provided the farmers keep a majority shareholding their interests are safeguarded. The same kind of argument could be made that the 50% threshold in employee-ownership is more significant than the number of wholly employee-owned businesses. Alternatively, advocates of worker co-ops say nothing less than complete employee-ownership will ensure that workers are in control and they are very much against having outside shareholders with voting rights. Yet they also have an issue to face concerning ownership; a worker co-op may be wholly owned by employees, but unless it is fully mutual not all workers are members; some may be serving a probationary period, or be working in subsidiaries where ownership is not on offer, and if the proportion who are members falls below say 50% it could be argued that it is no longer a worker co-op but some kind of partnership. These are complicated points, and so Table 8.1 sets it all out in a matrix.

There are some knotty problems concerning the ownership and control of worker co-ops that have inhibited their development, and it is useful to discuss these before we trace the history of this type. First there is the question of who owns the equity. The value of a business can be held in individual shares owned by employees or held in common (just as in the old urban and rural co-operative banks where Schulze's followers advocated a large member share while Raiffeisen's advocated a nominal share – see Chapter 7). Sometimes there is a mix of individual and common

Table 8.1   Proportion of employees who are owners, by whether outside investors are also owners

	Rest of owners are outside investors	*Only employees are investors*
Under 50% of employees are owners	Employee shareholding scheme (ESOP)	Partnership (deformedworker co-op)
Over 50% of employees are owners	Employee-owned business	Worker co-op

ownership, and so there are three types (corresponding quite closely to full equity, limited equity and non-equity housing co-operatives – see Chapter 5). The distinction matters because it affects the motivations of members, their ability to raise capital and the likelihood of the co-operative being demutualised.

Individual ownership is just like a large partnership, and unless longer serving members are rewarded it is likely to lead to existing members restricting entry rights so as to keep the equity to themselves, or eventually demutualising so as to have their shares revalued in the market. There are ways of rewarding long service that do not infringe the one person one vote principle: the issue of non-voting preference shares or the use of individual member accounts that accrue bonuses. *Common ownership* means new members have the same advantages as founder members, and it requires the latter to be highly committed to the idea and prepared to give up any advantages they may have earned through growth of the business. It is more likely to be found in worker co-ops providing public services; being dependent on government grants and operating in a restricted market, the co-op has little market value and tends to be non-profit distributing. *Mixed ownership* tends to be found in employee-owned businesses that have been sold to their employees by a previous owner. Here, some of the equity is put into an employee trust and some distributed to individuals so that it becomes more difficult for a group of members to force the sale of the company for profit.

This last point is related to the *problem of management*. A mixed ownership structure with some or all of the equity being put into a trust also insulates managers from interference by employee-members. When a worker co-operative is small it can operate with high levels of self-management and participatory democracy, and egalitarian rewards systems such as equal pay; for some people that is the major attraction of working in this type of MOB. When it grows it needs a separate function of management, exercised by specialist staff whose task is to co-ordinate the workforce and give them clear instructions. This is a major change and, as we shall see from the historical record, many experiments in worker control cannot not make the transition; workers who are also owners sometimes will not allow themselves to be 'managed'. The problem becomes acute in an economic downturn when the company has to cut employees' wages or make them redundant. It is particularly acute in 'rescue co-operatives' where the workforce has taken over a business with the help of trade unions. The adversarial culture of the union does not lend itself to the new co-operative culture of employee-ownership, and workers have to adjust to a completely new situation.

There is another problem related to ownership; that of *capital raising*. Often there is a need for fresh capital investment, in order to enter new markets or keep up with the technologies used by competitors. Because MOBs cannot issue shares on the stock market, they have to rely on built up reserves, the issue of preference shares to members and supporters, and on bank loans. Again, the history shows that this can result in MOBs lagging behind IOBs, becoming stuck in low-profit sectors, or going out of business. Where there is intense competition and they have to lower wages and ask members to work longer hours, there is the danger of 'self-exploitation' (Mellor et al, 1988).

The founding period

The origins of the worker co-operative can be found in France. Here, in the 19th century industrialisation affected the country differently than in Britain, with industrial production remaining small scale and geared to local markets, and with skilled craftsmanship holding out against mass production (Kemp, 1985). Because of the sluggish development of capitalism, the state was used to intervening to support new developments, in a very different attitude from the 'laissez-faire' capitalism that was driving the transformation of Britain. As in the development of consumer co-operatives in Britain and co-operative banks in Germany, there was no shortage of promoters. Charles Fourier was the French equivalent of Robert Owen, designing utopian communities that failed but also advocating co-operative solutions to contemporary problems (Lambert, 1963). Then there was Philippe Buchez, who like William King in Britain had practical experience and codified a set of principles that would give the movement direction and purpose. He advocated democratic governance, the return of surpluses proportionate to the work done, the indissoluble nature of co-operative capital (so that if a society dissolved its assets would transfer to another society), and full membership for all workers after a probationary period of one year (Birchall, 1997). These principles were remarkably similar to those of the Rochdale Pioneers. Buchez set up an association of cabinet-makers in 1831, and it was followed in 1833 by a series of workshops set up by striking workers who wanted to set up on their own. Unlike the Pioneers, Buchez saw a positive role for governments in providing investment finance. He was backed up in this by Louis Blanc who in 1839 wrote a book *l'Organisation du Travail* which advocated state aid for worker co-ops.

There was a second wave of worker co-ops after the 1848 revolution, with the aid of a provisional government that loaned them capital. But the 200 or more societies were short lived, and by 1855 there were only about a dozen left. Then during the 1860s there was another wave with a credit bank set up to fund them, but this faltered after the fall of the Paris Commune in 1871. Then an iron foundry owner called Godin introduced profit-sharing into his factory, and set up a system of co-partnership whereby the workers could gradually buy him out. This provoked a lot of interest, but it was essentially the gradual handover of a successful business to its workers by a talented owner-manager, which did not prove that workers could start up and run a business on such a scale independently (Fay, 1913). In fact, despite all the promotion, publicity, and government support, by 1906 there were only three large worker co-ops in France; the iron foundry, a spectacle manufacturer and a cab drivers' society (perhaps better classified as a producers' co-op). There were 340 smaller co-ops, but the three large societies were doing half the trade and it was not much to show for all the effort put in.

In Italy, the industrial revolution began late and then only in the North of the country, but as Putnam shows the Northern regions had plenty of the right kind of social capital and took to all types of co-operation with great enthusiasm (1994). The idea was introduced by the republican leader, Mazzini, who had met GJ Holyoake, chronicler of the Rochdale Pioneers and also an advocate of worker co-operation. He took back to Italy ideas that the English had, through a French-speaking Christian Socialist, JM Ludlow, recently imported from France (Birchall, 1997). From the 1860s onwards, worker co-ops began to be set up and by 1870 there were 878 societies, many of which also ran retail stores and provided social insurance. Then in the depression of the 1870s groups of landless rural labourers banded together in labour co-operatives, and were given contracts to clear land for local governments; by 1906 there were 454 'labour and public service societies' compared with only 153 other industrial societies (Fay, 1907). The idea was taken up in India, where this essentially simple form of co-operation became very successful (there are now nearly 30,000 labour co-ops in over 90 district federations, with 1.6 million members – Birchall, 2008).

In Britain, Godin's scheme was influential among promoters of worker co-ops who had set up a series of self-governing workshops in the 1850s (all of which had failed). They turned to labour co-partnership as a kind of watered down version of full worker ownership which mixed in owner-ship by employees with a more substantial ownership share by consumer co-operatives. This gave co-partnerships that specialised in basic con-sumer products such as hosiery, boots and shoes, buckets and fireguards, shirts and washing machines a source of ready investment capital and a guaranteed market. By 1903 there were 126 of them (Fay, 1913). Their survival rates were impressive, but once they had captured a niche in the consumer co-operative market they showed no ability to grow further. In the USA there was a brief flowering of worker co-operatives in the period after the civil war. At least 500 were formed and they were in a variety of trades, being particularly strong in shoe manufacture. However, they did not last long; there were co-operatively owned refuse companies in San Francisco in the 1920s, and worker buyouts of plywood factories in the 1940s, but this form of MOB never really took off (Rosen et al, 2005).

Explanations for the lack of growth

Why did worker co-ops make such slow progress? It was not from lack of supporters. In 1848, the great economist, JS Mill, devoted a large section of his *Principles of Political Economy* to the subject, seeing worker and consumer co-operatives as a kind of antidote to class conflict (in recent editions of the book, editors have tended to cut out this section and so his vigorous approval of worker control is not generally recog-nised). Unfortunately, unlike other types of MOB they had no particular organisational comparative advantages over the IOB type. They required members who were able and willing to co-operate in the difficult busi-ness of managing a complex production process, yet they often failed because they were careless in who they allowed in and could not main-tain quality and consistency in management. In 1899, Beatrice Potter in her history of the co-operative movement put it this way; on the one hand there was a tendency for workers to lack discipline and inter-fere with management, but on the other hand, if they succeeded they deformed into partnerships, denying membership to new employees and retaining the profits for themselves. Whether they failed or succeeded it seemed the workers could not win. Her argument was backed up by statistics. Of the 54 societies she could find, only eight approximated to the ideal of a genuine worker co-operative (Potter, 1899).

Since Mill set out the arguments, many influential thinkers have come upon the idea of worker control and for much the same reasons; it ought to counter class conflict and alienation at work, and encourage a fairer distribution of the economic results. However, there has been a disappointing lack of empirical evidence of success. During the 1970s, much hope was placed by non-Marxist socialists in the worker self-management system in Yugoslavia, but it turned out to be mostly a sham, permeated by party political influences and bolstered up by a state banking system that eventually collapsed under the strain. Also during the 1970s there was a movement for worker takeovers of bankrupt businesses all over Western Europe, and by the end of the decade there were 40,000 workers in France and around 10,000 in Britain in worker co-ops (Birchall, 1997). A similar flurry of activity took place in Argentina in an economic crisis from 2001, when around 200 failed enterprises were taken over by the workers (Howarth, 2007). The problems with such takeovers are that they inherit a weak business proposition and need a profound cultural adjustment on the part of the workers, and so there is a high failure rate. If it were not for the concentrations of worker co-operatives in North Italy and the Mondragon system in Spain, there would be few successful examples to cite.

The growth of worker co-operative systems in North Italy and the Basque region of Spain

In the Emilia Romagna region of Italy there is a concentration of around 8,000 independent worker co-operatives producing a wide variety of goods including fashion, ceramics and speciality cheeses. The largest is SACMI that has been a worker co-op since 1919, and is a world leader in manufacturing machines and complete plants for the ceramics, packaging and plastics industries. The key to their success is that they form a dense network of complementary business relationships that are mutually supportive. Though each co-op is relatively small, they have complementary skills and form consortia to bid for large projects. Also, they are part of a wider culture of co-operation that includes several types of co-op organized in three federations representing different political traditions: Legacoop has 1,000,000 members, employs 40,000 people and has an annual turnover of almost $8 billion, while Confcoop has 285,000 members, also employs 40,000 people and has a turnover of $13.5 billion. The Associazione has 75,000 members and an annual turnover of $2.2 billion. Also, as a result of an Act passed in 1990, now over

85% of the region's social services are provided by social co-operatives. Between them, co-ops generate around 40% of GDP, and two out of three citizens are members of a co-op. Per capita income has risen to second among Italy's 20 regions.

The Mondragon Corporation has grown out of a small group of worker co-ops in the Basque region of Spain to become the largest concentration of worker-owned businesses in the world. It now has 264 companies in membership, and has become Spain's seventh largest industrial company, with a workforce of over 100,000. Its bank, the Caja Laboral, uses the savings invested by local people to finance new ventures, so individual co-ops are not short of capital. In return, they bind themselves to the discipline of the group. A heavy investment in institution building has meant the group meets its own needs for technical and university training, research and development and business planning, and so its human capital is the best available. Workers have to make a significant investment, and in return receive a share of the profits and a pension based on their lifetime earnings; over 50% of profits are distributed to worker members. Their democratic structure is complex and allows worker-owners to oversee their co-op while accepting the right of management to manage and of the Bank and other institutions to influence business strategy. The Mondragon system is tighter than that of North Italy, but the effect is the same – to sustain a complex system of interconnected firms that overcome the weaknesses of worker-ownership while building on its strengths. Attempts to transplant the Italian and Spanish systems to other parts of the world have so far failed, though there seems no reason in principle why the Mondragon system should not work elsewhere. Certainly, it seems to have solved the persistent problems that have bedevilled this type of MOB, though it is now growing beyond national boundaries and causing controversy because it does not offer membership rights to workers in other countries: now only 38% of workers are members compared with 90% in 1990, and four jobs are being created abroad for every one created in Spain (MacLeod and Reed, 2009). It seems that Mondragon may after all be deforming into a kind of worker capitalism.

In other countries there is a small, interesting but not particularly important worker co-operative sector. Scotland is fairly typical. It has more than 50 wholly or largely employee-owned co-ops. The larger tend to be ones that were successful companies that were sold to their employees in a managed buyout after the owner decided to retire. John Lewis Partnership is the largest, a huge retail chain that was given to the workforce by its founder, and has a turnover of £605 million. Then there are businesses that were set up as worker co-ops – wholly owned and tending to have a more direct involvement of workers in day to day decision-making in the business. They include a bicycle retail co-operative, two wholefood wholesalers and a fair trade marketing co-op. After this comes a wide range of co-ops in sectors such as child care, social care, crafts, and professional services. Why are there so many small co-operatives? One reason is that they tend to thrive in niche markets where dedication, specialist knowledge and attention to detail are needed, and these are all complemented by employee control. Another reason is that their members want to work in small, more intimate settings. A less positive reason is that there may be dis-incentives to growth because a common ownership structure does not reward individual entrepreneurialism. Here, expertise in creating share incentive plans and internal share markets in co-ops is vital to the growth of the sector (Birchall, 2009).

Partial forms of employee-ownership

If we drop the requirement that only workers can be owners in an enter-prise, then there is another story to be told that begins in the USA in the 1880s. Here, the idea of employee-ownership was attractive not only to labour leaders but to some employers. In 1886, Leland Stanford, the railroad magnate who founded Stanford University, introduced a bill to encourage employee-ownership, and in 1919 John Rockefeller formed a commission that recommended that companies sell stock to their employees at a discount (Rosen et al, 2005). Several companies were already doing it, but after 1919 the pace picked up and by the late 1920s employees owned 6% of AT&T, 7% of Bethlehem Steel and 12% of Procter and Gamble. The 1930s depression stopped the whole movement dead, and the idea had to be revived anew by Louis Kelso who, in 1958, wrote a book advocating employee-ownership not as a means of gaining control of industry but as a way of distributing wealth more fairly. He discovered that in employee-buyouts the employees could pay for their shares out of the company's future earnings rather than having to borrow it from the banks; the leveraged buyout became known as a 'Kelso Plan'. Employee share ownership plans (ESOPs) became common, and were written into tax legislation so that they would remain attractive to both companies and their workers. Now there are 11,400 companies in the USA with ESOPs, stock bonus and profit-sharing plans, covering 13.7 million workers, and many more millions in stock-option plans and stock-purchase plans (NCEO, 2010). In Europe there are 9.3 million employees with some kind of ownership and 91% of companies have share-ownership plans, though the employees' share is extremely low at under 3% (EFES, 2010). However, in other parts of the world, employee-ownership plans are much less common.

Employee-ownership on its own does not guarantee anything; the collapse of United Airlines in 2002 shows that. However, there is compelling evidence that it provides a range of efficiency gains over conventionally-owned firms when it is in closely held companies and when combined with participatory management. Studies find it is associated with higher organisational commitment and identification with the company. Productivity improves by an extra 4–5% in the year an ESOP is adopted, and this higher productivity level is then maintained. It is also associated with greater employment stability, faster growth and higher rates of firm survival (NCEO, 2009).

Future prospects for producer- and employee-owned businesses

What is the future for producer- and employee-owned businesses? In the farmer co-operative sector, the recession will probably accelerate trends already occurring, such as the growth in co-operative conglomerates. Supply co-ops are facing new competition from internet sales, with farmers becoming less loyal and able to shop around among suppliers for farm inputs. Marketing co-ops are facing intense pressure on prices from the large supermarket chains that are engaged in fierce price competition, yet here there are signs that farmers are becoming more loyal, asking to join co-operatives in order to secure higher prices in the long run (Kuchler, 2010). Further down the value chain, processing co-operatives will continue to consolidate and expand internationally in order to maintain profitability, but with the unanswered question hanging over them of how to keep hundreds of thousands of farmers in hundreds of primary co-operatives engaged in their governance. However, the credit crunch may slow down the pace of change in the structure of farmer-owned businesses, giving time for reflection and perhaps a renewed commitment to maintaining farmer-ownership.

Retailer-owned businesses can also expect to benefit indirectly from the recession, as retailers become more loyal and appreciative of the benefits of joint-buying. They will face continued price competition from the multiple chains and, as often happens in a recession, even more pressure from discount chains. The trend towards joint-buying between retailer-owned and consumer-owned co-operatives will continue. Some consumer co-operatives may start to franchise stores to independent operators and so the distinction between these two types of retailer-owned business may become less clear. During the recession, the shared service co-operative sector can be expected to grow, as small businesses group together to lower costs and increase sales. It will also become better recognised, though it is uncertain what it will be called, whether shared service co-operatives, co-operative consortia or just business co-operatives.

In a recession, the advantages of employee-ownership become clearer. A recent study finds that in all countries there is a downturn in production and sale (CICOPA, 2010). Some sectors are more affected by the recession than others. The construction sector is affected everywhere, but other sectors are affected in particular countries: textiles in Eastern Europe, forestry in Canada, the metal industry in Brazil and so on. Everywhere there is a decrease in demand, and the crisis particularly affects recent start-ups where there is a lack of expertise and financial reserves. However, the reduction of jobs has so far been limited. The capacity of co-operatives to combine 'security with flexibility' and their commitment to remaining in their own local economies gives them a comparative advantage (CICOPA, 2010: 2). We can expect more worker takeovers of failing businesses. They are affected by the credit crunch, and there is a need to enter into partnerships with co-operative banks and credit unions so as to provide capital. In a crisis like this it helps to have your own bank; the Mondragon co-operative bank, the Caja Laboral, is keeping open a specific credit line for the Mondragon Group.

A recent UK study provides more grounds for optimism. In a comparative survey of employee-owned and non-owned businesses, it shows that EOBs generally outperform the non-EOBs, with employees being 'more committed to delivering quality service and more flexible in responding to the needs of the business' (Lampel et al, 2010). During the three years from 2004 (the period before the recession), EOBs experienced greater employment growth, then after the recession set in they continued to grow even faster, with increases of 12.9% compared to 2.7% in non-EOBs. If they can solve the problems that have bedevilled worker co-operatives in the past, then this type of MOB may be in for a renaissance.

9

The Peculiar History of 'Member-owned' Businesses in Developing Countries

Co-operatives in developing countries provoke contradictory images. I remember interviewing the manager of a district coffee marketing union in Tanzania. There is a photo on the wall from the 1950s. It is like one of those long black and white photos in which a school class line up to have their photo taken. Here, it is black and white in a different sense; there is a sea of white faces and one black face in the front row. I realise that I am looking at the staff of the coffee union fifty years ago, but it looks like a branch of the colonial service rather than a member-owned co-operative. Clearly, the running of a 'native' co-operative could not be left to its members, but had to be run by well-meaning white people from the English Home Counties.

Another image; I am visiting a multi-purpose co-operative in Sri Lanka. It is a long two storey building in the middle of a village, with a row of businesses on the ground floor and the rural bank upstairs. The whole building is painted a lurid yellow – the co-operative colour in Sri Lanka – and at intervals it has the rainbow flag of the International Co-operative Alliance painted on to it. I am given tea and cakes by the board of directors but I can't get them to talk about democracy. When asked what proportion of their members voted in the last election they assure me all the members voted. I wonder if this is a language problem. 'How much political influence is there in this co-operative?' I ask. They do not understand the question, but I get my answer; there is a huge banner of the current president draped over one end of the building, and it is not even election time.

Another, more positive image; a concrete shack two hours down a dirt road in the middle of the coffee growing area of Tanzania. There are coffee beans in sacks ready to be sent away to be cleaned and graded and then put into auction. The secretary greets me with a smile, and explains through an interpreter that her co-op has just given up membership of the district union and, along with a dozen other primary societies is marketing her own members' coffee directly on the open market. She is full of optimism about the future, asks if we can find her a computer and expresses a lot of interest in the potential of fair trade coffee. Newly freed from the shackles of the district union, her co-op is improving the quality of members' coffee plants and is teaching unemployed young people how to make bricks.

Another positive image; an education campus out in the country in Sri Lanka owned by the savings and credit co-operatives movement known as SANASA. I am shown around by Dr Kiriwandeniya, leader of the movement and a dedicated co-operator. He talks about the need for member-education, and shares his vision of a member-driven co-operative banking system that will do more than anything else to raise people out of poverty. Much of the campus is a building site, with new classrooms and residential blocks going up among rolling hills and dense forest. There is no political influence here; just a single minded focus on learning how to do co-operative banking really well, and a refusal to allow politicians to interfere.

In general, and with some notable exceptions, throughout the 20th century the performance of member-owned businesses in developing countries has been disappointing. Enormous investments have been made in financial and technical aid from donor countries, and support from first colonial governments and then nationalist governments for co-operative development. Yet after a century of efforts there is not much to show for all of this. Why has there been such a gap between promise and performance? There is one simple explanation; they have not been allowed to be autonomous businesses, owned and controlled by their members. They have not been allowed to *be* co-operatives. How could such a basic mistake have been made by so many people for so long, and why are we only just seeing the emergence of an autonomous member-owned business sector? To answer these questions we need to appreciate the peculiar history of co-operatives in developing countries.

The colonial period

Co-operatives were introduced into developing countries early in the 20th century and it is tempting to see their history as starting then. However, this would be to ignore the pre-existing forms of co-operation that indigenous people were already familiar with. There were two basic types: work groups and rotating savings and credit associations. In work groups, members work on each others' farms in rotation; examples include the naam groups in Burkina Faso and nnoboa groups in Ghana. In rotating savings and credit associations, members make contributions to a revolving fund and the total amount is given to individuals in rotation; examples include esusu groups in Nigeria, savings clubs in Zimbabwe, and tontines in practically all the countries in Africa. Also, as in England when the Rochdale Pioneers started their first store, in some parts of Africa burial societies existed as a kind of informal predecessor of the savings and loan societies (Muenkner and Shah, 1993).

Why, then, do we date the history of co-operatives to the beginning of the 20th century? If the new co-ops had been grafted on to the old as a kind of hybrid form then the history might have been different, but the new forms were transplanted complete, from Europe into Africa and Asia without much adaptation. Models that were transplanted included the Raiffeisen rural banking system that had begun in Germany in the 1860s, the Rochdale consumer co-operative system that had begun in England in the 1840s, and the producer association that had grown up everywhere that farmers were adapting to a market economy but had flowered dramatically in Denmark during the 1890s. There were several possibilities as to who would take the lead: white settlers, local leaders, aid agencies, missionaries and nationalist politicians were all important, but by far the most important influence was that of the *colonial administrators*. They believed that developing country economies needed modernising, and co-operatives provided the promise of economic development along similar lines to that experienced by France, Britain and Germany in a long period of growth during the second half of the 19th century. Co-operatives were seen as compatible with indigenous mutual aid practices and had demonstrated their ability to raise the incomes of low-income people 'back home'.

The earliest example of such a 'transplanting' was the Raiffeisen savings and credit co-operative in India. Colonial officials had identified the indebtedness of farmers to local money lenders as a major block on economic development, and in the 1890s Sir Frederick Nicholson was seconded to study the Raiffeisen system in Europe. His report of 1897 was influential; as an academic observer noted, it was a 'bible with which Indian co-operators worked for many years' (Fay, 1938: 375). It led to the first co-operative law, a Co-operative Credit Societies Act passed in 1904. It was very much a 'top-down' approach, based, as a later co-operative development expert described it, 'on an imported theoretical concept without practical experience with this form of organisation under socio-economic conditions prevailing in India' (Muenkner, 1989: 101). An Act of 1904 established the form, and then one of 1912 introduced limited liability and allowed for the formation of secondary and tertiary societies, but the resulting societies were seen more as state agencies for granting loans, and with only small amounts saved on deposit by members (Fay, 1938). The sector grew rapidly, and by the early 1930s there were 80,000 of them, but a quarter had to be liquidated. The system had become over-elaborate; in each province there was a registrar, a provincial bank and a co-operative union, and a long chain of accountability over four levels from province to primary society. Despite these disadvantages, the 'British-Indian' system was copied by colonial officials in every British colony.

The history of *white settler co-ops* was a continuation of farmer co-operation in Europe, with farmers having similar motives and using similar techniques. In Africa, the first co-ops were formed by European settlers who wanted to export cash crops such as coffee and cocoa. British settlers had laws enacted on their behalf in Tanzania (1925), Zimbabwe (1926) and Kenya (1931). French settlers in Tunisia organised wine growers' co-ops and then developed settlement co-ops to buy land to be turned into vineyards (Muenkner and Shah, 1993). Attempts by *local people* to develop their own co-operatives were often met with suspicion and either suppressed or brought under strict regulation. For instance, in India existing 'native' credit societies, such as that formed in 1892 in the Hoshiapur district of Punjab, were brought under the Registrar's regulation which inhibited their growth. In Tanzania, in 1925 native coffee growers formed the Kilimanjaro Native Planters Association to market their crops. At first, colonial officials encouraged it but became alarmed by conflicts of interest between the Association, European planters and local chiefs. The financial crisis in 1929 was a pretext for them to close it down and promote their own marketing co-operative sector that was integrated with the chieftaincy and guided by the state (Gibbon, 2001). However, because of the lack of democracy this was deeply unpopular, and in 1936 the British military had to quell protests against it. It is no wonder that, whenever there was agitation for freedom from colonial rule, indigenous co-operatives were seen as part of a liberation movement.

Missionaries and aid agencies sometimes saw the value of co-operatives. In North China, in 1919 an international famine relief commission began to promote credit co-ops, and by the mid-1930s an American commentator reported that there were 15,000 societies with five million members (Warbasse, 1936). Catholic missionaries in the Belgian Congo set up credit and savings unions and supported indigenous co-ops. When these got into trouble with colonial authorities for competing with Belgian businesses, the missionaries gave them support, and when the authorities refused to recognise co-ops they turned to other legal structures in order to continue in business. Sometimes co-operatives were formed by *nationalist politicians* keen to use them as an organising base. The Egyptian co-operative sector started in this way early in the 20th century. In Tanzania campaigns by nationalist politicians against cheating on weights and measures by Asian agents led to the formation of cotton co-ops. The colonial government promoted them and by 1958, 275 societies were taking 83% of the cotton crop. They were then given a marketing monopoly (Gibbon, 2001). In South Africa, during the 1930s the Afrikaaner nationalist movement promoted co-operatives to aid small farmers displaced by the growth of commercial agriculture (Theron, 2005).

The approach of each colonial power was different. It depended on the way that their policy towards co-operatives fitted into their wider economic development policies, and on the character of the MOB sectors in their home countries on which they could draw for legislation. The British approach was to develop a single co-operative 'movement' with a unified co-operative law. Colonial governments set up an elaborate structure of primary societies, district and provincial unions and national federations and, while paying lip service to the idea of autonomous co-operatives, in practice they regulated the sector as soon as it began. In each country, they set up a powerful co-operative department headed by a registrar who had much wider powers to intervene in the affairs of co-operatives than had the British Registrar of Friendly Societies on which the system was modelled. This 'British-Indian pattern' was copied throughout the British empire in Asian countries such as Sri Lanka (1911), Malaysia (1922) and Singapore (1925), and in African countries such as Ghana (1931), Kenya (1931), Tanganyika (1932) and Nigeria (1935); a Model Co-operative Societies ordinance passed in 1946 led to its transfer to all other British African colonies. This also influenced the Belgian and Dutch attitudes towards co-operative development in their colonies (Muenkner and Shah, 1993).

The French approach was to promote a variety of types of MOB, including co-operatives, mutuals and associations as part of a wider social economy. They did not go in for elaborate superstructures, nor did they focus their efforts through one co-operative registry. Co-operative development was done by general administrators rather than specialised personnel, and each type of co-op was under the supervision of a different ministry; agricultural co-ops under the ministry of agriculture, credit co-ops under the ministry of finance, and so on. However, they did try to impose their own ideal model, the Societe Indigene de Prevoyance (SIP) that had the same kind of function as large, multi-purpose agricultural co-ops (Muenkner, 1989). Starting in 1910, by 1915 the voluntary nature of the SIPs was already compromised, with compulsory membership of all adults in an area and compulsory financial contributions being collected annually. The presidents and directors were appointed by the governor, and management was carried out directly by colonial civil servants whose mission was mainly a technical one of introducing modern agricultural production and marketing techniques. They were described by one expert as 'centrally administered frameworks that had no relation to the existing traditional structures' (Develtere, 1994: 46).

In 1947, a French co-operative law was extended to the colonies that made possible the founding of autonomous co-operatives. However, it did not make anyone responsible for promoting them, and without any support many co-ops lasted only a few years. In 1955, a supervising authority similar to the British Registrar was introduced, though promotion was still carried out by general administrators (Muenkner and Shah, 1993). SIPs were transformed into 'mutual societies for rural development', and by the mid-1950s a process of 'accelerated co-operative development' was being promoted, but the government interest was still in harnessing mutual societies to centrally-designed rural development schemes (Develtere, 1994). Again, as in the British system, the basic pattern applied universally to all French colonies.

The Belgian approach in the Congo, Rwanda and Burundi was based on legislation in their home country for semi-public enterprises that were a kind of municipal-co-operative hybrid, and that became involved in a wide variety of activities such as dairy, construction and tribal industries such as pottery, oil pressing and tanning (Develtere, 2008: 9). After the Second World War, the government began to develop more along British-Indian lines, creating special co-operative departments at national and provincial level and introducing large agricultural co-ops. As in the French colonies, they were paternalistic, top-down structures;

provincial governors fixed the prices co-ops would pay their members for produce, appointed education committees and advisors and a controller who was responsible for financial inspection and had a right of veto, while the district commissioner appointed co-operative managers. The Portuguese approach in Mozambique and Angola was to encourage agricultural producer associations, but with a repressive regime at home that supported agriculture as part of a corporatist state-controlled system, they were hardly likely to allow greater freedoms to their colonies. Agricultural co-ops were set up for the export trade, but they were 'merely functional appendages of rural extension work of semi-public agencies' such as cotton and coffee marketing institutes (Develtere, 2008: 10).

A stocktake of the achievements of the colonial period

The main achievement of the colonial period was a system of producer co-operatives that organised agricultural processing and marketing for export crops: sugar, tea and cotton in Asia, coffee in Tanzania and Kenya, cocoa in Ghana, and so on. The co-ops were really collecting agents for parastatal marketing boards, and providers of necessary inputs such as fertiliser and farm credits. There was not much room for member involvement, nor was it encouraged, and in most cases farmers saw them as being an arm of government. In contrast, the savings and credit sector was quite strong and extensive, particularly where it was free of government control, benefitting from a cultural link with indigenous methods of saving and lending. Consumer co-ops were used in Asia to distribute essential supplies to the rural population. Their most extensive use was in Sri Lanka, where during the Second World War food shortages and rationing led to the government organising a comprehensive network of consumer co-ops. There were only 38 such societies in 1942, but by 1945 there were over 4000 with a membership of over a million people. One historian says 'More than half the population were being clothed and fed through Co-op stores' (Jayaweera, 1987). Again, they were quite weak as businesses and without much member involvement.

Some sectors were quite large; in the late 1950s Tanganyika had 617 societies with 325,000 members, Uganda 1598 societies with 158,000 members and Kenya 576 societies with 158,000 members (Birchall, 1997). In most British colonies they had a 'considerable penetration rate', though this only amounted to a small percentage of the population; Tanganyika had the most members, at 3.4% of the population. Uganda had 2.7% and Kenya 1.8%. In the Belgian colonies just over 1%, and in the French colonies, less than 1% of the population were involved (Develtere et al, 2008: 12).

What went wrong? The colonial administrators thought they could harness the economic development potential of co-operatives modelled on the ones they saw working well at home. Contractual co-operation was seen as a higher stage in the evolution of economic organisation, a way of enabling a transition from traditional to modern society. Margaret Digby, a well known British co-operative promoter, put it this way:

> *The value of co-operation is that it provides for a transition from the primitive to the modern economic and social worlds, which involves no violent disruption and prevents the exploitation of the less advanced.*

A more negative reading would be that co-ops were introduced as

> *A government instrument to maintain the existing relations, to introduce the natives gradually into the externally controlled, export-oriented money economy, and to develop local, modernised, indigenous structures* (Develtere, 1994: 40, 48)

There was meant to be an eventual transition from paternalistic oversight to takeover by indigenous co-operative members, but it was always being put off to another day. Perhaps it was part of the progressive evolutionary mindset that saw gradual democratisation as being inevitable given enough time. Certainly, that was how the British co-operative movement saw it, but they were fooling themselves.

The nationalist period

After independence, all the English speaking countries of Africa continued to follow the British-Indian pattern. Most of the French-speaking countries also continued to follow the 1955 Act that had promoted parastatals. It was a period of 'extravagant praise and great expectations for co-operatives' (Laidlaw, 1978: 64), and governments began to take an active role in promoting them. Nationalist leaders had grown up in the co-operatives and had a high regard for them; for instance, in Tanzania in 1961 a third of all members of the national assembly were active co-operators and four cabinet ministers were ex-co-operative officers (Spaull, 1965). In some places, co-operatives had been involved in the liberation struggle and so it was natural for the new governments to see them as a central part of their economic strategies. Aid agencies were also keen to promote them and did so extravagantly over the next 30 years until structural adjustment programmes forced a rethink. Co-operatives were helped by some ambiguity over their meaning; they could be 'read' as either a means towards a market society or towards a socialist society, and in both cases were seen as part of a project of modernisation (Birchall, 1997).

However, for co-operative members almost everywhere it was business as usual but with new officials in charge. Where genuine co-ops developed, 'the ruling party or the state quickly brought them under their control to create jobs for officials and to use them for political ends' (Muenkner and Shah, 1993: 16). A dependency relationship soon reasserted itself, with co-ops dependent on handouts from the state, and with political parties using them as an organising base, particularly in rural areas.

Everywhere there was a rapid growth in co-operatives. In Africa, the number of societies grew from 6637 in 1951 to 7342 in 1966, with a growth in membership from under 1.3 million to 1.8 million, mainly in the agricultural co-op sector (Develtere, 1994). In some countries this meant a brief flowering of independent societies. For instance, in Sri Lanka the new government started a drive to create agricultural production and sales societies, fishery societies and industrial co-operatives. By 1956 there were 995 agricultural societies which gained a predominant position in supply of fertilisers. Smallholders in the export sectors (rubber, coconut and tea) formed co-ops for inputs, marketing and processing. Dairy co-ops were also formed, selling to the government milk board. By the mid-1950s there were 75 different types of co-op, single purpose but reflecting the needs of the members. However, they were small and often not viable, with one village having seven or eight different types (Rajaguru, 1996). In Tanzania after independence there was a rapid expansion of rural co-ops in a wide range of sectors. In 1961 there were 275 cotton societies and 182 coffee societies. The first five year plan saw a drive to place all marketing of crops under control of co-ops, which were seen as the main vehicle of the government's effort to modernise the economy. By 1965 over 20 types of crops were being marketed through 1287 primary co-ops, and they controlled over 80% of agricultural production and marketing (Banturaki, 2000).

Rapid growth led in many cases to an over-supply of weak co-operatives that were badly managed and sometimes corrupt. Inevitably, governments began a period of intensification of control, culminating in some countries in the complete takeover of the sector. For instance, in Sri Lanka a radical Minister of Agriculture had envisaged a rationalised system where one multi-purpose village society would do everything: providing credit, distributing rationed foodstuffs, purchasing crops under a guaranteed price scheme, providing subsidised inputs of fertiliser and so on. By 1968 there were 5108 societies, with a membership of over a million. However, they were not multi-purpose, retail sales were inadequate, and there was inefficient and dishonest management. The target-oriented, time-limited approach to their promotion did not provide for orientation of members and so the 'MPCSs' had become simply distributors of rationed commodities. Only a few had created a real development role based on identification of members needs. In 1970, 5818 MPCS societies were amalgamated into 371, each covering 10–20 villages. As a local historian put it 'Co-operatives were born from the pen of the Registrar and not from voluntary association' (Rajaguru, 1996: 6).

In Tanzania also, rapid expansion of the sector was associated with a decline in efficiency. By 1966 there were rising complaints, and a Presidential commission of enquiry was set up to investigate charges of nepotism and corruption. The Commission urged the government to expand co-operative education, strengthen control over the movement, and increase the powers of the Registrar to fire incompetent and corrupt leaders. All these were enacted in a law passed in 1968, while 16 district and regional co-operative unions were taken over, their committees dismissed and government personnel put in. At this time, government interference was seen as beneficial, the argument being that government was using co-operatives to achieve the political aim of socialism, an aim which overrode any claims on the part of co-operative members to autonomy. After the Arusha Declaration of 1967, co-ops became recognised as 'instruments' for implementing the policy of socialism. From 1969 onwards, they were transformed to fit into Ujamaa villages as multipurpose co-operative societies. It is interesting to note that the policy was resisted; even after 'villagisation' was completed in 1974, rural primary societies persisted, and 'village multi-functional co-ops proved neither easy to constitute nor popular' (Gibbon, 2001).

Takeover by governments did not achieve the required results nor did it even get rid of corruption. Yet the answer to disappointment was seen to be even more centralised control (Hussi et al, 1993). For instance, in Sri Lanka, under an Act of 1970 co-op boards were to consist of 15 people, only five of whom were elected by the members; in many cases hardly any were elected, and unsurprisingly there was little interest among members to stand for election. Then in 1972 another act consolidated the Registrar's powers even further. The government's view was that large sums of its money were in co-operative hands and, with 46% of the societies either defunct or loss making it had to take control. However, despite increasing control by the Registrar, political patronage and corruption were still rife.

In Tanzania, in 1976 the President, Nyerere, declared that co-operatives could not cope with his 'quick march to socialism', as they were capitalist organisations. All co-operative unions were dissolved and replaced with crop authorities that were required to do marketing directly from the villages. There was resistance; the unions failed to die a natural death and had to be forcibly closed by the police. The decision to abolish them was not accepted by many in government and, after a crisis in rural production that was blamed on the poor performance of the crop boards, in 1984 Nyerere changed his mind. He admitted it was a wrong decision and the unions were to be re-established, but only 'to serve primarily political interests' as a mass organisation under the direction of the ruling party. At both higher and lower levels the movement was faced by government control. The district unions looked upwards to a national union that, in 1979 had been made a mass organisation of the ruling party. Looking down, their base was the compulsory government-led primary societies set up under Ujamaa. And the ruling party reserved the right to screen candidates for the district unions! As one historian describes it, co-operatives were officialised institutions in which the members were passive; 'Heavy government involvement and manipulation had systematically eroded and diminished the poverty reduction potential of co-operatives' (Sizya, 2001: 6). By 1989 the co-operative unions' debts had risen to 40 billion shillings, and the government confessed publicly that its policies were responsible for 87% of these.

Elsewhere, the pattern was similar. In Zimbabwe, the ZANU government kept the bureaucratic structure inherited from the British, but filled most of the committee places with party members. In Chad, Madagascar and Tunisia, co-operatives became 'heavy bureaucratic organisations' dominated by government or political parties, in Senegal multi-purpose co-ops were promoted as local agents of a state marketing board, and in Zaire the co-operative and mutual movement were linked to one national trade union which was a satellite of the single party in power (Develtere et al, 2008). However, there were exceptions: in Kenya the government did not have the resources to control the sector and so it remained comparatively independent, while in Mali from 1979 onwards independent village co-ops began to emerge based on older mutual traditions, and aided by a new community-based approach to development (Muenkner and Shah, 1993).

What did leaders of the Western European co-operative movements make of the way co-operatives were being developed in Africa? Generally, they were happy to see co-operatives given such a high status and seeming to achieve such a strong position. In 1954 the International Co-operative

Alliance began to organise 'movement to movement' assistance but without raising the question of who owned the co-operatives. In 1965, the journalist Hebe Spaull published a book on the worldwide co-operative movement and her reaction is probably typical. In a survey of African countries, she noted that Morocco was doing much to extend co-ops, but that they had 'come to depend to a considerable extent on Government aid and leadership' (1965: 78–79). She explained this in terms of illiteracy among the farmers, which would be solved with time. In Kenya, all African farmers were required by law to be in a co-op, but this was because they were dependent on technical advice; compulsion was necessary 'in order to maintain the high quality of the product' (1965: 97). She saw the French SIPs, with their compulsory membership, as a foundation on which the co-operative movement was being built, because a law passed in 1958 allowed them to turn from semi- into full co-ops. In the Ivory Coast, she described how a state controlled body, working through 52 district centres, had 'led to promising beginnings of co-operative organisation in the interior' (1965: 80). In Senegal, state organisations were 'intended to be converted into true co-operative societies' when they had completed their primary task. Clearly, she was assuming a progressive model of development in which co-operatives would emerge naturally... but always tomorrow.

The International Labour Organisation (ILO) had always had a watching brief for co-operatives; its first director, Albert Thomas, set up a Co-operative Branch that still works on international co-operative development issues. In 1966, it passed a Co-operatives (Developing Countries) Recommendation which called for governments to set up one central body that would be the instrument for developing co-operatives, but without affecting their independence and the voluntary nature of membership. Government tutelage was seen as a temporary measure, but by then, as the Canadian co-operative leader, Alex Laidlaw put it, the co-operative 'movement' had three masters: the civil service, government ministers and local politicians. The old colonial system had been taken over and then used vastly to increase control over co-operatives (1978).

By the mid-1970s, there was a growing awareness that 'the poor had not been reached' (Verhagen, 1984: 4). In 1975 a report by researchers from the United Nations Research Institute for Social Development (UNRISD) declared 'rural co-operatives have seldom achieved the development goals set for them by economic and social planners' and 'they bring little or no benefit to the masses of poor inhabitants' (UNRISD, 1975: 10, ix). The report drew on a large project carried out in the late 1960s that included 37 co-ops in three Asian, three Latin American and six African countries. Their methodology was to assess the performance of co-ops using their own declared economic and social goals. They found two problems. First, co-operatives were being promoted by external donors such as USAID and the World Bank, national governments, churches and so on. The result was that alien models were being imposed rather than evolving out of the felt needs and capacities of potential co-op members. The task of organising them fell almost exclusively to national governments, which meant that officials and politicians were too closely involved and would not let the co-operatives be independent. People were being forced to join because of direct compulsion, the granting of monopolies in farm inputs and marketing, and through inducements such as cheap credit (Fals-Borda et al, 1976). Second, the co-ops were found to be making little impact on the wider economy, with only a small proportion of farmers being involved. Instead of contributing to positive economic change, they reinforced existing patterns of inequality as richer farmers grabbed the opportunities available at the expense of the poor and of women (Develtere et al, 2008).

The UNRISD study was heavily criticised and provoked a debate about both the validity of its findings and, more seriously, about the nature of co-operation. The Canadian co-operative leader, Alex Laidlaw, charged the UN researchers with failing to understand the nature of co-operatives. He pointed out that equality is not one of the co-operative principles and that they cannot be held responsible for the unequal environment they operate in (Birchall, 2003: 9–10). They neglected the key issue of the need to educate and train members, and did not problematise the relationship with government. Nor did they provide a substitute for co-ops that might do the job better. What Laidlaw was saying was that co-operation had not really been tried, and so the failures were not those of member-owned businesses (Laidlaw, 1978). In a later, more academic critique, Holmen went further, pointing out that the 'immanent' approach of the UNRISD studies took as their starting point the goals of the co-operatives. He argued that these could not be taken for granted if they had been determined by external actors. They may even conflict with the goals desired by members, and so the important question is how these goals came to be proclaimed in the first place (Apthorpe and Gasper, 1982). To answer this question, we must see co-ops in the wider framework of a weak state that needs to co-opt other institutions to bolster its legitimacy and its capacity to act (Holmen, 1990).

In 1976, the United Nations restated its faith that co-operatives are expected to generate social and economic benefits to low-income groups; it recognised that there was no alternative. Also, by now a participatory methodology for project development was being tried by NGOs, and some genuine co-operatives were beginning to emerge (Verhagen, 1984). In the same year, the development expert Hans Muenkner wrote an interesting report on the question 'Co-operatives for the rich or poor?', admitting that co-operatives do attract the relatively rich farmers but could also strengthen the middle layer, and that if this happened it would release resources to enable governments to concentrate on helping the poor (Muenkner, 1976). The International Co-operative Alliance (ICA) then held an experts' consultation. The key questions asked of the experts were whether co-operatives had failed the people of developing countries and whether they could still become a decisive factor in conquering poverty. They found that the political structures within a country frequently prevented co-operatives from reaching their potential, because co-operative principles such as voluntary membership were being thwarted (ICA, 1978). Co-operatives were a very imperfect embodiment, and occasionally a caricature, of the ideals of co-operation. In particular, they failed to enlist people as active members and even when they did this they frequently failed to give them the full benefits of membership.

Yet the experts agreed that 'theoretically and in the long run' co-ops could solve the problems of development. They were a valuable means of generating wealth, but what they could not do was to *redistribute* wealth. They concluded that the pattern of ownership and power was 'seldom decisively altered through co-operative activities' (ICA, 1978: 14). There was no substitute for enlightened government policies, and co-operatives could only succeed in the right environment. The experts considered the question of whether to set up co-ops for the poor. They preferred the idea of having a mixed membership and educating the members to give the poor preferential treatment. The support for co-operatives continued. In a 1986 review of World Bank-assisted projects it was found that 50% of all agricultural projects in Africa included co-operatives (Develtere et al, 2008). This was a mixed blessing, as too often co-ops were seen merely as implementing agencies for externally-generated projects. Now, as well as being 'gov-operatives' they had become 'don-operatives' (Braverman, 1991).

At the same time, there were some developments that pointed towards a different kind of future. The most important of these was the *different trajectory of growth taken by savings and credit co-operatives*. In the mid-1990s there were more than 5400 of them in Africa with a market share of 1.6%. They built on the traditional forms of saving such as tontines and savings clubs, and because they were small tended to be outside of government and party control (Muenkner and Shah, 1993). In Asia, average growth during 1985–90 was nearly 8% in membership and 17% in savings, and by 1995 there were 14,500 unions in Asia affiliated to the World Council of Credit Unions (WOCCU), with over six million members. Again their market penetration was low at only 0.34%, but a low market share was not necessarily an indication of failure; it indicated that the poorest people were benefitting from small savings and loans (Birchall, 1997: 184–185).The range of types was large, from the informal credit circles called 'hui' groups in Vietnam to the Grameen Bank in Bangladesh which has pioneered lending to some of the poorest people in the world.

Here is a more detailed example. In Sri Lanka, the old savings and credit co-ops (called 'Sanasa societies') were small enough to escape the attention of government. However, the establishment of the multi-purpose co-ops affected them badly, as people visited the MPCs for their rice ration and used the co-operative rural banks that were attached to them; between 1964 and 1978 the number of Sanasa primary societies dropped from over 4000 to 1300 (Hulme et al, 1996). Then, in 1977 a community activist, Dr Kiriwandeniya, seeing the potential in these societies as a base for a potential social movement, reactivated the society in his home village. He then organised a seminar to publicise the results, and the movement began to grow. Between 1980 and 1985 the number of primary societies almost doubled and 19 district unions had been formed. Efforts were made to incorporate lower-income groups and women. By the mid-1980s the movement faced serious constraints on further growth due to lack of technical and managerial capacity, and there began a long association with international donors and NGOs that provide assistance. However, while the higher tier organisations became more dependent on grant aid, the primary societies remained financially independent. The secret of Sanasa's success is that the leadership consciously avoided contact with politicians, and it became a norm that those active in party politics could not be leaders.

Another positive development was – at long last – *a serious attempt by some agencies to invest in co-operative education.* Previously, the emphasis had been on training of government department staff and managers of co-op federations, but now the ICA and ILO began programmes that targeted managers, board members and ordinary members. Another development was the beginning of *a process of parallel promotion and strengthening* in which local co-op leaders and Northern co-operative development agencies began to work together. This was particularly important in the credit sector, where Desjardins International (DID) and the Canadian Cooperative Association (CCA) began to work in long-term programmes with credit movements in several countries.

Finally, there was *a shift of emphasis among donors towards non-cooperative and semi-cooperative forms* that were to some extent able to circumvent the government-regulated official sector and develop independently. The UN's Food and Agriculture Organisation was particularly active in developing alternatives to traditional farmer co-ops, calling them producer associations and using the new participatory development methodology (Rouse, 1996). The International Labour Organisation's ACOPAM programme worked in six countries in Sub-Saharan Africa, promoting over 2000 grassroots organisations benefitting 80,000 people. Also using a participatory methodology, the programme set up self-managed cotton markets, village grain banks, savings and credit schemes, village irrigation schemes, women's groups and so on. Before it ended in 2000, the programme helped to draw up new co-operative laws in these countries to create a favourable environment for these new forms of association (Birchall, 2004).

A period of liberalisation

During the 1980s, much of the infrastructure for sustaining the co-operative sector in developing countries began to fall apart, under the impact of internal budget constraints and external debt burdens and a structural adjustment policy that forced many governments to privatise their economies. Previously, agricultural co-ops had operated in a protected environment; granted monopolies, guaranteed prices, tax exemptions, financial assistance and support services, they did not have to be very good at doing business. They were not in a good condition to face the rigours of market liberalisation and structural adjustment. In 1994, a report for the ICA on co-operatives in Sub-Saharan Africa summed up the challenges: low business efficiency was 'the rule rather than the exception', there was a weak capital base, heavy indebtedness and limited credit-worthiness. Their managers and board members had limited entrepreneurial capability, while attempts to diversify had usually been unsuccessful, and members had little regard for them and no sense of affiliation. They were not prepared to change, and since members were already disillusioned it was difficult to see where the pressure for change would come from (Birgegaard and Genberg, 1994: 3–4).

Under the impact of budget cuts, introduction of market prices, and the collapse of the parastatal marketing boards, many co-operatives disappeared. Many continued but only at a survival level, while some, under strong leadership and good management, began to prosper in the new environment as the autonomous businesses they should always have been. One analyst describes it this way: 'liberalisation has produced a sieve for sifting the grain from the chaff in the co-operative sector' (Wanyama et al, 2009: 386).

In the early 1990s, naturally there was great concern among donors and co-operative developers about the impact of market liberalisation on co-operative sectors. A report was published by the World Bank that reviewed 25 of its projects that had involved co-ops. It was hopeful both about the development of new associative forms and about the ability of some of the previously government-controlled co-ops to transform themselves. However, it found that some African governments were still exerting control over co-ops and subsidising their operations. Their mental attitudes and the vested interests involved were highly resistant to change. The report also criticised the World Bank for not having a clear idea of what it wanted to achieve in working with co-ops, and for not paying attention to the need to strengthen them as institutions in the long term. It cited one instance in Senegal, where Bank staff had negotiated with government but not with the rural organisations who had refused to take part, preferring instead to keep their independence. More positively, the report found that, as a condition for disbursement of credit, the Bank had supported the passing of new co-operative laws in several countries (Hussi et al, 1993: 9). On the important question of whether aid agencies should work with existing co-ops or with the new formal and informal groups that were beginning to take their place, it was pragmatic. It found that in some countries the old co-ops were the only alternative, and in others, where negative attitudes towards co-ops hindered their reform, the new groups were preferable.

What was holding co-ops back was, on the one hand the lack of a conducive policy and legal framework, and on the other internal constraints such as lack of business experience and undercapitalisation. In between these was a new factor; the limited availability of markets. In Guinea, for example, fruit marketing co-ops were geared up to producing for a state-owned enterprise that closed, leaving them without export markets. Having saturated the local markets they had ceased to expand (Hussi et al, 1993: 22). The report found that governments were still using marketing co-ops in the old way, compelling them to be purchaser of last resort for crops, and subjecting them to legal restrictions that were not placed on other private sector businesses. The participation of members was still discouraged by local officials and political leaders. In some countries co-operative leaders were pessimistic about new laws that were meant to guarantee autonomy but still kept too much government control. Clearly, a co-operative reform process was still needed to allow co-ops to survive in the new privatised marketplace (Birchall and Simmons, 2010).

In 1995 the ICA completed an exhaustive survey of its members and came up with a clear set of values and principles on which to base the co-operative identity. The previous revision, in 1966, had not emphasised enough the autonomous and independent nature of co-operatives. Now, there was a new identity statement that all organisations claiming to be co-ops have to subscribe to, and new principles emphasising their autonomy and independence, the voluntary nature of their membership, democratic member control, member economic participation and so on (Birchall, 1997). This was the international lead that co-operative promoters had been waiting for. In 2001, the United Nations produced *Guidelines aimed at creating a supportive environment for the development of cooperatives* (UN, 2001). The aim was to provide advice to governments and set out broad principles on which national co-operative policies might be based. The message was that, in order to put co-operatives on an equal footing with other types of business organisation, governments have to recognise and take account of their special character. It encouraged governments to recognise publicly the contribution of co-operatives to their economies and civil societies. It pointed to the ICA principles as evidence that there should be co-operative laws that recognise this special character. Such laws would safeguard the autonomy of co-operatives, provide light regulation, and ensure a 'level playing field' with other types of business. The guidelines stated that the co-operative movement should be able to participate fully in the drafting of these laws. There was a sense of urgency here, of wanting to right past wrongs, when the document declared: 'This process should have as its purpose the early and complete disengagement by governments from the internal affairs of co-operatives' (UN, 2001: 18). There was a sense of impatience at not wanting to wait much longer before real co-operatives could be promoted. The guidelines suggested that even before a law was enacted 'discriminatory provisions should be rendered inoperative as quickly as possible'.

In 2002 the International Labour Conference adopted a new Recommendation (No. 193) concerning the promotion of co-operatives (ILO, 2001). This revised the ILO's previous Recommendation of 1966, which had reflected the concern of that time with co-operatives as a tool of development and was restricted to developing countries. Like the UN Guidelines, it drew explicitly on the work done by the ICA to reformulate the co-operative principles. It agreed that governments need to provide a supportive framework for co-operative development, and insisted that co-operatives are autonomous associations of persons that have their own values and principles. This means that promoting co-operatives as 'tools' of development is wrong; assistance has to be given to the members – to create income-generating activities, gain access to markets, improve their own social and economic well-being – while respecting their autonomy. It went further than the UN Guidelines in spelling out the kinds of support services governments should provide access to: human resource development, research and management consultancy, finance and investment, support for marketing, and so on.

Since 1990, new co-operative laws have been enacted and old ones repealed in many countries. The pressures of structural adjustment and democratic reforms led 15 sub-Saharan African states to revise their laws; others will follow. In 1995, an Act in Andra Pradesh introduced, for the first time, the concept of co-operative autonomy and self-reliance in India, and ten other states passed similar laws attempting to set the Indian co-operative movement free of state tutelage. Fiji, Indonesia, Jordan, Malaysia, Mongolia, Nepal, the Philippines, Thailand and Viet Nam have new laws, and several Latin American and Caribbean states are also revising their laws. Since 1995, the makers of these new laws have been helped by the new ICA statement of identity and principles, backed up by the UN Guidelines and the ILO's Recommendation 193. Where governments want to restrict the scope of co-operative sectors, co-operators can now appeal to these international standards for guidance and to the ICA and the ILO for help (the latter has helped the governments of over 60 countries with drafting new laws and guidance on co-operatives). A new, more sophisticated understanding of the relationship between governments and co-operatives is emerging that is beginning to undo some of the mistakes made in the past.

However, in one respect at least – the participation of women – there is much more work to do. Despite the new legislation, there are still factors that impede women's access to co-operatives. First, some laws still admit only one person per household to membership, on the grounds that voting rights should not be concentrated in large families, or that having more than one member would complicate matters when it comes to using family assets as guarantees. The Andra Pradesh law has removed this condition, and as a result thousands of women have joined. Second, under the wider legal system in several countries married women are considered to be minors, and not able to hold property or do business in their own right. Third, succession rules often prevent women from inheriting their deceased husband's assets held in the co-operative. More broadly, even in 'gender-perfect' legislation there are further barriers such as prejudiced application of the law by male lawyers and a lack of will to enforce it. Cultural inhibitions prevent women from using the law to gain their rights, and so the idea that a woman is under the 'guardianship' of her husband persists. Where the one-member-per-household rule operates, women have no option but to form their own co-operatives. Yet even here they face difficulties because they may not be able to own land or gain access to credit, they are more likely than men to be illiterate and have poor knowledge of their legal rights. In such cases, new co-operative legislation may be unknown to them and so may not help (Nippierd and Holmgren, 2002).

The current situation

The current situation is much more hopeful than it has ever been for co-operative development in the poorer countries of Africa and Asia. A recent project in 12 countries in Africa has shown how the sector is growing, finding that, despite all the problems they faced when liberalisation first began, 'cooperatives in Africa have survived the market forces and continued to grow in number and membership' (Wanyama et al, 2009: 374). Even in countries such as Uganda and Rwanda where the sector was on the verge of collapse due to conflicts it now seems to be growing again. The survey data shows that there are around 150,000 co-operative-type businesses in the sample countries (though if the dormant ones are subtracted the number reduces considerably – in respect of statistics, the tendency to inflate the numbers of co-ops has not changed). Around seven percent of the African population belong to co-ops. Old co-ops have reformed, while new ones have emerged.

They are no longer connected vertically in the old British system but are more inclined to seek horizontal linkages with other co-ops in order to gain the advantages of networks. Traditional apex bodies and regional unions are becoming irrelevant and sometimes, as in Uganda, simply collapsing. New federal bodies are being formed out of the needs of primary co-ops for shared services: in Ethiopia the Oromia Coffee Producers Federation, and in Kenya the Union of Savings and Credit Co-ops, are good examples. Everywhere, savings and credit co-ops seem to be seeking strength through federation. The survey points to substantial growth in several sectors: savings and credit, housing, non-traditional industries such as distilling, and even consumer co-operatives. They begin by being unifunctional and then, under pressure from members, take on other activities. They are increasingly market driven, seeking niches and marketable products. The old problem of poor management is being solved by their ability, as successful business, to afford to hire professional staff. The study finds that within this general upsurge in co-operative activity there are some outstanding examples such as Githunguri Dairy Farmers Co-operative in Kenya, Kuapa Kokoo in Ghana, the General Co-operative for Weaving and Spinning Workers in Egypt, the Union des Banques Populaires in Rwanda, and the Rooibos Tea Co-operative in South Africa.

A report this author has written for the ILO shows that the successful co-operatives contribute not only to poverty reduction but to the wider aims of the Millennium Development Goals (Birchall, 2004). The argument was based on case studies, which does not mean that co-operatives *in general* have this capacity. A larger study was then carried out in Tanzania and Sri Lanka, which included a survey of 450 co-operative managers. The results were quite clear; 87% of co-operative managers in Tanzania and 80% of those in Sri Lanka told us that they were effective at raising incomes and achieving a wide range of other benefits for members (Birchall and Simmons, 2009). We might expect managers to be biased, but their judgement was echoed in a survey of board members, and they were able to give good examples to support their optimism. Many reasons were given for the organisational advantages of co-peratives. In *multi-purpose* and *credit* co-operatives, a widely-identified factor was the ability for members to receive small loans to support their self-employment, enable buildings to be repaired, electricity and telecommunications to be installed, and essential equipment to be purchased. These loans are difficult for people to obtain elsewhere – these businesses would never get off the ground without the co-operative. They are aware of the risks of supporting new businesses and so provide training in entrepreneurship. *Agricultural/fishing* and *industrial/craft* co-operatives are also able to support their members through knowledge and training, providing up-to-date technical information and supplying inputs at low prices or on credit. A major benefit of industrial and craft co-operatives is the shared facilities provided.

Another role was to help members sell their outputs. Dairy co-operatives collect milk from their members for sale, while agricultural marketing co-operatives collect rice, grains, tea, coffee, cashew nuts, mushrooms, and tomatoes. The co-operative is able to offer a higher price than members would be able to get from private traders, and also provides market information so that members know when their produce will fetch the best price. However, the complexity of the co-operative payment system, with a first payment on delivery and a second payment once the produce has been sold, means that sometimes smallholder farmers are tempted to take the single payment offered by the private traders, even though this is at a lower price. The co-operatives also contribute to skill development and education, promote gender equality and the empowerment of women, help when members suffer illness, and help to improve their shelter and living standards. They also take seriously their central role in communities, and are particularly good in solving common problems in the community and helping to create 'good citizens'.

Our study also included historical analysis and interviews with key informants in both countries that made us realise that there is still a need for a reform of the conditions under which co-operatives do business. A superficial reading of the recent history would lead one to expect that the reform process that began in the early 1990s is just about complete, and that co-operative sectors are now free from government control. We found a strong contrast between Sri Lanka where there is continuing political control of multi-purpose co-operatives and resistance to reform, and Tanzania where there is a genuine reform programme that is setting agricultural co-operatives free (Birchall and Simmons, 2010).

A new paradigm of co-operative development

Related to the issue of reform is the question of what is the best way to promote MOBs in developing countries. It has become clear by now that one development paradigm has not just given way to another. State-controlled co-ops have not just turned into an autonomous movement, and in some countries governments, officials and politicians still have an interest in blocking the reform process. Also, other competing ways of understanding the subject have emerged. It is possible to identify at least five models through which donors, development agencies and governments have come to view the idea of member-owned businesses in developing countries.

1. The old parastatal model

Has the old top-down, government-driven model, which was universal from the 1960s through to the end of the 1980s, really been superseded? Yes, for the most part, sometimes as part of a conscious legal reform (such as occurred in Kenya in 1997, Tanzania in 2002, Vietnam in 2002, and China in 2007), sometimes because government regulatory organisations and apex co-operatives have collapsed (for instance in Cape Verde (Mendonca, 2008), Uganda (Mrema, 2008), and among cotton co-ops in Tanzania – Gibbon, 2001). However, in some countries there have been no legal reforms and a lot of resistance to change; our own research in Sri Lanka shows that the nationwide network of multi-purpose co-ops is still essentially government-controlled (Birchall and Simmons, 2009), while in Indonesia a new co-operative law was recently rejected, and in Egypt a bureaucratic regime is still in place (Aal, 2008). In others, such as Ghana and South Africa, new co-operative laws are only just being written (Tsekpo, 2008; Theron, 2008). Despite the efforts of ICA and ILO, as Develtere et al put it 'many African countries still rely on an outdated and often dysfunctional or obsolete legal framework' (Develtere et al, 2008: 23).

2. A community development model

During the late 1970s, a participatory alternative began to be developed challenging the dominant top-down model of development and emphasising the value of community development and grassroots democracy (see Verhagen, 1984). This is still a powerful model, being promoted for instance by UN agencies and the World Bank. Here farmers and other small business people are seen as part of a wider geographical community, and economic development is meant to benefit the community as a whole. This model can work well among indigenous people such as the Inuit of Northern Canada, or tribal peoples in India (Rajagopalan, 2003) but because it assumes a more inclusive form of organisation and social rather than economic benefits it is not good at promoting strong, sustainable producer associations. Even in promotion of savings and credit co-ops, the assumption that the organisation is part of a community can hold back the realisation that it is actually a bank and that members have to learn how to do banking effectively.

3. A reformed co-operatives model

In the reformed co-operatives model, members take control of their co-operatives as part of a reform process based on the enactment in law of the principle of autonomy and recognition of international co-operative principles. This is quite an exacting model as it requires simultaneous application of several important kinds of reform (Birchall and Simmons, 2010). Changes in the law are not enough. If people do not know about the new law, or assume it is just for new co-ops, there will be no change (for India see Rajagopalan, 2003). New co-operative laws are not necessarily less controlling, when they arise out of the chaos that occurred during the liberalisation period; in Kenya a 2004 act gave great powers to the Commissioner to regulate co-ops (Wanyama, 2008). Even where a new agricultural co-operative sector is created under a reformed law, it can be dominated by political interests and freer in some regions than others (for Vietnam, see Fforde and Huan, 2001). Government pro-motion brings new dangers of incorporation into national policy priorities. In Ethiopia the government has set an ambitious target of 24,000 primary co-ops and 600 co-operative unions, but the setting of such targets brings the dangers inherent in the old state-planning approach. Already, the registration process overseen by a Federal Co-operative Agency under a new law has proved not to be flexible enough (Lemma, 2008), and secondment of agency personnel to co-op unions can bring a new form of dependency. In China, one study found that officials had taken the lead in starting 84% of farmer associations (Shen and Zhang, 2005; World Bank, 2006). A new law passed in 2007 provides protection for their autonomy through co-operative principles, but does not give them specific powers to federate and allows for membership of up to 20% from government-affiliated agencies (Zhao, 2009). In most African countries co-operative policy development has been erratic and a climate of uncertainty has resulted (Develtere et al, 2008). Yet there are some success stories and the reform process is continuing; it needs to be better understood and made more systematic.

4. A civil society interest group model

In the civil society interest group model, people organise in associations in order to gain a voice and representation as part of a rural civil society agenda. Alongside the co-operative reform process this is a separate, parallel development of representative bodies for farmers, women or ethnic groups, which then becomes the focus of development aid for wider purposes. In particular, it sees farmers as a potential social movement rather than an economic interest group. This way of looking at producer organisations is exemplified in a report sponsored by IFAP and the World Bank (Rondot and Collion, 2001). Despite defining POs as members organising themselves in order to raise farm incomes, the main interest is in how to channel resources so as to strengthen them as bodies that can meet the needs of the donors. Their needs are to develop primary associations that can be used to channel extension services to farmers, and secondary and apex organisations that can take part in national policy-making. While donors recognise that they should not 'turn these groups into extended arms of themselves' (Rondot and Collion, 2001: 1) in practice this danger is often overlooked. The economic benefits of farmer associations are played down. For example, the above report places advocacy and provision of public services alongside 'economic and technical functions', and sees improved access to markets as being a result of representative and advocacy activities 'as well as their combined financial clout' (Rondot and Collion, 2001: 2). The ultimate objective of strengthening POs is to 'make them capable of analysing their own needs, formulating their requests...and negotiating', rather than organising farm inputs, marketing and processing so as to add value to their products. This is naive. Farmers do not increase their incomes through advocacy but through trading.

The resulting relationship between POs and donors is a paternalistic one, with donors contributing to operational costs, 'allowing POs to manage their own funds', and so on. The language is of empowerment, access to services, negotiating with service providers, and managing 'activities'. This is a long way from the language of the next model, which restores the basic idea of POs as economic associations.

5. An economic association model

In this comparatively new, uncompromising, economic model, farmers are seen simply as entrepreneurs running small businesses. The focus is sectoral, analysing the demand for particular farm products and connecting the producers up to markets. The approach is pragmatic; if in a particular locality co-operatives have a bad name, promoters of this type will call them farmer associations and register them under whatever laws are most supportive. This approach is not yet fully codified, but is illustrated by agencies such as Technoserve and Agriterra working in several countries with funding by, among others, USAID. Here, capacity building is conceptualised in economic terms as training in bookkeeping, business-planning, strengthening the capital base, and technical assistance in product development (Rouse, 1996). This model converges at some points with the co-operative reform model; for instance, in Tanzania and Kenya primary co-ops are beginning to operate commercially outside their district unions, while in Uganda the collapse of the unions has allowed primary co-ops to shift to new crops such as vanilla and oil-seed. In this approach, top priority is given to promoting economically viable and independent producer groups. To do this, donors have to be careful not to put in too much external capital, as this distorts the incentives for membership and leads to the enterprise responding more to the demands of external providers than to member needs. The main focus is on an income-generating activity that members identify. Similarly, in relation to savings and credit co-ops, in this model members are seen as joint-owners of a bank rather than of a community organisation.

Conclusion

Throughout this book we have seen MOBs as businesses whose main purpose is to bring tangible economic benefits to their members, and so it will come as no surprise that our argument favours this last, *economic association* model for developing countries. The achievement of a reformed environment for MOBs is incomplete, and its completion will not be easy. It will only be achieved if genuine member-controlled businesses are driving the reform. The process is meant to stop co-operatives from being 'gov-operatives', but as we can see from the *civil society interest group model* there is still a danger of their being promoted as 'don-operatives', subject to the interests and priorities of donors, NGOs and development experts. In the economic association model, aid for MOBs is provided in the form of technical assistance and human capacity building, and is delivered by the international aid agencies of Northern MOB sectors such as Desjardins International and ACDI-VOCA, who know how to build genuine member-owned businesses. Charitable help is only necessary in times of natural disaster, and then it is given from movement to movement; after the Tsunami agencies such as the Italian Legacoop and the Canadian Co-operative Association helped their counterparts in Sri Lanka to rebuild. In normal times, financial help is confined to business loans that are part of a sound business plan, just as in any situation in the developed world where an MOB plans to grow or diversify. As in Germany in the 1860s, so in Tanzania in the 21st century, credit unions provide the capital enabling other types of MOB to expand their business. The message from the peculiar history of MOBs in developing countries is a simple one; allow member-owned businesses to be member-owned, and to be businesses.

10
The Idea of Membership

In this book the main emphasis has been on the member-owned business as a *business* but the question of what is meant by membership has kept on cropping up. The *member-owned* aspect needs to be explored more carefully, as membership is both necessary to MOBs and problematic. One key finding has been that a business with members at its centre has comparative advantages over other types of business. We can see that from the way in which IOBs are continually trying to persuade their customers that they also offer membership – of clubs that provide trade discounts, loyalty incentives and other kinds of privileged treatment. MOBs have a great advantage here; they can show that they provide a real share in ownership that goes way beyond what the IOBs can offer their 'members'. It is becoming easier to persuade boards of directors and managers that their businesses have this built-in advantage, because they see the benefits of member-loyalty in the 'bottom line'. Yet membership comes at a cost; it brings with it the right to take part in governance, and the more members exercise this right the more their leaders are likely to be challenged and their managers called to account.

A conventional economic analysis would start from the assumption that boards and managers have their own separate interests and that there will be no incentive to involve members. Some co-operative theorists reflect this when they say the organisation consists of two separate entities, an association of members and a business, and that the two will always be in an uncomfortable relationship. This is a mistake; those MOBs that have given priority to membership have found that it is good for business; it creates high trust relations, cements loyalty, and acts back on the business strategy to make it more successful, but also less risky. When boards and managers are persuaded that it is in the interest of the business, then a membership strategy literally pays dividends.

What does a successful membership strategy look like? It begins with a broad-minded view of what motivates people to participate. First, it makes sure the business provides economic rewards to members that are not available to non-members. This taps into people's *self-interest* and makes it easier to recruit new members. Second, it demonstrates that only an MOB can do this, and that were it not for the strength in numbers that it provides the needs of people as individuals would not be met. This taps into people's *self-interest collectively expressed*, and makes it easier to get members interested in the business. They will experience a sense of personal satisfaction from learning about it and may occasionally take part in social events and member activities. Third, it taps into some people's sense of *collective interest*, and makes it easier to identify those who want to become more actively involved. It finds routes for them to follow in order to participate in the MOB's governance, either directly through being elected or indirectly through providing support and member feedback. We can expect people who participate to respond to 'collectivistic incentives' such as a sense of community, shared values and shared goals. Sometimes members want to focus on their local community and sometimes on a wider community of interest; in a consumer co-operative, for instance, they may want to promote both local food networks and fair trade. In implementing the strategy, managers should seek to find the most cost-effective ways of connecting with members, and this includes creative use of websites, blogs, and internet chat rooms as well as face to face activities such as member forums and special interest groups. Those who get it right cease to think of member relations *just* as a cost on the business, because it brings tangible benefits to the 'bottom line'. Some theorists over-complicate this by talking of 'triple bottom lines' but there is one simple measure that provides a test of whether an MOB is successful or not – member benefits.

From the point of view of boards the membership strategy ought to link into the governance strategy. We have seen how in recent years MOBs have had to run to catch up with their IOB competitors in ensuring compliance with corporate governance codes. The best of them are now going beyond this to do active succession planning for non-executive directors and ensure that member interests remain at the centre of decision-making. For membership to be revitalised, there need to be opportunities to participate. There also needs to be a way of enabling members with different interests to appreciate different points of view and come to a common understanding; otherwise the costs of governance will be too high and the business may as well demutualise. The solution to both of these issues might be the two-tier board whereby a larger group of elected members supervises a smaller management board. Arguably, if a two tier board had been operating, some of the big governance failures we have found in mutual insurers and agricultural co-operative would not have happened. For a complex business with members whose interests are not homogeneous, the Anglo-Saxon system of unitary boards may just be too simple.

This does not mean that MOBs can easily overcome differences of interest. Among co-operative theorists there is talk of multi-stakeholding, and some MOBs that deliver public services have embraced this with enthusiasm; social co-operatives in Italy have employees, service users, carers and volunteers on the board. In a service whose quality depends on the relationship between the stakeholders it may be right to take them all into governance. Yet to make a business work with such a wide range of interests all claiming ownership and control rights, the range of decision-making has to be narrowed. Reliance on government funding and restrictive conditions such as a lock on the assets and a non-distribution rule make it easier. However, a business that operates in a real market could never be run in this way. Even in public services, if there is competition for contracts and a clearly defined service, the single stakeholder model of a worker co-operative is probably more efficient.

It is important that the idea of membership is not diluted. Sometimes MOBs are mistaken for 'CBOs', community-based organisations that have everyone in a geographical area in membership. There is a simple way to tell the difference; in an MOB people can opt out of membership, and if they opt out they cannot receive any of the benefits. Sometimes MOBs are associated with a social movement. This provides powerful reinforcement, ensuring member commitment and participation through associating the business with issues that they care about. However, this cannot be the distinguishing feature of an MOB: other types of business are also concerned with issues such as climate change, the environment and fair trade. Also, if members are more interested in outside issues than in the business the MOB is in, this can divert the governance process into unprofitable channels. In some consumer co-ops in Europe, for instance, there used to be a political struggle over which party got to run the 'co-op', but everywhere this occurred the business suffered; politicians make poor retailers.

The task of engaging the interest of members is made much more difficult by the growing complexity of MOBs that are at the cutting edge in regional and global markets. The choice of a mixture of MOB and IOB status provides confused signals to members and should be avoided; there are plenty of other ownership structures that preserve the MOB intact. Another confusing signal to member is the venture into foreign markets. Here the ethical issue of whether to offer membership to people in other countries combines with the practical issue of how to engage a multi-national membership in governance. Given that many of the structural changes and acquisitions in banking, insurance, retailing and food processing have been unsuccessful, it is probably time for MOB boards to begin to consider whether the next step is a step too far. If they care about member involvement, perhaps they should begin to design the organisation with members in mind, rather than just following their competitors down the same road. The traditional alternative of setting up a federal body or joint venture between MOBs is still being well used.

Members have to find ways of challenging managers who argue that 'there is no alternative' to actions that make MOBs follow IOBs into new territory, or in some cases try to get there first. Just like any other type of business, MOBs can fail. When they do, the results can be serious for the livelihoods of people whose own businesses depend on them. Member involvement should produce a board that can challenge management, but there are issues concerning the kind of knowledge the board members have, and the extent to which they have access to independent sources of information. This is particularly important in calculating risk. The aim of good governance is sometimes set against the aim of involving members, particularly in the board; it is said that a board cannot afford to have directors whose main interest is in representing members, because this takes away from the skill set needed. This is a mistake. At least one member of the board should be tasked with the specific job of keeping in touch with members. Preferably that person should arise naturally out of the process of member participation rather than being imposed by the board. Arguably, a two-tier board offers a better alternative of a skill-based management board overseen by a member council.

In reports on the promotion of MOBs, analysts often blame the wider environment for their shortcomings, citing ignorance among business advisers, legal impediments, tax disincentives and other outside influences. Yet we have come across many instances of successful MOB sectors clearing the way of impediments: putting resources into education and training, promoting new laws, arguing for favourable tax regimes and so on. There *are* serious threats to MOB status, notably the recent attempt by an international accounting body to impose rules that would turn assets into liabilities and undermine their comparative advantages. These threats have to be met head on by the international bodies that represent each MOB sector. However, the environment will never be conducive until MOB sectors establish their distinctive identity and communicate it to the wider public.

Some evolutionary biologists and psychologists have suggested that, just as genes replicate themselves, there are mental equivalents called memes that are replicated from one mind to another. There is a kind of survival of the fittest of the memes; the more successful of them replicated quickly and effortlessly into the consciousness of millions of people. The best examples are popular songs that, suddenly, everyone starts to sing. The consumer co-operative movement used to have one of these. Gracie Fields sang 'Stop and shop at the Co-op' and everyone listened. Another meme was the dividend number that millions of people knew by heart in the days when, as children, they were sent on errands by their parents and had to chant out the number at the checkout. Among MOBs, Latin American credit union and co-operative movements still have this kind of cultural resource; songs and cultural events that reinforce the idea of membership. The rest of us have to make do with marketing messages that are carefully crafted to stick in the mind. The best of the consumer-owned businesses are beginning to tell their customer-members that they are the owners, and ask questions such as 'Why do business with anybody else?' When combined with an ethical stance concerning the product this can be a powerful message. The best of the farmer-owned businesses are beginning to tell their customers that the farmers are the members, and that this guarantees a pure, unadulterated product. When consumer- and producer-owned businesses come together, they have an even more powerful message concerning sustainability and fairness at both ends of the value chain.

Some social theorists have described a process of individualisation that is affecting people under conditions of late modernity, cutting them loose from collective identities such as class and religious affiliation and making them reluctant to participate in civil society. Analysts who observe failures in MOBs sometimes point to this underlying shift in people's consciousness. Yet psychologists tell us that there are different kinds of individualism, and that it can be compatible with collectivistic attachments. *Possessive individualists* probably are too calculating to get involved as members, but *solidaristic individualists* make an individual choice about which causes to belong to. Their commitment may be less habitual than it was in the past but, when they make it, it can be just as strong.

However, there are profound cultural shifts taking place that are affecting MOBs; the decline of the Japanese *han* groups in retail and health co-operatives shows this. Also, there has been a decline in the numbers of young people becoming members and taking part in MOBs, and evidence of an alarming ignorance about what it means to be a member. A member-strategy has to address this directly by promoting youth forums and school co-operatives and providing opportunities for participation in governance. There are plenty of causes that younger people do believe in; it is just a matter of linking these to the idea of membership.

Finally, a word of warning about the meaning of member-ownership. There have often been theorists who, on discovering the idea of a member-based economy become excited about its potential to cure many ills. They see it as a replacement for capitalism, a solution to globalisation, a way of creating sustainable economies, a key to unlocking the economic potential of developing economies, and so on. At its best it may contribute to all of these, and it is a vital part of some important social movements, but it is not in itself a movement. We have to appreciate the potential of member-ownership but not put more weight on it than it can bear.

If we want to know how important the member-owned business sector is, instead of straining to envisage what it might achieve if it were more successful, perhaps we should ask what our world would look like without it.

Bibliography

Aal, A (2008) 'The Egyptian cooperative movement: between state and market', in Develtere, Pollet and Wanyama (eds) (2008) *Cooperating Out of Poverty: The Renaissance of the African Co-operative Movement*, Geneva: International Labour Organisation

All-Party Parliamentary Group for Building Societies and Financial Mutuals (2006) *Windfalls or Shortfalls: The True Cost of Demutualisation*, London: Mutuo

Apthorpe, R and Gasper, D (1982) 'Policy evaluation and meta-evaluation: The case of rural co-operatives', *World Development*, 10(8): 651–668

Armitage, S and Kirk, P (1994) 'The performance of proprietary compared with mutual life offices', *Service Industries Journal*, 14(2): 238–261

Attwood, D and Bhaviskar, B (1988) *Who Shares? Co-operatives and Rural Development*, Oxford: Oxford University Press

Aubrun, R (1915) *Mutual Aid Societies in France*, Exposition Universelle de San Francisco

Axelrod, R (1984) *The Evolution of Co-operation*, New York: Basic Books

Banturaki, J (2000) *Cooperatives and Poverty Alleviation*, Dar es Salaam: Tema Publishers

Baron, M-L (2007) 'Defining the frontiers of the firm through property rights allocation: The case of the French retailer co-operative Leclerc', *Review of Social Economy*, LXV, 3: 293–317

Beito, D (1990) 'Mutual aid for social welfare: The case of American fraternal societies', in *Critical Review*, 4(4): 709–736

Beveridge, W (1948) *Voluntary Action: A Report on the Methods of Social Advance*, London: George Allen and Unwin

Bibby, A and Shaw, L (eds) (2005) *Making a Difference: Co-operative Solutions to Global Poverty*, Manchester: Co-operative College

Birchall, J (1987) *Save Our Shop: The Fall and Rise of the Small Co-operative Store*, Manchester: Holyoake Press

—— (1988) *Building Communities: The Co-operative Way*, London: Routledge

—— (1994) *Co-op: The People's Business*, Manchester: Manchester University Press

—— (1995a) 'The hidden history of housing co-operatives in Britain', in Heskin and Leavitt op cit

—— (1995b) *The Rochdale Pioneers*, speech at the 150th Anniversary of the Co-operative Movement, Manchester: Co-operative Union

—— (1997) *The International Cooperative Movement*, Manchester: Manchester University Press

—— (2000) 'Some theoretical and practical implications of the attempted takeover of a consumer co-operative society', *Annals of Public and Co-operative Economics*, Vol 71(1): March, pp29–54

—— (ed.) (2001) *The New Mutualism in Public Policy*, London: Routledge

—— (2002) *A Mutual Trend: How to Run Rail and Water in the Public Interest*, London: New Economics Foundation

—— (2003) *Rediscovering the Co-operative Advantage: Poverty Reduction through Self-help*, Geneva: ILO

—— (2004) *Co-operatives and the Millennium Development Goals*, Geneva: ILO

—— (2005) 'Business ethics and the Co-operative Bank', in Tsuzuki, C (ed.) *The Emergence of Global Citizenship: Utopian Ideas, Co-operative Movements and the Third Sector*, Tokyo: Robert Owen Association of Japan

—— (2008) *An Introduction to Co-operatives*, New York: UNDESA Division of Social Policy and Development

—— (2009) *A Comparative Study of Co-operatives in Scotland, Finland, Sweden and Switzerland*, Glasgow: Co-operative Development Scotland

Birchall, J and Hammond Ketilson, L (2009) *Resilience of the Co-operative Business Model in Times of Crisis*, International Labour Organisation Responses to the Global Economic Crisis, Geneva: International Labour Organisation

Birchall, J and Simmons, R (2004a) 'The involvement of members in the governance of large-scale co-operative and mutual businesses: A formative evaluation of the co-operative group', *Review of Social Economy*, 42(4): 487–515

—— (2004b) 'What motivates members to participate in co-operative and mutual businesses: a theoretical model and some findings', *Annals of Public and Co-operative Economics*', 75.3, 465–495

—— (2008) *Final report to the ESRC: Co-operatives and Poverty Reduction Project*, ESRC Non-governmental Public Action Programme, September

—— (2009) *Co-operatives and Poverty Reduction: Evidence from Sri Lanka and Tanzania*, Manchester: Co-operative College

—— (2010) 'The co-operative reform process in Tanzania and Sri Lanka', *Annals of Public and Co-operative Economics*, forthcoming

Birgegaard, L and Genberg, B (1994) *Co-operative Adjustment in a Changing Environment in Sub-Saharan Africa*, Geneva: International Co-operative Alliance

Bonner, A (1970) *British Co-operation*, Manchester: Co-operative Union

Braverman, A, Guasch, J and Huppi, M (1991) *Promoting Rural Co-operatives in Developing Countries: The Case of Sub-Saharan Africa*, World Bank Discussion papers 121, Washington: World Bank

Brazda, J and Schediwy, R (eds) (1989) *Consumer Co-operatives in a Changing World*, Geneva: International Co-operative Alliance

Brazda, J (1989) 'The consumer co-operatives in Germany', in Brazda, J and Schediwy, R (eds) *Consumer Co-operatives in a Changing World*, Geneva: International Co-operative Alliance

Buchmueller, T and Couffinhal, A (2004) *Private Health Insurance in France*, Paris: OECD Health Working Papers no.12

Building Societies Association (2010) *Conversations with Members: Member Engagement at Building Societies*, fourth edition, London: BSA

Burgan, R (ed.) (2010) *Fair and Square: Ethical Shopping Matters*, Manchester: Co-operative College Paper 16 (Manchester: Co-operative College)

Burnett, J (1989) *Plenty and Want: A Social History of Food in England from 1815*, London: Routledge

CECODHAS (2008) www.cecodhas.org, accessed 1.4.10

Chaddad, F and Cook, M (2004) 'Understanding new cooperative models: An ownership-control rights typology', *Review of Agricultural Economics*, 26(3): 348–360

CICOPA (2010) www.cicopa.coop, accessed 30.3.10

Cole, GDH (1944) *A Century of Co-operation*, London: George Allen and Unwin

Commission on Co-operative and Mutual Housing (2009) *Bringing Democracy Home*, London: CCMH

Cook, M and Chaddad, F (2004) 'Redesigning co-operative boundaries: The emergence of new models', *American Journal of Agricultural Economics*, 86(5): 1249–1253

Co-op City (2010) *History*, found at en.wikipedia.org/wiki/co-op_city,_bronx

Co-op Village (2010) *website*, www.coopvillage.coop

Co-operative Commission (2000) *Report*, Manchester: Co-operative Union

Co-operative Independent Commission (1958) *Report*, Manchester: Co-operative Union

Co-operatives UK (2010) Trading for mutual benefit: A guide to co-operative consortia, Manchester, downloaded from www.cooperatives-uk.coop on 19.5.10

Cote, D and Luc, D (1996) *Profile of World Agricultural Co-operation*, Montreal: Centre de Gestion des Cooperatives, Ecole des Haute Etudes Commerciales

Cowen, N (2008) *Swedish Lessons: How Schools with More Freedom Can Deliver Better Education*, London: Civitas

Danish Agricultural Council (2007) *Agriculture in Denmark: Facts and Figures 2007*, found at www.landbrug.dk, accessed 19.5.10

Davies, K (2005) *Cooperative Principles and International Expansion: The Example of NTUC Fairprice*, Stirling University Institute for Retail Studies

Davies, K and Burt, S (2006) *Consumer Co-operatives and Retail Internationalisation: Problems and Prospects*, Stirling University Institute for Retail Studies

Davis, D (1966) *A History of Shopping*, London: Routledge and Kegan Paul

Davis, K (2007) 'Australian credit unions and the demutualisation agenda', *Annals of Public and Co-operative Economics* 78(2): 277–300

Delisted (2010) www.delisted.com.au/Demutualised.aspx, accessed 18.5.10

Dept for Children, Schools and Families (2009) *Co-operative Schools: Making a Difference*, London: UK Government

Develtere, P (1994) *Co-operation and Development*, Leuven: ACCO

Develtere, P (2008) 'Chapter One – Co-operative development in Africa up to the 1990s', in Develtere, P, Pollet, I and Wanyama, F (eds) (2008) *Cooperating Out of Poverty: The Renaissance of the African Co-operative Movement*, Geneva: International Labour Organisation

Doe, H (2010) *Mutual Marine Insurance Clubs*, at www.helendoe.co.uk, accessed 6.3.10

Drake, L and Llewellyn, D (2001) 'The economics of mutuality: A perspective on UK building societies', in Birchall, J (ed.) (2001) *The New Mutualism in Public Policy*, London: Routledge

Emery, H (2010) *Fraternal Sickness Insurance*, http://eh.net/encyclopaedia, accessed 5.3.10

Equitable Life (2010) *The History of Equitable Life*, found at www.equitable.co.uk, accessed 8.3.10

European Co-operative Banking Association (2008) *Statistics*, found at www.euro-coopbanks.coop on 23.3.10

European Federation of Employee Ownership (EFES) (2010) *Statistics for 2009*, found at www.efesonline.org, accessed 18.5.10

Fals-Borda, O, Apthorpe, R and Inayatullah (1976) 'The crisis of rural co-operatives: Problems in Africa, Asia and Latin America', in Nash, J, Dandler, J and Hopkins, N, *Popular Participation in Social Change*, The Hague: Mouton

Fay, C (1907) *Co-operation at Home and Abroad* (first edition) London: PS King
—— (1913) *Co-partnership at Home and Abroad*, Cambridge: Cambridge University Press
—— (1938) *Co-operation at Home and Abroad* (fourth edition in two volumes), London: PS King
Federal Deposit Insurance Corporation (FDIC) (1999) *History of the Eighties: Lessons for the Future*, Vol.1, Washington: FDIC
Federation National de la Mutualite Francaise (2010) website www.mutualite.fr, accessed 5.3.10
FForde, A and Dinh Huan, N (2001) *Vietnamese Rural Society and Its Institutions: Results of a Study of Cooperative Groups and Cooperatives in Three Provinces*, Final report (financed by SIDA)
Franklin, N and Lee, W (1988) 'Demutualisation', *Journal of the Staple Inn Actuarial Society*, 31: 89–125
Fulton, M and Larson, K (2009) 'Overconfidence and hubris: The demise of agricultural co-operatives in Western Canada', *Journal of Rural Co-operation*, 37(2): 166–200
Gibbon, P (2001) 'Cooperative cotton marketing, liberalisation and "civil society" in Tanzania', in *Journal of Agrarian Change*, 1(3): 389–439
Girard, J-P (2000) 'Co-op activities in the health and social care sector in Quebec', in Fairbairn, B, MacPherson, I and Russell, N (2000) *Canadian Co-operatives in the Year 2000*, Saskatoon: University of Saskatchewan
Goldblatt, M (2000) 'Canada's nonprofit co-operative housing sector: An alternative that works', in Fairbairn, B, MacPherson, I and Russell, N (2000) *Canadian Co-operatives in the Year 2000*, Saskatoon: University of Saskatchewan
Gosden, P (1973) *Self-help: Voluntary Associations in Nineteenth Century Britain*, London: Batsford
Government of Canada (2010) *Co-operatives in Canada: Situation 2005*, accessed from www.coop.gc.ca on 19.5.10
Green, D (1993) *Reinventing Civil Society: The Rediscovery of Welfare Without Politics*, London: Institute of Economic Affairs
Green, D and Cromwell, L (1984) *Mutual Aid or Welfare State: Australia's Friendly Societies*, Sydney: George Allen and Unwin
Green, D and Irvine, B (2001) *Health Care in France and Germany: Lessons for the UK*, London: Civitas
Group Health (2010) website, www.ghc.org, accessed 29.3.10
Halpern, D (2005) *Social Capital*, pp269–271, Cambridge: Polity Press
Ham, C and Hunt, P (2008) *Membership Governance in NHS Foundation Trusts*, Mutuo/University of Birmingham
Hannan, M and Freeman, J (1989) *Organisational Ecology*, Cambridge Mass: Harvard University Press
Hansmann, H (1985) 'The organization of insurance companies: Mutual versus stock', *Journal of Law, Economics and Organisation*, 1: 125–153
Hansmann, H (1996) *The Ownership of Enterprise*, Harvard: Harvard University Press
Heffernan, S (2005) 'The effects of uk building society conversion on pricing behaviour', *Journal of Banking and Finance*, 29(3): 779–797
Hino, S (1996) *Health Co-operatives in Japan*, Tokyo: Japanese Consumer Co-operatives Union

Hirschmann A (1970) *Exit, Voice and Loyalty*, Cambridge Mass: Harvard University Press

Hogeland, J (2002) *The Changing Federated Relationship Between Local and Regional Co-operatives*, US Dept of Agriculture RBS Research Report 190

Holmen, H (1990) *State, Co-operatives and Development in Africa*, Uppsala: Scandinavian Institute of African Studies

Holyoake, GJ (1857, and third edition 1907) *Self-help by the People: The History of the Rochdale Pioneers*, London: Swan Sonnenschein

Hopkins, E (1995) *Working-class Self-help in Nineteenth Century England*, London: UCL Press

Howarth, M (2007) *Worker Co-operatives and the Phenomenon of Empresas Recuperadas in Argentina*, Manchester: Co-operative College

Hussi, P, Murphy, J, Lindberg, O and Brenneman, L (1993) *Development of Co-operatives and Other Rural Organisations: The Role of the World Bank*, Washington: World Bank

Hulme, D, Montgomery, R and Bhattacharya, D (1996) 'Mutual finance and the poor: A study of SANASA in Sri Lanka', Ch.13 of Hulme, D and Mosley, P (1996) *Finance Against Poverty*, Vol.2, London: Routledge

International Co-operative Alliance (ICA) (1978) *Cooperatives and the Poor: Report of an Experts' Consultation*, London: ICA

—— (1995) 'Statement on the Co-operative Identity, Report to the 31st Congress', in *Review of International Co-operation*, 88(3)

—— (2010) website, ica.coop and linked websites of ICA Housing etc

International Co-operative and Mutual Insurance Federation (ICMIF) (2009) *Mutual Market Share and Global 500*, Bowdon: ICMIF

—— (2010) *About Us*, available at www.icmif.org, accessed 8.3.10

International Labour Organisation (ILO) (2001) *Recommendation 193 Concerning the Promotion of Co-operatives*, Geneva: ILO

Jayaweera, P (1987) *The Role of Co-operatives in Poverty Alleviation*, unpublished report

Jeffreys (1954) *Retail Trading in Britain 1850–1950*, Cambridge: University Press

Johnstad, T (2000) 'Mutual maritime insurance clubs: Co-operation and competition', *Annals of Public and Co-operative Economics*, 71(4): 525–555

Kemp, T (1985) *Industrialisation in Nineteenth Century Europe*, Harlow: Longman

Kennedy, J (1999) *Not by Chance: A History of the International Co-operative and Mutual Insurance Federation*, Manchester: Holyoake Books

Kuchler, H (2010) 'Farmers club together in struggle to survive', *Financial Times*, April 16

Kuisma, M, Henttinen, A, Karhu, S and Pohls, M (1999) 'The Pellervo story: A century of Finnish co-operation 1899–1999', Pellervo Federation, Ch.1 by Kuisma, M 'We have no Rockefellers, but we have cooperatives', Helsinki: Pellervo Federation

Kurimoto, A (1999) 'Renewing the membership basis for raising investment and patronage', *Journal of Co-operative Studies* 32.1, 50–60

—— (ed.) (2010) *Toward Contemporary Co-operative Studies: Perspectives from Japan's Consumer Co-ops*, Tokyo: Consumer Co-operative Institute of Japan

Kuustera, A (1999) *Niche of Co-operative Banking in Finland During the First Half of the Twentieth Century*, Helsinki: Pellervo

Lacey, S (2009) *Beyond a Fair Price: The Co-operative Movement and Fair Trade*, Manchester: Co-operative College Paper 14

Laidlaw, A (1978) 'Co-operatives and the poor: A review from within the co-operative movement', in International Co-operative Alliance *Co-operatives and the Poor; report of an experts consultation*, London: ICA
—— (1980) *Co-operatives in the Year 2000*, Geneva: International Co-operative Alliance
Lambert, P (1963) *Studies in the Social Philosophy of Co-operation*, Manchester: Co-operative Union
Lampel, J, Bhalla, A and Jha, P (2010) *Model Growth: Do Employee-owned Businesses Deliver Sustainable Performance?* Published by John Lewis Partnership, Employee Ownership Association and Cass Business School, downloaded from www.employeeownership.co.uk on 19.5.10
Lemma, T (2008) 'Growth without structures: The co-operative movement in Ethiopia', in Develtere, P, Pollet, I and Wanyama, F (eds) (2008) *Cooperating Out of Poverty*: *The Renaissance of the African Co-operative Movement*, Geneva: International Labour Organisation
Llewellyn, DT and Holmes, M (1991) 'In defence of mutuality: A redress to an emerging conventional wisdom', *Annals of Public and Co-operative Economics*, 62(3)
Lundquist, LJ, Elander, I and Danermark, B (1990) 'Housing policy in Sweden – still a success story?', *International Journal of Urban and Regional Research*, 14: 445–467
Mabbett, D (2001) 'Mutuality in insurance and social security: Retrospect and prospect', in Birchall (ed.) (2001)
MacLeod, G and Reed, D (2009) 'Mondragon's response to the challenges of globalisation', in Reed, D and McMurtry, J (eds) *Co-operatives in a Global Economy*, Newcastle upon Tyne: Cambridge Scholars
MacPherson, I (1999) *Hands Around the Globe: A History of the International Credit Union Movement*, Victoria Canada: Horsdal and Schubart
Margolis, S and Liebowitz, S (2009) *Path Dependence*, paper available from www.utdallas.edu accessed 12.5.10
Mason, D (2003) 'Savings and loan industry, US', in Whaples, R (ed.) *EH.Net Encyclopaedia, URL:* http://eh.net/encyclopedia/article/mason.savings.loan.industry.us
Mellor, M, Hannah, J and Stirling, J (1988) *Worker Co-operatives in Theory and Practice*, Milton Keynes: Open University Press
Mendonca, JG (2008) 'Surviving on the islands: Cooperatives in Cape Verde', in Develtere, Pollet and Wanyama (eds) (2008) *Cooperating Out of Poverty*: *The Renaissance of the African Co-operative Movement*, Geneva: International Labour Organisation
Mercer, T (1947) *Co-operation's Prophet: Life and Letters of Dr William King*, Manchester: Co-operative Union
Merrett, C and Walzer, N (eds) (2001) *A Cooperative Approach to Local Economic Development*, Westport CT: Quorum Books
Mrema, H (2008) 'Uganda: Starting all over again', in Develtere, Pollet and Wanyama (eds) (2008) *Cooperating Out of Poverty*: *The Renaissance of the African Co-operative Movement*, Geneva: International Labour Organisation
Muenkner, H-H (1976) *Co-operatives for the Rich or for the Poor?* Marburg: Institute for Co-operation in Developing Countries
Muenkner, H-H (ed.) (1989) *Comparative Study of Co-operative Law in Africa*, Marburg: Marburg Consult

Muenkner, H-H and Shah, A (1993) *Creating a Favourable Climate and Conditions for Cooperative Development in Africa*, Geneva: International Labour Organisation

Murphy, S (2010) *Life Insurance in the United States through World War 1*, www.eh.net/encyclopaedia, accessed 7.3.10

Mutual Assurance (2010) Mutual assurance; its beginning in America, www.mutual-assurance.com accessed 6.3.10

Myners, P (2004) *Final Report: Myners Review of the Governance of Life Mutuals*, London: HM Treasury

National Center for Employee Ownership (NCEO) (2009) *Employee Ownership and Corporate Performance*, note on www.nceo.org/library/corpperf.html 168 Annual Economic Survey of employee ownership

—— (2010) statistics from www.nceo.org, accessed 18.5.10

National Fraternal Congress of America (NFCA) (2010) replies to questions in an email exchange

National Rural Electricity Co-operative Association (NRECA) International (2010) website, www.nreca.org, accessed 12.4.10

Nickson, A (2000) *Organisational Structures and Performance in Urban Water Supply: The Case of Saguapac Water Co-operative in Santa Cruz, Bolivia*, Birmingham: International Development Department, Birmingham University

Nilsson, J (2001) 'Co-operative organisational models as a reflection of the business environment', in Birchall, J (ed.) (2001) *The New Mutualism in Public Policy*, London: Routledge

Nilsson, J and Ohlsson, C (2007) 'The New Zealand co-operatives' adaptation to changing market conditions', *Journal of Rural Co-operation*, 35(1): 43–70

Nippierd, A-B and Holmgren, C (2002) *Legal Constraints to Women's Participation in Cooperatives*, Geneva: ILO

OBOS (2010) website www.obos.no, accessed 3.4.10

Organisation of Brazilian Co-operatives (2010) *Agricultural Co-operative Statistics*, found at www.ocb.org.br, accessed 19.5.10

Olson, M (1971) *The Logic of Collective Action*, Cambridge Mass: Harvard University Press

Overseas Cooperative Development Council (OCDC) (2007) *Cooperatives: Pathways to Economic, Democratic and Social Development in the Global Economy*, at www.coopdevelopmentcentre.coop, accessed 4.4.10

Parnell, E (1995) *Reinventing the Co-operative: Enterprises for the 21st Century*, Oxford: Plunkett Foundation

Pellervo Federation (2000) *The Pellervo Story*, Helsinki: Pellervo Federation

Penn South Housing Co-operative (2010) *website*, www.pennsouth.coop, accessed 6.4.10

Pestoff, V (2009) 'Towards a paradigm of democratic participation: Citizen participation and co-production of personal social services in Sweden', *Annals of Public and Co-operative Economics*, 80(2): 197–224

Polanyi, K (1957) *The Great Transformation: The Political and Economic Origins of Our Time*, Boston: Beacon Press

Potter, B (1899) *The Co-operative Movement in Great Britain*, London: Swan Sonnenschein

Putnam, R (1994) *Making Democracy Work: Civic Traditions in Modern Italy*, Princeton: Princeton UP

—— (2000) *Bowling Alone*, New York: Simon and Schuster

Quarter, J (1992) *Canada's Social Economy*, Toronto: James Lorimer
Rabobank Group (2009) *Co-operative Banks in the New Financial System*, self-published report
Rajagopalan, S (2003) *Tribal Co-operatives in India*, New Delhi: ILO
Rajaguru, RB (1996) *Survival in the Open Market: A Critical Study on the Co-operative Movement of Sri Lanka Within the Market Economy*, New Delhi: International Co-operative Alliance
Redfern, P (1938) *The New History of the CWS*, London: JM Dent
Rhodes, R (1995) *The International Co-operative Alliance During War and Peace*, Geneva: International Co-operative Alliance
Rondot, P and Collion, M-H (2001) *Agricultural Producer Organisations: Their Contribution to Rural Capacity Building and Poverty Reduction*, Washington: Rural Development Department, World Bank
Rosen, C, Case, J and Saubus, M (2005) *Equity: Why Employee Ownership is Good for Business*, Boston: Harvard Business School Press
Rouse, J (1996) *Rural People's Organisations in a Liberalised Market Economy: Recent FAO Experience*, SD Dimensions series, FAO
Sandler, S, Paris, V and Polton, D (2004) *Health Care Systems in Transition, France*, Geneva: World Health Organisation
Schediwy, R (1989) 'The consumer co-operatives in Sweden', 'The consumer co-operatives in Finland', and 'The consumer co-operatives in France', in Brazda, J and Schediwy, R (eds) *Consumer Co-operatives in a Changing World*, Geneva: International Co-operative Alliance
—- (1996) 'The decline and fall of Konsum Austria', in *Review of International Co-operation* 89(2): 62–68
Setzer, J (1989) 'The consumer co-operatives in Italy', in Brazda, J and Schediwy, R (eds) *Consumer Co-operatives in a Changing World*, Geneva: International Co-operative Alliance
Shah, T (1996) *Catalysing Co-operation: Design of Self-governing Organisations*, New Delhi: Sage
Siddeley, L (1992) 'The rise and fall of fraternal insurance organisations', *Humane Studies Review*, 7(2)
Shen, R and Zhang (2005) 'Farmers; professional associations in rural China; state dominated or new state-society partnership?', Stanford University Working Paper
Sizya, J (2001) 'The role co-operatives play in poverty reduction in Tanzania', paper presented at *United Nations International Day for Eradication of Poverty*, 17 Oct
Smith, L (1961) *The Evolution of Agricultural Co-operation*, Oxford: Blackwell
Smith, S and Ross, C (2006) *Organising out of Poverty: How the Syndicoop Approach has Worked in East Africa*, Manchester: Co-operative College
Smith, SC (2003) 'Network externalities and cooperative networks: A comparative case study of mondragon and la lega with implications for developing and transition countries', ch. 8 of Laixiang Sun (ed.) *Ownership and Governance of Enterprises*, Basingstoke: Palgrave Macmillan
Spaull, H (1965) *The Co-operative Movement in the World Today*, London: Barrie and Rockcliffe
Standard Life (2010) *Demutualisation*, found at www.standardlife.com/about/demutualisation accessed 8.3.10
Stryjan, Y and Wijkstrom, F (1996) 'Cooperatives and non-profit organisations in Swedish social welfare', *Annals of Public and Co-operative Economics*, 67(1): 5–37

Sudradjat, S (2010) "The German co-operative and Raiffeisen system: A brief overview', available from www.dgrv.de accessed 18.5.10

Supporters Direct (2010) Website, www.supportersdirect.co.uk, accessed 17.5.10

Svendsen, GL and Svendsen, GT (2004) *The Creation and Destruction of Social Capital: Entrepreneurship, Co-operative Movements and Institutions*, Cheltenham: Edward Elgar

Svensson, K (1995) 'Not the middle way but both ways: Co-operative housing in Sweden', in Heskin, A and Leavitt, J (1995) *The Hidden History of Housing Co-operatives*, Davis CA: University of California

Theron, J (2005) *The Co-operative Tradition in South Africa and Namibia: Essential Research for a Co-operative Facility* (mimeo), Geneva: ILO

—— (2008) 'Coooperatives in South Africa: A movement re-emerging, in Develtere, Pollet and Wanyama (eds) (2008) *Cooperating Out of Poverty: The Renaissance of the African Co-operative Movement*, Geneva: International Labour Organisation

Thompson, EP (1968) *The Making of the English Working Class*, Harmondsworth: Penguin

Tsekpo, A (2008) 'The cooperative sector in Ghana: Small and big business', in Develtere, Pollet and Wanyama (eds) (2008) *Cooperating Out of Poverty: The Renaissance of the African Co-operative Movement*, Geneva: International Labour Organisation

United Nations Economic and Social Council (UNESCO) (2001) *Co-operatives in Social Development*, Report of the Secretary-General, New York

—— (2003) *World Water Development Report 2003*, Geneva: UN

United Nations Research Institute for Social Development (UNRISD) (1975) *Rural Co-operatives as Agents for Change,* a research report and a debate, Geneva: UNRISD

United Nations Department for Economic and Social Affairs (1997) *Co-operative Enterprise in the Health and Social Care Sectors: A Global Survey*, New York: UNDESA

US Department of Agriculture (USDA) (2007) *Farmer Co-operative Statistics, 2006*, Service Report 67, Washington: USDA

Vacek, G (1989) 'The consumer co-operatives in Japan', in Brazda, J and Schediwy, R (eds) *Consumer Co-operatives in a Changing World*, Geneva: International Co-operative Alliance

Verhagen, K (1984) *Co-operation for Survival: An Analysis of an Experiment in Participatory Research and Planning*, Amsterdam: Koninklijk Instituut voor de Tropen

Wanyama, F (2008) 'The qualitative and quantitative growth of the cooperative movement in Kenya', in Develtere, Pollet and Wanyama (eds) (2008) *Cooperating Out of Poverty: The Renaissance of the African Co-operative Movement*, Geneva: International Labour Organisation

Wanyama, F, Develtere, P and Pollet, I (2009) 'Reinventing the wheel? African cooperatives in a liberalised economic environment', in *Annals of Public and Co-operative Economics*, 80(3): 361–392

Warbasse, J (1936) *Co-operative Democracy*, New York: Harper

West, T (1986) *Horace Plunkett: Co-operation and Politics*, Gerrards Cross: Colin Smythe

Wisconsin (2010) *User-owned Comprehensive Health Insurance*, accessed on 2.3.10 from www.uwcc.wisc.edu

Wolff, H (1907) *Co-operative Banking: Its Principles and Practice*, London: PS King

—— (1893) *People's Banks: A Record of Social and Economic Success*, London: PS King

World Bank (2006) *China: Farmers' Professional Associations, Review and Policy Recommendations*, Beijing: China Agricultural Press
—— (2007) *Financial Deepening Report*, Washington
—— (2008) *Development Report*, Washington
—— (2009) *Finance for All*, Washington
World Council of Credit Unions (2010) *International Credit Union System*, found at www.woccu.org/memberserv on 22.3.10
Zhao, J (2009) 'Farmer-controlled organisations in China: Pushed forward or taking off?', paper for *ICA International Co-operatives Research Conference*, Oxford, September

Index